	Past		meaning
Positive	Negative		
学生だった 学生でした	学生　じゃ／では　なかった 学生　じゃ／では　ありませんでした 学生　じゃ／では　なかったです		*to be a student*
便利だった 便利でした	便利　じゃ／では　なかった 便利　じゃ／では　ありませんでした 便利　じゃ／では　なかったです		*convenient*
重かった 重かったです	重くなかった 重くありませんでした 重くなかったです		*heavy*

d adjectives

dverbial f.	-te f.	-tara f.	-ba f.	meaning
i	de	dattara	nara	
学生に	学生で	学生だったら	学生なら	*to be a student*
便利に	便利で	便利だったら	便利なら	*convenient*
ku	-kute	-kattara	-kereba	
重く	重くて	重かったら	重ければ	*heavy*
大きく	大きくて	大きかったら	大きければ	*large*
安く	安くて	安かったら	安ければ	*cheap*
よく	よくて	よかったら	よければ	*good*

The shaded parts show the material covered in this volume.

D0472045

SITUATIONAL FUNCTIONAL JAPANESE

VOLUME *1* : NOTES
SECOND EDITION

TSUKUBA LANGUAGE GROUP

BONJINSHA CO.,LTD.

Published and distributed in Japan by BONJINSHA Co., Ltd.,
1F Ryōshin Hirakawachō Building, 1-3-13, Hirakawa-cho, Chiyoda-ku, Tokyo
    03-3263-3959
Copyright © 1991, 1995 by Tsukuba Language Group. All rights reserved.
Printed in Japan

First edition, 1991
Second edition, 1995   ISBN4-89358-312-3 C3081

ACKNOWLEDGEMENTS

We would like to express our thanks to the many people who have contributed to making this textbook.

First of all, we would like to thank the students of Tsukuba University Japanese Language Course who, on being exposed to the trial version of this book, made constructive criticisms and comments on its shortcomings. On completion of the course a student compelled to fill out vast sets of questionnaires, nevertheless encouraged us by reporting that Tsukuba University should be proud of having produced these teaching materials. Having abandoned familiar ground and having decided to go for something radically new, such encouragement was much welcomed. Our goal was to try to provide students with an understanding of the structure of the language while ensuring that this would not be at the expense of giving them communicative competence. Without the students' co-operation, we would not have been able to achieve this balance.

In addition, we should like to thank the students of SOAS, London University, whose reactions are reflected in the grammatical explanations. The students of Wollongong University gave this book the delightful nickname of "Sitfun." Like the Tsukuba students here, these groups of students who used this book in draft form abroad helped to ease our fears and gave us the courage to persevere.

The University of Hawaii at Manoa decided to use SFJ from August 1993, and another new relationship is in the process of developing. Professor Gerald Mathias was kind enough to send us a list of suggested amendments, most of which were taken on board for the second edition; we look forward to more reactions from both staff and students in order to make further improvements to SFJ.

Special thanks are due to three postgraduate students of Tsukuba University, James Ford, Ronald Craig and Ted Johnson. Far beyond simply translating Japanese into English, they gave us valuable insights and ideas that would never have occurred to native speakers of Japanese.

We also have to thank the book itself; the experience of writing it has helped us grow as human beings, and has given us confidence in our work: if you really put your mind to something, you can do it!

Lastly, we would like to express our thanks to Ohashi Makiko, Ueno Masafumi and Kon Mitsuko. Without their enduring encouragement this book would never have seen the light of day so speedily and handsomely.

The authors

PREFACE

Situational Functional Japanese is a series of textbooks and drillbooks which aims primarily to enable you to acquire a basic ability to communicate with Japanese people in Japanese. Knowledge grammar is not enough to communicate smoothly: you must know in what kind of situation to use the grammar or expressions you have learned. This is why Situational Functional Japanese takes a different approach from traditional grammar-oriented textbooks.

Situational Functional Japanese (SFJ) has two main objectives: providing grammatical knowledge and communication skills. The purpose of the 'grammar' part of SFJ is as follows:

(1) To give you the Japanese grammar necessary for everyday communication
(2) To provide the basis from which you go on to increase your Japanese language abilities according to your individual needs and objectives

The purpose of the 'conversation' part of SFJ is as follows:
(1) To provide knowledge about Japanese culture, customs, and interpersonal relations needed for everyday communication
(2) To provide communication skills for your individual needs

Classroom work can only give you a basis for successful communication; you should attempt to use the Japanese language in real life and actively communicate with Japanese people as much as possible.

CONTENTS

TABLE OF CONTENTS

Lesson Title	Grammar Notes
L 1 紹介する Introducing people P. 1～26	I. ～です II. は and も〈1〉: discourse particles III. Question sentences IV. の〈1〉: modifying nouns V. と〈1〉*and*: connective particle
L 2 郵便局で At the post office P.27～50	I. Verbs in the polite form: [V(base)]-masu II. が〈1〉; を〈1〉; に〈1〉; へ: structure particles III. は and も〈2〉: discourse particles and structure particles IV. で〈1〉*at*; と〈2〉*with*: structure particles V. なに *what?* and いくら *how much?*: question words VI. ～まい and ～えん: counters VII. Numbers
L 3 レストランで At a restaurant P.51～74	I. に〈2〉*from/to*: structure particle II. です substituting for a verb III. ～にします and ～になります: する verbs and なる verbs〈1〉 IV. いつ *when?*: question word V. ～ましょう and ～ませんか VI. ひとつ, ふたつ, ……: counter for things ひとり, ふたり, ……: counter for people VII. は and も〈3〉: more about discourse particles
L 4 場所を聞く Asking the whereabouts P.75～98	I. The こ/そ/あ/ど system〈1〉 II. Expressions of existence III. ～から〈1〉: *because～* IV. ～なら〈1〉: *if you mean～* V. や and とか *and*: connective particles
まとめ1(L1～4)	A. Grammar

Conversation Notes

⟨General Information⟩ ⟨Strategies⟩

1. Formal introductions
2. Addressing people
3. Short questions and responses
4. *Aizuchi*

S-1. How to start a conversation —1.
At a party
S-2. How to introduce yourself or others
S-3. How to end a conversation —1.
After a meeting

---

1. Post office services in Japan
2. Letters and postcards
3. Paying and receiving money

S-1. How to start a conversation —2.
On the street
S-2. How to start a conversation —3.
Introducing a request
S-3. How to send mail at the post office
S-4. How to buy something at the post office

---

1. At a restaurant
2. Expressions used in restaurants and shops
3. Fast food shops

S-1. How to ask for something you need
S-2. How to give and receive something
S-3. How to order
S-4. How to deal with problems in a restaurant
S-5. How to pay the cashier

---

1. Location

S-1. How to start a conversation —4.
Introducing a question
S-2. How to ask the whereabouts of things /people
S-3. How to get something you didn't catch repeated
S-4. How to confirm information —1.
S-5. How to gain time to collect your thoughts
S-6. How to end a conversation —2. After asking a question

B. Conversation

Lesson Title	Grammar Notes

(4)

Conversation Notes

⟨General Information⟩	⟨Strategies⟩
1. Katakana words	S-1. How to introduce a main topic —1. S-2. How to ask for information about a word S-3. How to make sure you have understood S-4. How to end a conversation —3. When the listener does not give the required explanation
1. Office instructions 2. Delivery service	S-1. How to introduce a main topic —2. S-2. How to ask for instructions S-3. How to correct others' mistakes S-4. How to ask for advice implicitly S-5. How to give an alternative
1. Telephones 2. Telephone numbers	S-1. How to ask for a telephone number S-2. How to make a telephone call S-3. How to deal with a wrong number S-4. How to introduce a question politely S-5. How to ask about office hours S-6. How to make an appointment
1. The relationship between seniors and juniors in Japan 2. A report for leave of absence	S-1. How to start a conversation —5. Asking for permission S-2. How to introduce a main topic —3. S-3. How to ask for permission S-4. How to give a warning

B. Conversation

How to Use This Book

Situational Functional Japanese is designed for complete beginners as well as those who have already studied a little Japanese. It consists of 3 volumes each with textbooks (Notes) and drillbooks. Each volume contains 8 lessons, making a total of 24 lessons.

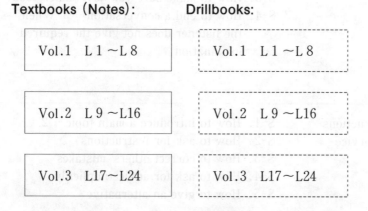

Textbooks (Notes):

Vol.1   L 1 ~L 8

Vol.2   L 9 ~L16

Vol.3   L17~L24

Drillbooks:

Vol.1   L 1 ~L 8

Vol.2   L 9 ~L16

Vol.3   L17~L24

The lessons in the textbook are divided into the following five sections:

Ⅰ. Model Conversation
Ⅱ. Report
Ⅲ. New Words and Expressions
Ⅳ. Grammar Notes
Ⅴ. Conversation Notes

Before Lesson 1, there is an Introduction and a Pre-session. You are advised to read the Introduction part by yourself before starting the first lesson.

The Pre-session is a warm-up section, designed to make you aware of the differences between the formal style and the casual style which are both commonly used in everyday conversation, and help you to acquire natural-sounding Japanese as soon as possible.

The Pre-session practice uses tapes to help you to distinguish between affirmative and negative, past and non-past forms, as well as speech styles (casual/formal), by making you aware of differences in shape, sound and intonation at the end of sentences.

Textbook:

I. Model Conversation

The 24 model conversational situations represent frequently encountered situations for foreign students or researchers in Japan, and are set in a communication network between an Indian student, Anil Sharma, Lisa Brown from the United Kingdom, and their Japanese friends, seniors, and professors. The Model Conversations are written in as"natural" Japanese as possible. The characters use formal expressions with their seniors or strangers at the beginning and gradually start to use casual expressions as their psychological distance diminishes. You should listen to the Model Conversations several times and try to understand the kind of communication procedure that is possible in a given situation. This will enable you to remember the Model Conversations when you encounter a similar situation.

II. Report

The Reports, which are placed after the Model Conversation, sum up the content of the conversations and related material in the written language in the form of reports and diaries, etc. Conversational exchanges, which are often shortened, are expressed in full sentences to show the sentence structure, and create a basis for future study of the written language.

III. New Words and Expressions

Here you find explanations of new words and expressions used in the Model Conversations and the Reports, including references to the Grammar Notes and the Conversation Notes.

IV. Grammar Notes

The Grammar Notes are designed as follows:

(1) They cover the grammatical items needed for the elementary level.
(2) Grammatical items are selected and arranged on the basis of the Model Conversations.
(3) Grammatical points are introduced and explained in a detailed and systematic manner, to enable you to form your own sentences.
(4) The introduction and explanation of grammar is done in an enjoyable, easy-to-understand manner through the use of pictures and cartoons and copious example sentences.

(5) Important items concerning sentence structure are covered and expanded over the course of several lessons. (**wa** and **ga**, *keego*, **suru/naru** verbs, noun modification, etc.)

(6) In this textbook, emphasis is placed on distinguishing between structure particles and discourse particles. The former expresses the basic (grammatical) relationships among words in a structure, while the latter expresses the speaker's feelings. In actual conversation, structure particles are used with discourse particles such as **wa** and **mo**.

(7) The Grammar Notes for Lessons 1 to 4 use romanization (the example sentences are in Kana and Kanji but with romanized transcriptions), but from Lesson 5, Kana and Kanji are used, although romanization is used where it helps to clarify grammatical explanations, etc..

(8) After every 4 lessons, there are review and summary sessions (まとめ).

You should read the Grammar Notes before using the drillbooks.

V. Conversation Notes

The Conversation Notes act as a compact guide to Japanese culture. Before practising the drills and the Model Conversations, you should read them to prepare yourself for the new material. The Conversation Notes are made up of General Information (GI) and Strategies (S):

1. General Information

Linguistic expressions that are based on interpersonal relations are a key factor in Japanese language communication, making it necessary to give information on society and interpersonal relations, to overcome the communication gap between cultures.

2. Strategies

For successful communication with the Japanese, you will need an understanding of the appropriate strategies that the Japanese use in order to achieve the aim of interpersonal communication, such as getting someone to do you a favour.

After every 4 lessons there are review and summary sessions (まとめ). The conversation まとめ includes a summary of conversational strategies and additional information.

1. Summary of conversational strategies

Here, the strategies of the Conversation Notes in the four lessons are divided into 6 functions. Using the check list of "What I am able to do now", check it first by yourself, then have it confirmed by a teacher. If you cannot do something satisfactorily, do further practice.

2. Additional information

Under this heading, all the meanings of an item explained over several lessons are summed up and reviewed.

At the end of the text, there are two appendices:

Ⅰ. Grammar Check

Ⅱ. Answers for Grammar Check and Model Conversation Check

The Grammar Check Sheets are designed to check that you have correctly understood the material after reading the Grammar Notes. The correct answers are also given, so you can check your answers as you work through the checksheet, and reread the Grammar Notes if necessary. Language practice becomes much easier if you proceed to the structure drills after having completed the checksheet first.

The Model Conversation Check is recorded on tapes after every Model Conversation to enable you to check whether you have understood the situations in the Model Conversations and the uses of the expressions in the Conversation Notes. The correct answers are given in Appendix Ⅱ.

Drillbook:

The lessons in the drillbook are divided into the following four sections:

Ⅰ. New Words in Drills

Ⅱ. Structure Drills

Ⅲ. Conversation Drills

Ⅳ. Tasks and Activities

Ⅰ. New Words in Drills

(1) The New Words are divided into Basic Words and Additional Words. Basic words include basic vocabulary items which appear in the Structure Drills and in the Conversation Drills.

(2) You should check through the vocabulary before beginning the Structure Drills.

II. Structure Drills

The Grammar Notes only convey knowledge; to become able to use the language, you need to do the Structure Drills. The Structure Drills are designed to accomplish the following:

(1) To consolidate the items covered in the Grammar Notes
(2) To give practice in using the correct forms
(3) To guide you beyond mechanical practice to become able to make your own sentences
(4) To make possible enjoyable, easy-to-understand practice through the inclusion of pictures and illustrations

III. Conversation Drills

The Conversation Drills are oral practice items to internalize the expressions in the strategies through repetition and to achieve accuracy and fluency.

There are many different types of practice in the Conversation Drills, the main ones being the following:

1. Substitution drills
2. Response drills
3. Communication drills
4. Role plays

IV. Tasks and Activities

The tasks are a central element of SFJ; the explanations and drills in the Grammar and Conversation Note, are developed by the tasks, which are designed as real-life tasks.

The tasks are designed to achieve the following:

(1) To cover the four basic skills, in particular, reading and writing practice
(2) To give information on life and culture in Japan
(3) To improve learner's motivation through the incorporation of games

Note: Several of the listening and reading tasks include some new vocabulary and constructions as preview material for later study.

Supplementary aids:

Audio tapes are available for the drillbooks, corresponding to the Structure Drills (except the ones marked with ☆), the Conversation Drills, and the listening tasks with the tape mark. There is a teacher's manual for the drillbooks with a script for the listening tasks. Video tapes for Model Conversations and CAI (Computer Assisted Instruction) programs for this textbook are due to be published.

Abbreviations and Notations

This is a list of main symbols used in this book:

	discourse particles
	structure particles
	connective particles
▼	Be careful!
○	correct
×	wrong
[N]	noun
[A]	-i adjective
[NA]	na adjective
[V]	verb
[V(base)]	verb base
[V-(r)u]	-(r)u form of verb
[V-te]	-te form of verb
[V-ta]	-ta form of verb
[V-nai]	-nai form of verb
[V-nakatta]	-nakatta form of verb
《＋を verbs》	verb with を（object particle）
《－を verbs》	verb without を（object particle）
{S}	sentence
⇨	Refer
MC	Model Conversation
GN	Grammar Notes
CN	Conversation Notes
lit.	literally
🄴	formal/polite speech
Ⓒ	casual/plain speech
⬆	speaking to a Higher
⬇	speaking to a Lower
➡	speaking to an Equal
🕈	spoken by male
🕇	spoken by female

Introduction
to
Japanese

I. GRAMMAR

1. **Nihongo** is like a train.
2. Predicates
3. The classification of Japanese words
4. Particles (＝**joshi**)
5. The Japanese language and social relationships

II. PRONUNCIATION

1. Mora
2. Accent and Intonation

III. WRITING SYSTEM

1. Hiragana
2. Katakana
3. Katakana words
4. Hiragana exercises

I. Grammar

1. Nihongo is like a train

The Japanese language, **Nihongo**, can be compared to a train.

1) Look at the following illustration:

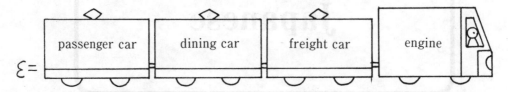

The engine of the train is pulling a passenger car, a dining car and a freight car. The order of the cars can change, but the engine always comes in furthest right.

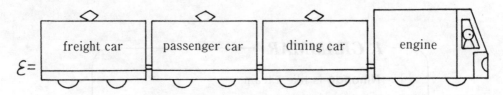

A train can run without a freight car, a passenger car or a dining car, but not without the engine. However, the engine can run on its own:

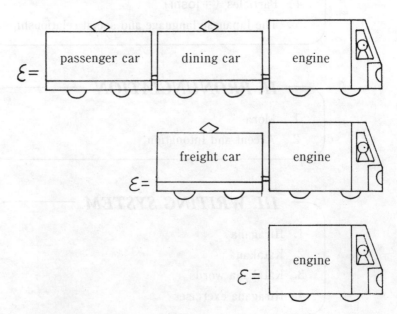

2) The idea *I will go to Tokyo tomorrow* is expressed in Japanese as:

Watashi wa	ashita	Tookyoo e	iku.
I	*tomorrow*	*to Tokyo*	*(will) go*

You can express the same idea by changing the order of the sentence:

Tookyoo e	watashi wa	ashita	iku.
to Tokyo	*I*	*tomorrow*	*(will) go*

You can also abbreviate, mentioning only those parts you want to focus on.

Watashi wa	iku.	*I will go.*
Ashita	iku.	*(I) will go tomorrow.*
Tookyoo e	iku.	*(I) will go to Tokyo.*
	iku.	*(I) will go.*

You can thus change the order of words or phrases, or omit them if they are understood from the context, but you cannot change the position of **iku** *to go*, or omit it, as it is the predicate of the sentence. The predicate is the most important element in a Japanese sentence. Just as the engine is the driving force of the train, the predicate is the driving force of the sentence.

2. Predicates

There are four types of predicate in Japanese.

　　　(1) verb
　　　(2) **-i** adjective
　　　(3) **na** adjective
　　　(4) noun + **da**

A predicate inflects according to whether it is

　　　(1) plain (non-polite) or polite,
　　　(2) non-past or past,
　　　(3) positive or negative.　　　　　　　　⇨ Pre-session

See the table of plain and polite forms below:

	Plain form	Polite form
verb	iku	ikimasu
	(I) go.	
-i adjective	omoshiroi	omoshiroi desu
	(It) is interesting.	
na adjective	genki da	genki desu
	(I) am in good health.	
noun + **da**	Yamada-san da	Yamada-san desu
	(He) is Yamada-san.	

One cannot always tell the subject of a sentence from the predicate alone, but it can be understood from the context or the situation. (In the translations in this textbook, subjects that are not explicit are normally in rounded brackets.)

3. Classification of Japanese words

Japanese words are divided into several groups such as nouns, verbs, adjectives and adverbs. Look at the following illustration to form an idea of each group. (The abbreviations are given in square brackets, while the Japanese terms are given in rounded brackets.)

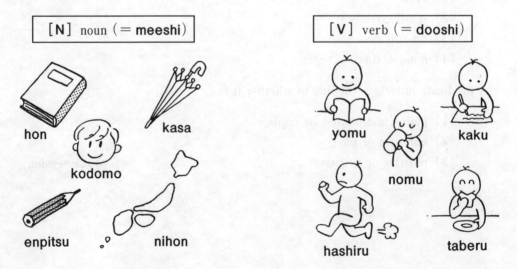

[N] noun (= **meeshi**)

hon
kodomo
kasa
enpitsu
nihon

[V] verb (= **dooshi**)

yomu
kaku
nomu
hashiru
taberu

adjective（**keeyooshi**）

（There are two types of adjectives, **-i** adjectives and **na** adjectives. **-i** adjectives end in **-i**（not **-ri, -ki**, etc.）, while **na** adjectives don't.）⇨ L6GN（＝ Grammar Notes）I

[A]（＝ **-i** adjective）

atsui
tanoshii
kurai
itai
nemui

[N A]（＝ **na** adjective）

genki（na）
kirai（na）
suki（na）
heta（na）

adverb（＝ **fukushi**）

zenshi
yukkuri
slowly
zen
all
dandan
gradually
itsu
always

Others

demo
o
ba
dake
ga
keredo
sorekara

Try to identify the group to which the words（underlined）in the following sentences belong.

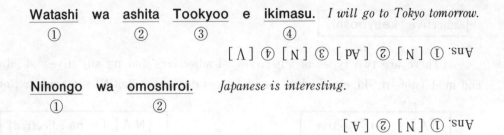

Watashi **wa** **ashita** **Tookyoo** **e** **ikimasu.** *I will go to Tokyo tomorrow.*
① ② ③ ④

Ans. ① [N] ② [Av] ③ [N] ④ [v]

Nihongo **wa** **omoshiroi.** *Japanese is interesting.*
① ②

Ans. ① [N] ② [A]

---

4. Particles (＝joshi)

Did you manage to label each word in the above sentences?

Well done! But what shall we do with **wa** or **e**?

Let's call this group 'particles' (**joshi** in Japanese). Particles can be divided into three sub-groups:

1) Structure particles

Attached to a noun, a structure particle indicates the grammatical relationship between that noun and its predicate.

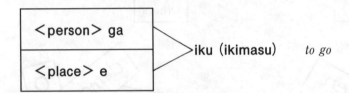

In this structure, <person> **ga** shows the subject of the sentence and <place> **e** indicates the destination or direction. We can call **ga** a subject particle and **e** a direction particle.

You will become familiar with the eight main structure particles in this textbook: **ga, o, ni, e, de, to, kara** and **made**

is our symbol for structure particles, because these particles show the bones (the grammatical structure) of the sentence.

2) Discourse particles

Discourse particles do not express grammatical relationships; they convey the speaker's attitude expressed by marking out a word as a topic contrasting it with others, omitting or emphasizing it.

Discourse particles are dependent on the context or the situation in which they are used.

There are two groups of discourse particles.

(1) Topic particles: **wa** and **mo**

The topic particles **wa** and **mo** make a word the topic of the sentence. For instance, **watashi**, *I* and **Tanaka-san**, *Miss Tanaka* are the topics in the following sentences.

Watashi <u>wa</u> Tookyoo e ikimasu.   *As for me, I will go to Tokyo.*

Tanaka-san <u>mo</u> Tookyoo e ikimasu.   *As for Tanaka-san, she will go to Tokyo, too.*

(2) Final particles

Added to the end of the sentence, final particles express the speaker's emotions of doubt, emphasis, caution, hesitation, wonder, admiration and the like.

Tookyoo e ikimasu <u>ka</u>.   *Are (you) going to Tokyo?*

Tookyoo e ikimasu <u>ne</u>.   *(You) are going to Tokyo, aren't you?*

Tookyoo e ikimasu <u>yo</u>.   *(I) will go to Tokyo, you know.*

Ka is used to signal a question, **ne** for soliciting the listener's agreement or confirmation, and **yo** to indicate that the listener is being informed of something.

is our symbol for discourse particles. The contrast between the live fish and the skeleton illustrates how discourse particles are used to enrich the basic sentence structure with substance and feeling.

3) Connective particles

Connective particles link nouns or sentences:

Tookyoo <u>to</u> Yokohama e ikimasu.
I will go to Tokyo and Yokohama.

Ashita nichiyoobi na <u>node</u>, Tookyoo e ikimasu.
I will go to Tokyo, as tomorrow is Sunday.

is our symbol for connective particles.

5. The Japanese language and social relationships

In Japan, as in many other parts of the world, language can be used to indicate social position. The Japanese language has certain words and forms (grouped together under the label 'levels of speech') which are used to express the social distance between the speaker and the other participants in a conversation. This distance has two dimensions: vertical and horizontal.

1) Vertical distance (Social status)

Traditional Japan was a strictly stratified society, with social status based upon seniority and rank. While modern Japanese society has undergone profound changes, resulting in a significant reduction of the privileges and power derived from social status, expression of social status in speech is still taken seriously, even when the subject of the conversation is not within earshot.

Both seniority and rank contribute to social status; in this book, we will, for the sake of easy reference, refer to a 'person of higher social status' as a Higher, and a 'person of lower social status' as a Lower. Where appropriate, 'senior' and 'junior' will also be used. Persons of equal social status/age will be referred to as Equals.

'Honorific and humble forms' (called **keego** in Japanese ⇨ L9, L10, L18, L19 Grammer Notes for details) can be matched with either style of speech when referring to one's interactions with a Higher.

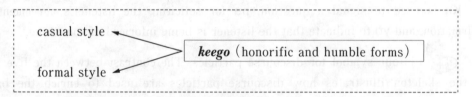

For example, a university student will normally use casual speech when talking with a student in a junior year or a close friend of approximately the same age or year, but will use formal speech when addressing an older student or a teacher. Honorific and humble forms combine with casual or formal speech when a teacher is referred to, regardless of whether that teacher is present or not.

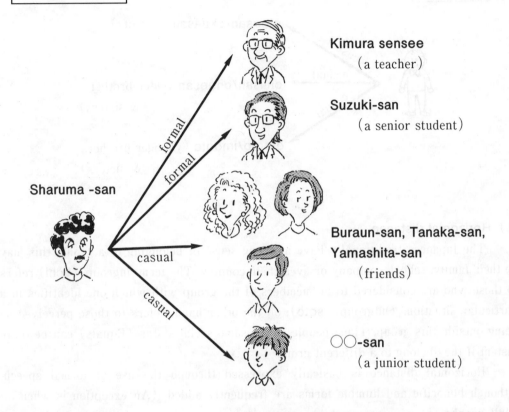

Similar usage can be observed in companies and most other social groups in Japan. The major exception is the family, where during the past decades the use of formal speech when addressing older siblings or parents has generally been abandoned. However, honorific elements such as **o-** or **-san** are still used for addressing senior family members only.

In a company

jooshi（superiors）

dooryoo（colleagues）

buka（subordinates）

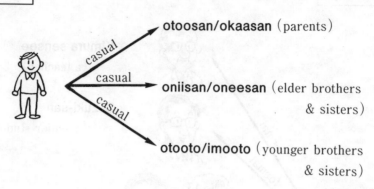

otoosan/okaasan（parents）

oniisan/oneesan（elder brothers
& sisters）

otooto/imooto（younger brothers
& sisters）

2）Horizontal distance

The Japanese traditionally have a strong sense of belonging to a group; this may be their family, school, company or even their country. The term 'ingroup' (**uchi**) refers to those who are considered to be members of the group with which one identifies in a particular situation. 'Outgroup' (**soto**), on the other hand, refers to those perceived as being outside this group. Thus, people of the same social status (Equals) can be quite distant if they belong to a different group.

Horizontal distance is basically expressed through the use of formal speech, although honorific and humble forms are frequently added. (An exception is when an adult speaks to an outgroup child, a situation where casual speech is normally used because of the marked difference in seniority.)

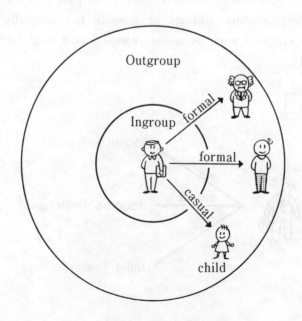

In Japan group consciousness takes precedence over social status. Thus, honorific forms are never used to refer to an ingroup person when speaking to an outsider, even if the ingroup person is a Higher. Conversely, humble forms are used for referring to members of one's own group when talking to outsiders. For example, an employee will normally refer to his company president using honorific forms when talking to a fellow employee of the same company, but when speaking to an employee from another company, he will use humble forms for his company president.

Depending on the ingroup/outgroup relationship between speaker and listener, therefore, the same person can be accorded high or low social status.

Besides social status and the **uchi/soto** relationship, there are other factors contributing to the choice of the speech level. These include the formality of the situation in which the conversation takes place, the topic, and even the speaker's emotional state. Speech levels are not predetermined but change in accordance with various combinations of these factors.

II. Pronunciation

Compared with other aspects of learning the Japanese language, pronunciation is relatively easy. This is because the language uses only five vowels, and each consonant is generally followed by a vowel to form a basic unit of sound called a mora (a syllable-like unit).

Pronouncing Japanese like a native speaker, however, requires a mastery of the Japanese sounds and moras as well as of pitch accent and intonation that only comes with much time and patience. To achieve this goal, it is important that you make a conscious effort to listen to as much Japanese as possible and constantly imitate what you hear.

Here are some suggestions to help you learn the correct pronunciation. First, listen carefully and repeatedly to the Japanese sounds until you are aware of the differences between the sounds of Japanese and those of your mother tongue.

1. Mora

The basic unit of Japanese pronunciation is called a mora. You may wonder what a mora is: each mora corresponds to one beat in the regular staccato rhythm that characterizes the pronunciation of Japanese words or sentences, and therefore takes roughly the same amount of time to pronounce.

① **One-mora words:**

1. ●   2. ●   3. ●
ha   te   me
は   て   め

② **Two-mora words:**

1. ● ●   2. ● ●   3. ● ●
i   nu   to   o   ha   na
い   ぬ   と   お   は   な

③ **Three-mora words:**

1. ● ● ●   2. ● ● ●   3. ● ● ●
ta   ba   ko   ri   n   go   ki   t   te
た   ば   こ   り   ん   ご   き   っ   て

④ **four-mora words:**

1. ● ● ● ●   2. ● ● ● ●   3. ● ● ● ●
   a   i sa tsu   da i ga ku   to sho ka n
   あ い さ つ   だ い が く   と し ょ か ん

Note that the examples above include such diverse one-mora units as the second **o** in **too**, the **n** in **ringo**, the **sho** in **toshokan**, the first **t** in **kitte**, and the **i** in **aisatsu**.

Since the words in each example have an equal number of beats, they take about the same length of time to pronounce.

The standard dialect of Japanese can be written with about 100 distinct moras (given below). Moras can be divided into six groups according to their structure:

1. Single vowels: **a, i, u, e, o**
2. A consonant + a vowel: **ka, ki, ku, ke, ko......**
3. A semi-vowel that is /y/ or /w/ + a vowel: **ya, yu, yo, wa**
4. A consonant + a semi-vowel + vowel: **kya, kyu, kyo......**
5. The single nasal consonant /N/:   **n** in **ringo, hantai**
6. The first (voiceless) consonant of a double consonant:
   The first **t** in **kitte**, **k** in **gakkoo**, **p** in **shippai**

1) The five single vowels

The Japanese vowel system is rather simple with its five vowels, whose sounds remain unchanged regardless of their environment. How many vowels does your own language have?

First listen carefully to the pronunciation of your teacher, then try imitating it. Can you hear the differences between Japanese vowels and those in your own language? Rely on your auditory impression of each sound for learning the Japanese vowels.

「あ」   /a/ is pronounced approximately like [a] in 'up'
「い」   /i/ is pronounced approximately like [i] in 'ear'
「う」   /u/ is pronounced approximately like [u] in 'look' but without rounding the lips.
「え」   /e/ is pronounced approximately like [e] in 'pen'
「お」   /o/ is pronounced approximately like [o] in 'short' (but shorter, than when pronounced in British English)

Note that two vowels and long vowels consist of two moras.

1.● ●   2.● ●   3.● ●   4.● ●   5.● ●   6.● ●
  a i   i e   u e   o i   o o   i i
  あ い   い え   う え   お い   お お   い い

2) Consonants with vowels

A Japanese consonant is usually followed by a vowel; together, these make up one mora. Listen carefully to each mora, then try to imitate it as closely as you can. The traditional order is as follows:

Chart 1. The 5 vowels and 63 consonant/vowel combinations

（including the 4 semi-vowel/vowel combinations）

	1	2	3	4	5	6	7	8	9	
a	ka	sa	ta	na	ha	ma	ya	ra	wa	
i	ki	shi (*si)	chi (*ti)	ni	hi	mi	-	ri	-	
u	ku	su	tsu (*tu)	nu	fu (*hu)	mu	yu	ru	-	
e	ke	se	te	ne	he	me	-	re	-	
o	ko	so	to	no	ho	mo	yo	ro	(*o)	n

* alternative form of romanization

10	11	12	13	
k→g	s→z	t→d	h→b→p	
ga	za	da	ba	pa
gi	ji (*zi)	-	bi	pi
gu	zu	-	bu	pu
ge	ze	de	be	pe
go	zo	do	bo	po

3) Semi-vowel/vowel combinations

See Chart 1. Column 7.

4) Consonant/semi-vowel/vowel combinations

Chart 2.　33　C + S + V

k→g	s→z	t	n	h	p→b	m	r
kya	sha (*sya)	cha (*tya)	nya	hya	pya	mya	rya
kyu	shu (*syu)	chu (*tyu)	nyu	hyu	pyu	myu	ryu
kyo	sho (*syo)	cho (*tyo)	nyo	hyo	pyo	myo	ryo
gya	ja (*zya)	-	-		bya	-	-
gyu	ju (*zyu)	-	-		byu	-	-
gyo	jo (*zyo)	-	-		byo	-	-

5) The single nasal consonant /N/

The single nasal consonant /N/ makes up one mora by itself. Pronounced on its own, /N/ is similar to the 'ng' sound in words like 'going' or 'spring' although it is longer than the English sound.

Used only in combination with other sounds, /N/ is never found at the beginning of a word; it is pronounced in different ways depending on the sound following it as [m], [n], [ŋ], or a nasal vowel.

(In the alternative Hepburn Romanization system, this sound is written as 'm' when followed by 'p'··'b'··'m', and as 'n' when followed by other consonants. In this textbook, we use 'n' in romanization and ん in Hiragana).

1.　Pronounced as [m]

When followed by /p/, /b/ or /m/, /N/ is pronounced as [m].

[sampo]	さんぽ	*a walk*
[gambaru]	がんばる	*to do one's best*
[tʃmmoku]	ちんもく	*silence*

2. Pronounced as [n]

When followed by /t/, /d/, /n/ or /r/, /N/ is pronounced as [n]. When followed by /s/, it also sounds quite close to [n].

[hontoo]	ほんとう	*true*
[honda]	ほんだ	*person's name*
[honno]	ほんの	*a little*
[honrai]	ほんらい	*originally*

3. Pronounced as [ŋ]

When followed by /k/ or /g/, it is pronounced as [ŋ].

[kaŋgaeru]	かんがえる	*to think*
[deŋki]	でんき	*electricity*

4. When followed by a vowel or semi-vowel, /N/ gives the preceding vowel a nasal quality.

[seNeN]	せんえん	*1,000 yen*
[kaNyo]	かんよ	*intervention*

6) Double consonants

Double consonants are written as 'pp', 'tt', 'ss', 'kk' in romanization, but in hiragana the first consonant is written with a small っ. This first consonant is not released and makes up one mora itself.

Double consonants should be pronounced with special care, because in Japanese the distinction between single and double consonants is very important, there being many pairs of words that are distinguished only by this feature.

Listen carefully to the pronunciation of your teacher. If you find double consonants difficult to pronounce, try making a slight pause directly before the double consonant to give yourself time to get ready for it.

shippai	しっぱい	*failure*
matte	まって	*wait!*
shikkari	しっかり	*firmly*
massugu	まっすぐ	*straight on*

2. Accent and intonation

1) Accent

Unlike English, which uses stress accent, Japanese uses pitch accent, which is based on the two relative pitch levels of high and low.

Try to establish a habit of listening closely to your teacher's pronunciation to pick up the pitch levels.

In standard Japanese, there are four accent patterns:

1) Only the first mora of a word is low ; from the second mora onwards, all moras are given high pitch.
   When a word is followed by a particles such as **ga**, this particle too stays on a high pitch.
2) The first mora is low and all following moras are high; however, a following particle such as **ga** comes down to a low pitch.
3) The first mora is low, one or more following moras high, and further moras low.
4) Only the first mora is high; all ensuing moras are low.

On this page the mark 「 is used to indicate where the pitch rises within a word and the mark ¬ to show where it falls.

ni「hongo	にほんご	*Japanese*
ni「hongo de	にほんごで	*in Japanese*
yu「ubi¬nkyoku	ゆうびんきょく	*post office*
yu「ubi¬nkyoku e	ゆうびんきょくへ	*to the post office*
yu「ubi¬nkyoku desu ka	ゆうびんきょくですか	*(Is it) the post office?*

2) Intonation

Intonation plays an important role in communicating the speaker's feelings and intentions toward the listener.

Falling intonation usually conveys the finality of a statement, while rising intonation generally indicates a question.

In this book, the mark ↗ indicates rising intonation, whereas ↘ is used to show a fall in intonation as illustrated in the examples below:

A: Tookyoo e ikimasu ka.↗	とうきょうへいきますか。	*Will you go to Tokyo?*
B: Ee, ikimasu.↘	ええ、いきます。	*Yes, I will.*
A: Soo desu ka.↘	そうですか。	*Really.*

Further explanation on intonation will be given in まとめ1BⅡ-2.

III. Writing System

Japanese is written in a combination of three scripts, Hiragana, Katakana and Kanji. The Roman alphabet (Roomaji) is also sometimes used, largely for the convenience of foreigners. Look at the following examples:

Hiragana:	ひがし
Katakana:	ヒガシ
Kanji:	東
Roomaji:	higashi

All of the above can be used to represent the Japanese word **higashi**, *east*.

Like Roomaji, both Hiragana and Katakana represent sounds. In theory, Japanese sentences can be written in either Hiragana or Katakana only, but except for some special cases such as childrens' books or telegrams, Japanese is usually written in a combination of Hiragana and Kanji, with an admixture of Katakana (and occasionally Roomaji).

私の名前は山下です。

Watashi no namae wa Yamashita desu.

My name is Yamashita.

The underlined parts in the above sentence are Kanji. Whereas the letters of the Roman alphabet generally represent a single sound, Hiragana and Katakana represent moras or syllables. Kanji generally express even larger units, which can be equated with basic units of meaning.

For example, the two-Kanji word **漢字** represents the sound **kanji**, which can be analyzed into **kan** *China/Chinese* and **ji** *character;* the combination meaning *Chinese character(s)*. Kanji are therefore best understood as representing the sound of blocks of meaning.

Roughly speaking, Kanji represent blocks of meaning, whereas Hiragana express the grammatical relations between them.

Because of their different visual impact, this way of combining Kanji and Hiragana in running text without any spaces between them (you may have already noticed this from the above example) enables readers of Japanese to recognize word boundaries even without spacing.

Katakana are used to express words of foreign origin, much like italics or underlining in European languages. Look at the following example:

彼の名前はシャルマです。

Kare no namae wa Sharuma desu.

His name is Sharma.

The underlined part ～～ is in Katakana because Sharma is an Indian name. Broadly speaking, Katakana are used for foreign words from countries other than those also using Chinese characters, with the vast majority stemming from English.

Nearly 2000 years ago, Kanji were introduced to Japan from China. Several centuries later, Hiragana and Katakana developed from Kanji were to express Japanese syllables phonetically. The following is an example of how Hiragana and Katakana were derived from Kanji:

Kanji 加 [ka]／[kuwa-(eru)] *add*

Katakana カ　Hiragana か

Katakana were often formed from a part of a Kanji, whereas Hiragana resulted from cursive abbreviation of an entire Kanji.

We suggest that before you start this book you learn the 46 basic letters and sounds of Hiragana, and learn how they are used in combination. Thereafter, you can start learning the Katakana set.

In order to familiarize you with the way Japanese is written in Japan, Kanji and Kana are used in this book. However, Kanji readings are indicated in Hiragana alongside the Kanji. By way of a warm-up, the sentences in the Grammar Notes and Conversation Notes are given in Kanji and Kana followed by romanization for the first four lessons only.

If you wish to become proficient in reading and writing Japanese, you will have to learn Kanji. Although thousands more are found in dictionaries, the number of Kanji for daily use in Japan is now about 2,000; the basic 1,000 are sufficient to read about 90% of the Kanji used in a newspaper.

1. Hiragana

☆ **The basic 46**

	A	I	U	E	O
	あ a	い i	う u	え e	お o
K	か ka	き ki	く ku	け ke	こ ko
S	さ sa	し shi	す su	せ se	そ so
T	た ta	ち chi	つ tsu	て te	と to
N	な na	に ni	ぬ nu	ね ne	の no
H	は ha	ひ hi	ふ fu	へ he	ほ ho
M	ま ma	み mi	む mu	め me	も mo
Y	や ya	い	ゆ yu	え	よ yo
R	ら ra	り ri	る ru	れ re	ろ ro
W	わ wa	い	う	え	を o
N	ん n				

☆ **Combination with small や、ゆ、よ**

ya	yu	yo
きゃ kya	きゅ kyu	きょ kyo
しゃ sha	しゅ shu	しょ sho
ちゃ cha	ちゅ chu	ちょ cho
にゃ nya	にゅ nyu	にょ nyo
ひゃ hya	ひゅ hyu	ひょ hyo
みゃ mya	みゅ myu	みょ myo
りゃ rya	りゅ ryu	りょ ryo

Hiragana（Handwritten shapes）

☆ **The basic 46**

	A	I	U	E	O
	あ a	い i	う u	え e	お o
K	か ka	き ki	く ku	け ke	こ ko
S	さ sa	し shi	す su	せ se	そ so
T	た ta	ち chi	つ tsu	て te	と to
N	な na	に ni	ぬ nu	ね ne	の no
H	は ha	ひ hi	ふ fu	へ he	ほ ho
M	ま ma	み mi	む mu	め me	も mo
Y	や ya	い	ゆ yu	え	よ yo
R	ら ra	り ri	る ru	れ re	ろ ro
W	わ wa	い	う	え	を o
N	ん n				

☆ **Combination with small や、ゆ、よ**

	ya	yu	yo
	きゃ kya	きゅ kyu	きょ kyo
	しゃ sha	しゅ shu	しょ sho
	ちゃ cha	ちゅ chu	ちょ cho
	にゃ nya	にゅ nyu	にょ nyo
	ひゃ hya	ひゅ hyu	ひょ hyo
	みゃ mya	みゅ myu	みょ myo

りゃ rya	りゅ ryu	りょ ryo

Hiragana

☆ **With two dots** ゛

G	が ga	ぎ gi	ぐ gu	げ ge	ご go
Z	ざ za	じ ji	ず zu	ぜ ze	ぞ zo
D	だ da	ぢ ji	づ zu	で de	ど do
B	ば ba	び bi	ぶ bu	べ be	ぼ bo

ぎゃ gya	ぎゅ gyu	ぎょ gyo
じゃ ja	じゅ ju	じょ jo

びゃ bya	びゅ byu	びょ byo

☆ **With a small circle** ゜

P	ぱ pa	ぴ pi	ぷ pu	ぺ pe	ぽ po

ぴゃ pya	ぴゅ pyu	ぴょ pyo

* Be specially careful with the following Hiragana and sounds:

じ and ぢ＝are the same sound **ji**.

ず and づ＝are the same sound **zu**.

を＝**o**, not **wo**

じゃ，じゅ，じょ＝**ja, ju, jo**

Small っ shows double consonants

e.g. きって＝**kitte**

きっぷ＝**kippu**

きっさてん＝**kissaten**

* Printed shapes and handwritten shapes are slightly different.

Hiragana （Handwritten shapes）

☆ **With two dots** ゛

G	が ga	ぎ gi	ぐ gu	げ ge	ご go	ぎゃ gya	ぎゅ gyu	ぎょ gyo
Z	ざ za	じ ji	ず zu	ぜ ze	ぞ zo	じゃ ja	じゅ ju	じょ jo
D	だ da	ぢ ji	づ zu	で de	ど do			
B	ば ba	び bi	ぶ bu	べ be	ぼ bo	びゃ bya	びゅ byu	びょ byo

☆ **With a small circle** ゜

P	ぱ pa	ぴ pi	ぷ pu	ぺ pe	ぽ po	ぴゃ pya	ぴゅ pyu	ぴょ pyo

* Be careful about the following differences:

Printed shapes　vs.　Handwritten shapes

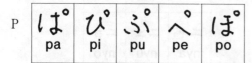

き ⟶ き
さ ⟶ さ
ふ ⟶ ふ
り ⟶ り

2. Katakana

☆ The basic 46

	A	I	U	E	O
	ア a	イ i	ウ u	エ e	オ o
K	カ ka	キ ki	ク ku	ケ ke	コ ko
S	サ sa	シ shi	ス su	セ se	ソ so
T	タ ta	チ chi	ツ tsu	テ te	ト to
N	ナ na	ニ ni	ヌ nu	ネ ne	ノ no
H	ハ ha	ヒ hi	フ fu	ヘ he	ホ ho
M	マ ma	ミ mi	ム mu	メ me	モ mo
Y	ヤ ya	イ	ユ yu	エ	ヨ yo
R	ラ ra	リ ri	ル ru	レ re	ロ ro
W	ワ wa	イ	ウ	エ	ヲ o
N	ン n				

☆ Combination with small ヤ、ユ、ヨ

ya	yu	yo
キャ kya	キュ kyu	キョ kyo
シャ sha	シュ shu	ショ sho
チャ cha	チュ chu	チョ cho
ニャ nya	ニュ nyu	ニョ nyo
ヒャ hya	ヒュ hyu	ヒョ hyo
ミャ mya	ミュ myu	ミョ myo

リャ rya	リュ ryu	リョ ryo

☆ **With two dots** ゛

G	ガ ga	ギ gi	グ gu	ゲ ge	ゴ go		ギャ gya	ギュ gyu	ギョ gyo
Z	ザ za	ジ ji	ズ zu	ゼ ze	ゾ zo		ジャ ja	ジュ ju	ジョ jo
D	ダ da	ヂ ji	ヅ zu	デ de	ド do				
B	バ ba	ビ bi	ブ bu	ベ be	ボ bo		ビャ bya	ビュ byu	ビョ byo

☆ **With a small circle** ゜

P	パ pa	ピ pi	プ pu	ペ pe	ポ po		ピャ pya	ピュ pyu	ピョ pyo

* Katakana can be used in different combinations. See the next section.

3. Katakana words

Katakana are mainly used to write foreign words and sometimes onomatopoeia (sound symbolism). They can also be used for emphasis, like italics or underlining in English.

In this section, we will look at the characteristics of loanwords, which represent the majority of words written in Katakana.

Modern Japanese, just like modern English, has a large number of loanwords from foreign languages. About 60% of the Japanese vocabulary comes from Chinese, while many other words can be traced back to other languages.

The majority of Chinese borrowings is fully integrated into the Japanese language and is written in Kanji (or Hiragana). Others, however, are relatively recent imports, which are still perceived as 'foreign words'; these are written in Katakana.

Most Katakana words (Katakana-go) have come from European languages such as

English, French, Italian, German, Dutch, Spanish and Portuguese; the majority of them are taken from English today. However, katakana-go are often difficult to recognize for English speakers, because their sounds and meanings have changed (some have even been *made up* in Japan!).

Fortunately, such changes do not occur at random, but conform to certain rules; the most important ones are given below:

1) Changes in pronunciation:

A typical Japanese syllable consists of a vowel, or a consonant + vowel. Therefore, an English word like *ice-cream*, which has only two syllables, becomes 'アイスクリーム (a-i-su-ku-ri-i-mu)', If you ask a Japanese speaker to pronounce this word very slowly, s/he will divide it into 7 segments instead of 2. Most consonants take '-u' as the added vowel (e.g. ライス raisu <*rice*, テープ teepu <*tape*, ミルク miruku < *milk*)while 't' and 'd' take '-o'(e.g. プレゼント purezento <*present*, カード kaado < *card*) and some others like 'ch' (and sometimes 'k') take '-i' (e.g. ランチ ranchi < *lunch*、マッチ matchi <*match*).

You can see other basic patterns of sound change below:

[1], [r]	→Japanese /r/		(e.g. ルール ruuru *rule*)
[b], [v]	→b		(e.g. ビーバー biibaa *beaver*)
[ei]	→ee		(e.g. テープ teepu *tape*)
[ou]	→oo		(e.g. コート kooto *coat*)
[ti]	→ti, chi	ティ、チ	(e.g. ティー tii *tea*, チーム chiimu *team*)
[di]	→di, ji	ディ、ジ	(e.g. ディスク disuku *disk*, エジソン ejison *Edison*)
[si]	→Shi	シ	(e.g. シール shiiru *seal*)
[zi]	→ji	ジ	(e.g. ジグザグ jiguzagu *zigzag*)

2) Changes in the writing system

We saw above that the pronunciation of loanwords is often adapted to the Japanese sound system. However, occasionally the writing system of katakana changes to accommodate loanwords.

For example, modern Japanese didn't have the sound **ti**, which consequently was approximated by using **chi**, as in チケット chiketto *ticket*. But today most Japanese speakers can pronounce this foreign sound, and will say, for instance, パーティー **paatii** (*party*) rather than **paachii**.

For such 'non-Japanese' sounds, there are some special Katakana combinations which are used only for loanwords and therefore do not have Hiragana equivalents:

ヴァ va	ヴィ vi	ヴ vu	ヴェ ve	ヴォ vo
		ヴュ vyu		
ツァ tsa	ツィ tsi		ツェ tse	ツォ tso
ファ fa	フィ fi	フュ fyu	フェ fe	フォ fo
	ウィ wi		ウェ we	ウォ wo
	ティ ti	トゥ tu	テュ tyu	
	ディ di	ドゥ du	デュ dyu	
	スィ si			
クァ kwa	クィ kwi		クェ kwe	クォ kwo
			シェ／ジェ	
			チェ che	
			イェ ye	

* As for the change of meaning and form of Katakana word, ⇨L5GI

4. Hiragana exercises

[Exercise 1]　あ　い　う　え　お
　　　　　　　　a　i　u　e　o

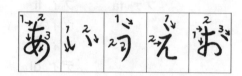

1. **あい** _love_ 　　　 2. **いえ** _house_ 　　　 3. **うえ** _above_
4. **おう** _to chase_ 　 5. **あう** _to meet_ 　 6. **あおい** _blue_
7. **え** _picture_ 　　 8. **おおい** _many_ 　 9. **いい** _good_
10. **いいえ** _no_

[Exercise 2]　か　き　く　け　こ
　　　　　　　　ka　ki　ku　ke　ko

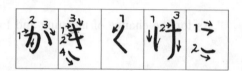

1. **きく** _to hear_ 　 2. **かく** _to write_ 　 3. **ここ** _here_
4. **あかい** _red_ 　　 5. **えき** _station_ 　 6. **おか** _hill_
7. **いけ** _pond_ 　　 8. **こえ** _voice_ 　　 9. **き** _tree_
10. **かう** _to buy_

[Exercise 3]　さ　し　す　せ　そ
　　　　　　　　sa　shi　su　se　so

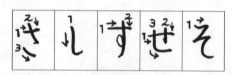

1. **すし** _sushi_ 　　 2. **あさ** _morning_ 　 3. **いす** _chair_
4. **うそ** _lie_ 　　　 5. **おかし** _sweets_ 　 6. **かさ** _umbrella_
7. **せかい** _world_ 　 8. **すき** _like_ 　　 9. **すこし** _a little_
10. **しお** _salt_

[Exercise 4]　た　ち　つ　て　と
　　　　　　　　ta　chi　tsu　te　to

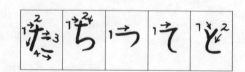

1. **て** _hand_ 　　　 2. **とち** _land_ 　　 3. **たつ** _to stand up_
4. **あつい** _hot_ 　　 5. **ちかい** _near_ 　 6. **たかい** _expensive_
7. **てつ** _iron_ 　　 8. **つくえ** _desk_ 　 9. **した** _under_
10. **ちかてつ** _subway, underground (train)_

[Exercise 5]　な　に　ぬ　ね　の
　　　　　　　na　ni　nu　ne　no

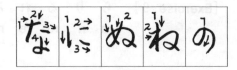

1. なな　*seven*　　　2. に　*two*　　　　　3. なに　*what?*
4. あなた　*you*　　　5. おかね　*money*　　6. さかな　*fish*
7. にく　*meat*　　　　8. いぬ　*dog*　　　　9. ねこ　*cat*
10. ぬの　*cloth*

[Exercise 6]　は　ひ　ふ　へ　ほ
　　　　　　　ha　hi　hu　he　ho

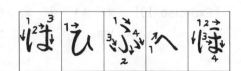

1. はは　*mother*　　　2. ひ　*day/fire*　　3. ほほ　*cheek*
4. ひと　*person*　　　5. はい　*yes*　　　　6. ふね　*ship*
7. はこ　*box*　　　　　8. ほし　*star*　　　9. はち　*eight*
10. はな　*flower/nose*

[Exercise 7]　ま　み　む　め　も
　　　　　　　ma　mi　mu　me　mo

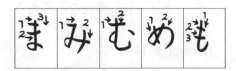

1. め　*eye*　　　　　　2. みみ　*ear*　　　　3. いま　*now*
4. なまえ　*name*　　　5. うみ　*sea*　　　　6. のむ　*to drink*
7. あめ　*rain*　　　　　8. みせ　*shop*　　　9. さむい　*cold*
10. ねむい　*sleepy*

[Exercise 8]　や　い　ゆ　え　よ
　　　　　　　ya　　yu　　yo

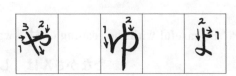

1. やま　*mountain*　　2. ゆき　*snow*　　　3. よむ　*to read*
4. ゆめ　*dream*　　　　5. へや　*room*　　　6. ふゆ　*winter*
7. やすい　*cheap*　　　8. つよい　*strong*　9. やすみ　*holiday*
10. やさしい　*easy/gentle*

[Exercise 9] らりるれろ
ra ri ru re ro

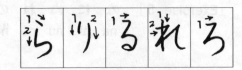

1. **そら** *sky*   2. **かれ** *he*   3. **ねる** *to sleep*
4. **これ** *this*   5. **くすり** *medicine*   6. **さくら** *cherry*
7. **はる** *spring*   8. **くろい** *black*   9. **しろい** *white*
10. **ふろ** *bath*

[Exercise 10] わ い う え を
wa   o

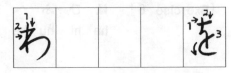

1. **わたし** *I*   2. **かわ** *river*   3. **にわ** *garden*
4. **おわり** *end*   5. **わるい** *bad*   6. **わかい** *young*
7. **なまえを かく** *to write* (one's) *name*
8. **くすりを のむ** *to take* (some) *medicine*
9. **くつしたを かう** *to buy* (a pair of) *socks*
10. **うたを うたう** *to sing a song*

[Exercise 11] ん
n

1. **ほん** *book*   2. **しけん** *test*   3. **おんな** *woman*
4. **きん** *gold*   5. **にほん** *Japan*   6. **せんせい** *teacher*
7. **たなかさん** *Mr/Ms. Tanaka*   8. **しんせつ** *kind*
9. **せんもん** *field of study*   10. **てんき** *weather*

* Be careful with the reading of **は** [wa] and **へ** [e] when they are used as particles.

1. **たなかさんは しんせつです。** *Mr. Tanaka is kind.*
2. **これは はこではありません。** *This is not a box.*
3. **せんもんは なんですか。** *What is your field of study?*
4. **こうえんへ いきます。** (*I'm*) *going to the park.*
5. **いつ にほんへ きましたか。** *When did you come to Japan?*

[Exercise 12]　が　ぎ　ぐ　げ　ご
　　　　　　　ga gi gu ge go

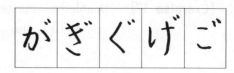

1. かぎ　*key*　　　2. げか　*surgery*　　3. ご　*five*
4. にほんご　*Japanese language*　　5. かぐ　*furniture*
6. がいこく　*foreign country*

[Exercise 13]　ざ　じ　ず　ぜ　ぞ
　　　　　　　za ji zu ze zo

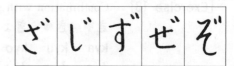

1. じこ　*accident*　　2. かぜ　*wind*　　3. しずか　*quiet*
4. くじ　*9 o'clock*　　5. かぞく　*family*　　6. ひざ　*knee*

[Exercise 14]　だ　ぢ　づ　で　ど
　　　　　　　da ji zu de do

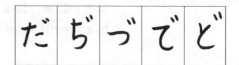

1. どこ　*where?*　　2. だれ　*who?*　　3. どうぞ　*please*
4. うで　*arm*　　5. でぐち　*exit*　　6. だいがく　*university*

[Exercise 15]　ば　び　ぶ　べ　ぼ
　　　　　　　ba bi bu be bo

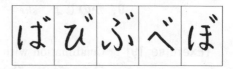

1. そば　*noodle*　　2. ぶた　*pig*　　3. かべ　*wall*
4. しんぶん　*newspaper*　　5. ぼこくご　*native language*
6. げつようび　*Monday*

[Exercise 16]　ぱ　ぴ　ぷ　ぺ　ぽ
　　　　　　　pa pi pu pe po

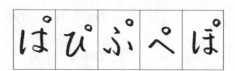

1. えんぴつ　*pencil*　　　2. かんぱい　*toast*
3. さんぽ　*a walk*　　　4. さんぷん　*3 minutes*
5. ぺこぺこ　*hungry*

[**Exercise 17**] Double consonants っ
-ss-/-tt-/-kk-/-pp-

1. **ざっし** *magazine*   2. **きって** *stamp*
3. **にっき** *diary*   4. **けっこん** *marriage*
5. **きっぷ** *ticket*

[**Exercise 18**] Combination with small や、ゆ、よ：

きゃ	きゅ	きょ	ぎゃ	ぎゅ	ぎょ
kya	kyu	kyo	gya	gyu	gyo
しゃ	しゅ	しょ	じゃ	じゅ	じょ
sha	shu	sho	ja	ju	jo
ちゃ	ちゅ	ちょ			
cha	chu	cho			
にゃ	にゅ	にょ			
nya	nyu	nyo			

1. **きゃく** *guest*   2. **きょねん** *last year*
3. **いしゃ** *doctor*   4. **しゅみ** *hobby*
5. **じしょ** *dictionary*   6. **おちゃ** *tea*
7. **ちょっと** *a little*   8. **こんにゃく** *a kind of Japanese food*
9. **かのじょ** *she*   10. **ぎょせん** *fishing boat*

[**Exercise 19**] Combination with small や、ゆ、よ（continued）：

ひゃ	ひゅ	ひょ	びゃ	びゅ	びょ	ぴゃ	ぴゅ	ぴょ
hya	hyu	hyo	bya	byu	byo	pya	pyu	pyo
みゃ	みゅ	みょ						
mya	myu	myo						
りゃ	りゅ	りょ						
rya	ryu	ryo						

1. **ひゃく** *100*   2. **さんびゃく** *300*
3. **ろっぴゃく** *600*   4. **さんみゃく** *mountain range*
5. **りゃく** *abbreviation*   6. **どりょく** *effort*
7. **りゅうこう** *fashion*   8. **りょかん** *Japanese inn*

[Exercise 20]　　Long [ee] sound:

えい	けい	せい	てい	ねい	へい	めい	れい
ee	kee	see	tee	nee	hee	mee	ree
げい	ぜい	でい		べい			
gee	zee	dee		bee			
				ぺい			
				pee			

1. えいご　*English*
2. とけい　*watch/clock*
3. せんせい　*teacher*
4. ていねい　*polite*
5. へいわ　*peace*
6. めいし　*name card*
7. きれい　*beautiful*
8. げいじゅつ　*art*
9. ぜいきん　*tax*
10. なんべい　*South America*

Exceptions：ええ　*yes*　／おねえさん　*elder sister*

[Exercise 21]　　Long [oo] sound:

おう	こう	そう	とう	のう	ほう	もう	ろう
oo	koo	soo	too	noo	hoo	moo	roo
ごう	ぞう	どう		ぼう			
goo	zoo	doo		boo			
				ぽう			
				poo			

1. がっこう　*school*
2. そうじ　*cleaning*
3. ありがとう　*thank you*
4. きのう　*yesterday*
5. ほうりつ　*law*
6. いもうと　*younger sister*
7. ろうか　*corridor*
8. にちようび　*Sunday*
9. ぞう　*elephant*
10. でんぽう　*telegram*
11. ばんごう　*number*
12. ぼうし　*hat, cap*

Exceptions：おおい　*many*　／おおきい　*big*
　　　　　　こおる　*to freeze*　／こおり　*ice*
　　　　　　とおる　*to pass by*　／とおい　*far*
　　　　　　おおさか　*Osaka*　／etc.

Pre-Session

1. Predicates
2. Actual use of predicates

1. Predicates

Predicates conjugate according to whether they are

(1) plain (= non-polite) or polite,
(2) positive or negative,
(3) non-past or past.

This can be illustrated as follows.

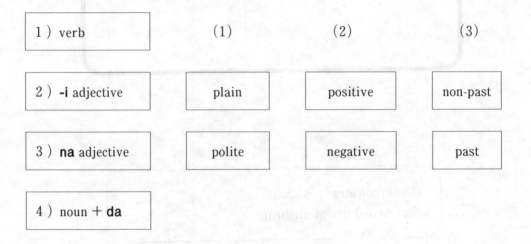

1) verb	(1)	(2)	(3)
2) **-i** adjective	plain	positive	non-past
3) **na** adjective	polite	negative	past
4) noun + **da**			

Let's take a verb as an example. In step (1), you choose between the plain (= non-polite) and polite forms. There are two speech styles in Japanese, casual (= informal) and formal, from which you make a choice according to the relationship between yourself (the speaker) and the listener.

The plain form is used in casual style sentences, while the polite form is used in formal style sentences. ⇨Introduction I. Grammar

In step (2), you choose between the positive and negative forms.

In step (3), you choose either the non-past or the past form. Use non-past for describing a habitual action or state, or an action/state in the future. Use past for actions or states that have already taken place.

1) verb: iku (*I*)(*will*) *go.*

		Positive	Negative
Casual style (Plain)	Non-past	**iku**	**ikanai**
	Past	**itta**	**ikanakatta**
Formal style (Polite)	Non-past	**ikimasu**	**ikimasen**
	Past	**ikimashita**	**ikimasen deshita**

<verb>　Formal style indicator:　　**-mas-**

　　　　　　Negative indicator:　　**-na(i)-**　（casual style）

　　　　　　　　　　　　　　　　-masen-　（formal style）

　　　　　Past indicator:　　　　**-ta-**

2) -i adjective: omoshiroi (*It*) *is interesting.*

		Positive	Negative
Casual style (Plain)	Non-past	**omoshiroi**	**omoshiroku nai**
	Past	**omoshirokatta**	**omoshiroku nakatta**
Formal style (Polite)	Non-past	**omoshiroi desu**	**omoshiroku arimasen** **omoshiroku nai desu**
	Past	**omoshirokatta desu**	**omoshiroku arimasen deshita** **omoshiroku nakatta desu**

<**-i** adjective>

　　　Formal style indicator:　　　**-des-**

　　　　　　　　　　　　　　　　-mas-　　　（negative）

　　　Negative indicator:　　　　**-na(i)-**　（casual style）

　　　　　　　　　　　　　　　　-arimasen-（formal style）

　　　　　Past indicator:　　　　**-ta**

3) **na** adjective: **genki da** (*I*) *am well.*

		Positive	Negative
Casual style （Plain）	Non-past	**genki da**	**genki ja nai**
	Past	**genki datta**	**genki ja nakatta**
Formal style （Polite）	Non-past	**genki desu**	**genki ja arimasen** **genki ja nai desu**
	Past	**genki deshita**	**genki ja arimasen deshita** **genki ja nakatta desu**

4) noun + **da**: **Yamada-san da** *It is Yamada-san.*

		Positive	Negative
Casual style （Plain）	Non-past	**Yamada-san da**	**Yamada-san ja nai**
	Past	**Yamada-san datta**	**Yamada-san ja nakatta**
Formal style （Polite）	Non-past	**Yamada-san desu**	**Yamada-san ja arimasen** **Yamada-san ja nai desu**
	Past	**Yamada-san deshita**	**Yamada-san ja arimasen** **deshita** **Yamada-san ja nakatta desu**

＜**na** adjective＞／＜noun + **da**＞

Formal style indicator:	**-des-** **-mas-**	
Negative indicator:	**-ja na(i)-**	（casual style）
	-ja arimasen-	（formal style）
Past indicator:	**-ta**	

2. Actual use of predicates

Now that you are familiar with Japanese predicates, let's study them in natural conversation.

1) Verb sentences (sentences which end in a verb)

【*Examples*】

Non-past

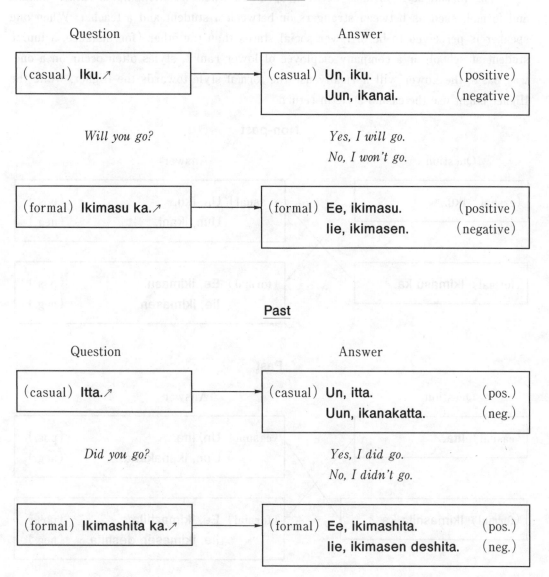

Question	Answer
(casual) **Iku.**↗	(casual) **Un, iku.** (positive)
	Uun, ikanai. (negative)
Will you go?	*Yes, I will go.*
	No, I won't go.
(formal) **Ikimasu ka.**↗	(formal) **Ee, ikimasu.** (positive)
	Iie, ikimasen. (negative)

Past

Question	Answer
(casual) **Itta.**↗	(casual) **Un, itta.** (pos.)
	Uun, ikanakatta. (neg.)
Did you go?	*Yes, I did go.*
	No, I didn't go.
(formal) **Ikimashita ka.**↗	(formal) **Ee, ikimashita.** (pos.)
	Iie, ikimasen deshita. (neg.)

【*Explanation*】

The final particle **ka** is added to the end of a formal question. In a casual question, **ka** is omitted; instead, rising intonation is used to signal the question. Avoid using plain form + **ka**, as in **iku ka**—it sounds rude.

Both **un** and **ee** mean *yes*. **Ee**(sometimes **hai**) is more polite than **un**.

Uun and **iie** mean *no*, but **iie** (sometimes pronounced **ie**) is politer than **uun**.

The casual style is used between people who are close, such as family members or good friends.

The formal style is used between speakers whose relationship is rather distant and formal, such as between strangers or between a student and a teacher. When one speaker is perceived to be of lower social status than the other (for instance, a junior student at school, or a company employee of lower rank), styles often occur on a one-way basis: the Lower will normally use the formal style towards the Higher, while the Higher might use the casual style in return.

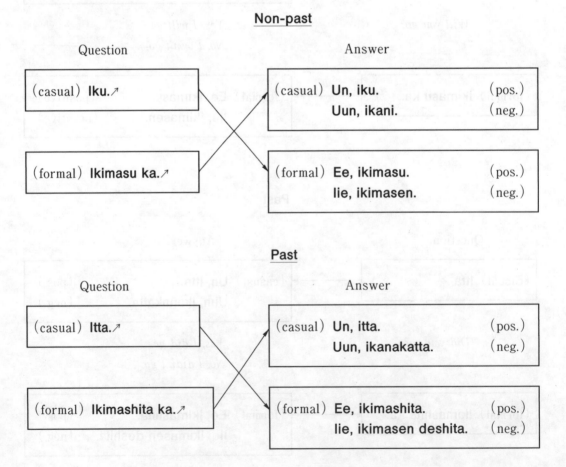

Non-past

Question	Answer

(casual) **Iku.**↗

(formal) **Ikimasu ka.**↗

(casual) **Un, iku.** (pos.)
Uun, ikani. (neg.)

(formal) **Ee, ikimasu.** (pos.)
Iie, ikimasen. (neg.)

Past

Question	Answer

(casual) **Itta.**↗

(formal) **Ikimashita ka.**↗

(casual) **Un, itta.** (pos.)
Uun, ikanakatta. (neg.)

(formal) **Ee, ikimashita.** (pos.)
Iie, ikimasen deshita. (neg.)

2) **Adjective sentences** (sentences ending in an **-i** adjective or a **na** adjective

(1) **-i** adjectives

【*Examples*】

Non-past

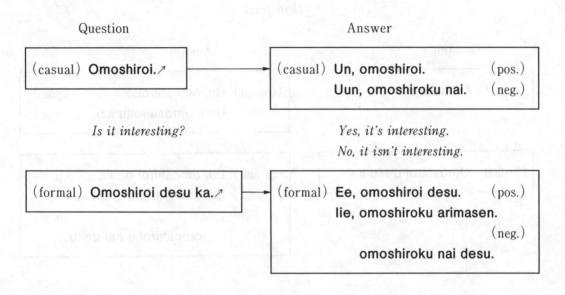

Question

(casual) **Omoshiroi.**↗

Is it interesting?

(formal) **Omoshiroi desu ka.**↗

Answer

(casual) **Un, omoshiroi.** (pos.)
Uun, omoshiroku nai. (neg.)

Yes, it's interesting.
No, it isn't interesting.

(formal) **Ee, omoshiroi desu.** (pos.)
Iie, omoshiroku arimasen.
(neg.)
omoshiroku nai desu.

Past

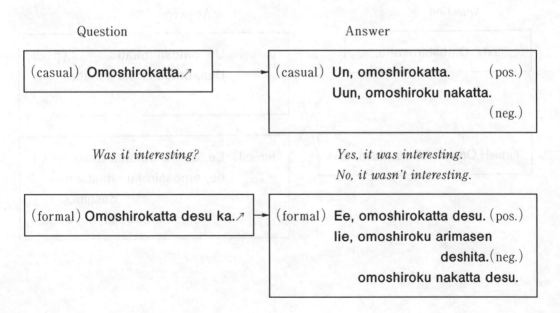

Question

(casual) **Omoshirokatta.**↗

Was it interesting?

(formal) **Omoshirokatta desu ka.**↗

Answer

(casual) **Un, omoshirokatta.** (pos.)
Uun, omoshiroku nakatta.
(neg.)

Yes, it was interesting.
No, it wasn't interesting.

(formal) **Ee, omoshirokatta desu.** (pos.)
Iie, omoshiroku arimasen
deshita. (neg.)
omoshiroku nakatta desu.

【*Explanation*】

Just as with verb sentences, **ka** is usually omitted in a casual question using an adjective sentence, too.

Desu is added to the plain form of an **-i** adjective to make the polite form.

The casual and formal styles can occur together as follows:

Non-past

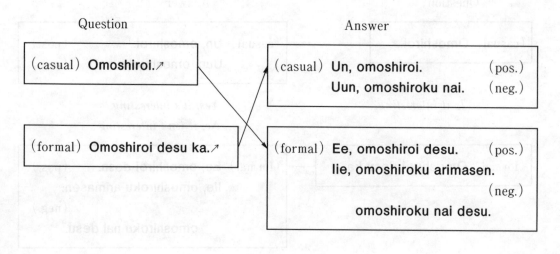

Question	Answer
(casual) **Omoshiroi.**↗	(casual) **Un, omoshiroi.** (pos.) **Uun, omoshiroku nai.** (neg.)
(formal) **Omoshiroi desu ka.**↗	(formal) **Ee, omoshiroi desu.** (pos.) **Iie, omoshiroku arimasen.** (neg.) **omoshiroku nai desu.**

Past

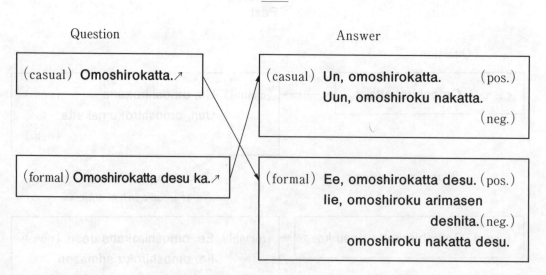

Question	Answer
(casual) **Omoshirokatta.**↗	(casual) **Un, omoshirokatta.** (pos.) **Uun, omoshiroku nakatta.** (neg.)
(formal) **Omoshirokatta desu ka.**↗	(formal) **Ee, omoshirokatta desu.** (pos.) **Iie, omoshiroku arimasen deshita.** (neg.) **omoshiroku nakatta desu.**

(2) **na** adjectives

【*Examples*】

Non-past

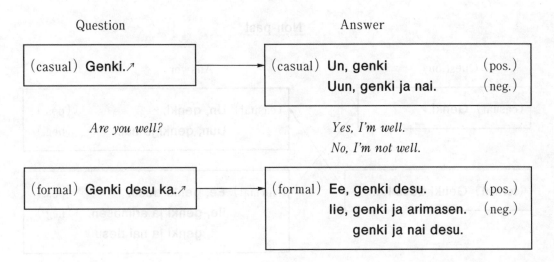

Question	Answer
(casual) **Genki.**↗	(casual) **Un, genki** (pos.) **Uun, genki ja nai.** (neg.)
Are you well?	*Yes, I'm well.* *No, I'm not well.*
(formal) **Genki desu ka.**↗	(formal) **Ee, genki desu.** (pos.) **Iie, genki ja arimasen.** (neg.) **genki ja nai desu.**

Past

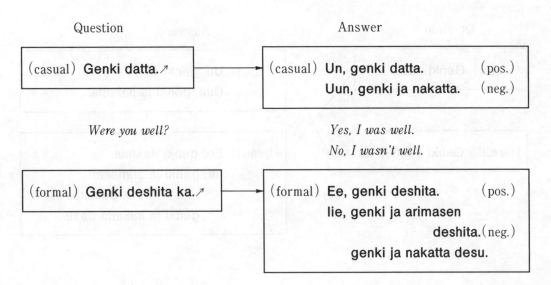

Question	Answer
(casual) **Genki datta.**↗	(casual) **Un, genki datta.** (pos.) **Uun, genki ja nakatta.** (neg.)
Were you well?	*Yes, I was well.* *No, I wasn't well.*
(formal) **Genki deshita ka.**↗	(formal) **Ee, genki deshita.** (pos.) **Iie, genki ja arimasen** **deshita.** (neg.) **genki ja nakatta desu.**

【*Explanation*】

Do not use **genki da ka**↗ or **genki ka**↗ in a casual question, because it sounds very rude. **Da** is also normally omitted in casual positive answers.

Casual and formal styles occur together as follows.

Non-past

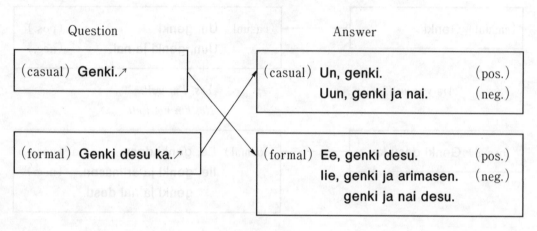

Question		Answer	
(casual) **Genki.**↗		(casual) **Un, genki.**	(pos.)
		Uun, genki ja nai.	(neg.)
(formal) **Genki desu ka.**↗		(formal) **Ee, genki desu.**	(pos.)
		Iie, genki ja arimasen.	(neg.)
		genki ja nai desu.	

Past

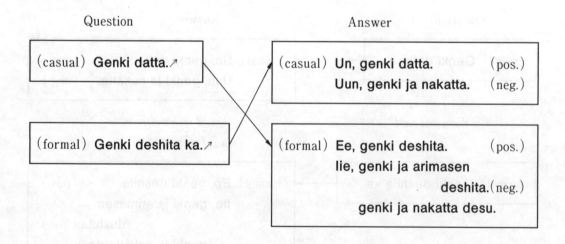

Question		Answer	
(casual) **Genki datta.**↗		(casual) **Un, genki datta.**	(pos.)
		Uun, genki ja nakatta.	(neg.)
(formal) **Genki deshita ka.**↗		(formal) **Ee, genki deshita.**	(pos.)
		Iie, genki ja arimasen	
		deshita.	(neg.)
		genki ja nakatta desu.	

3) Noun sentences (sentences ending in noun + **da**)

Noun + **da** works in the same way as a **na** adjective in both the casual and the formal styles.

【*Examples*】

Non-past

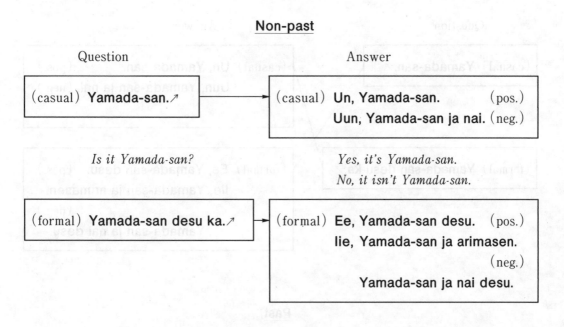

Question

(casual) **Yamada-san.**↗

→ (casual) **Un, Yamada-san.** (pos.)
Uun, Yamada-san ja nai. (neg.)

Is it Yamada-san?

Yes, it's Yamada-san.
No, it isn't Yamada-san.

(formal) **Yamada-san desu ka.**↗

→ (formal) **Ee, Yamada-san desu.** (pos.)
Iie, Yamada-san ja arimasen. (neg.)
Yamada-san ja nai desu.

Past

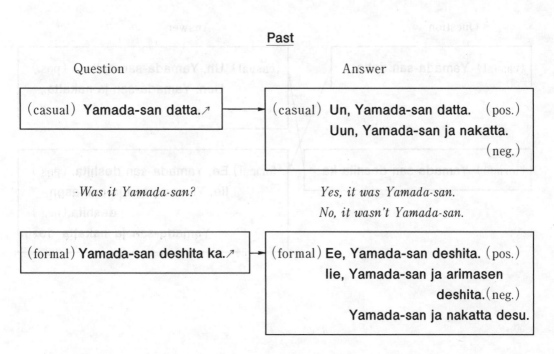

Question

(casual) **Yamada-san datta.**↗

→ (casual) **Un, Yamada-san datta.** (pos.)
Uun, Yamada-san ja nakatta. (neg.)

Was it Yamada-san?

Yes, it was Yamada-san.
No, it wasn't Yamada-san.

(formal) **Yamada-san deshita ka.**↗

→ (formal) **Ee, Yamada-san deshita.** (pos.)
Iie, Yamada-san ja arimasen deshita. (neg.)
Yamada-san ja nakatta desu.

【*Explanation*】

Casual and formal styles occur together as follows.

Non-past

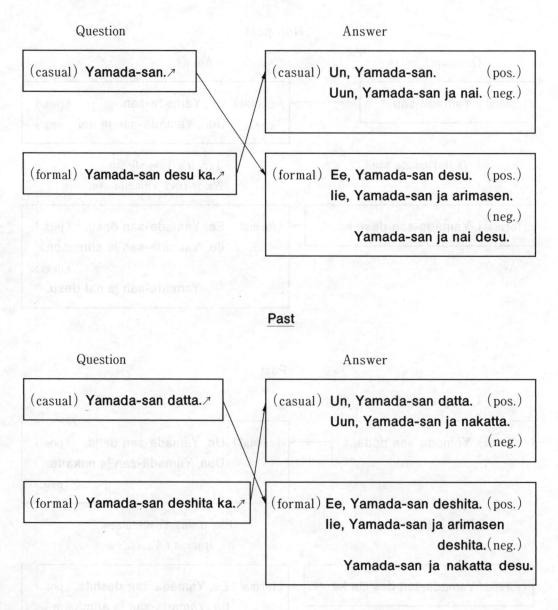

Question

(casual) **Yamada-san.**↗

(formal) **Yamada-san desu ka.**↗

Answer

(casual) **Un, Yamada-san.** (pos.)
Uun, Yamada-san ja nai. (neg.)

(formal) **Ee, Yamada-san desu.** (pos.)
Iie, Yamada-san ja arimasen.
(neg.)
Yamada-san ja nai desu.

Past

Question

(casual) **Yamada-san datta.**↗

(formal) **Yamada-san deshita ka.**↗

Answer

(casual) **Un, Yamada-san datta.** (pos.)
Uun, Yamada-san ja nakatta.
(neg.)

(formal) **Ee, Yamada-san deshita.** (pos.)
**Iie, Yamada-san ja arimasen
deshita.** (neg.)
Yamada-san ja nakatta desu.

Characters in Model Conversations

Ichiro Kimura

He is a professor in the Department of Computer Science at the University of Matsumi. He is Yamashita and Sharma's academic advisor. He is 54 years old and married. He has two daughters.

Kazuo Yamashita

He is in the first year of the Ph.D. course in Computer Science. He is 25 years old and single. He is reliable and hardworking. He lives in an apartment house near the university.

Anil Sharma

He is a research student now and going to sit for the entrance examination for the Ph.D. course in Computer Science next year. He is 27 years old and married. His wife and one year-old baby are now in their country, India. He is a hardworking and logical type. He lives in the dormitory.

Midori Tanaka

She is in the first year of the M.A. course in Business Administration, but she is using computers for statistical analysis and comes to Prof. Kimura's office. She is 23 years old and single. She is frank, active and cheerful. She likes Yamashita-san. She lives in the dormitory.

Lisa Brown

She is British and she is in the first year of the M.A. course in Business Administration. She is learning statistical analysis by using computers together with Tanaka-san. She is 24 years old and single. She is a quiet and naive woman, so she sometimes feels puzzled when Suzuki-san forces his attentions on her.

Tadashi Suzuki

He is an assistant in the Department of Computer Science and Yamashita's senior. He is 30 years old and single. He is aggressive and sometimes overconfident but good-natured and optimistic. He likes Lisa. He is a member of the university chorus club.

Human Relationships and Situations
in the Model Conversations

University

Reception party L1
Dormitory L4, L5
Dormitory office L6
Professor's office L8
Library L15
Seminar room L20, L23, L24

Professor Kimura

Prof. Kimura's wife

Assistant Suzuki

Prof. Kimura's home L19

Landlady
Apartment house L21

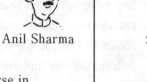

Lisa Brown   Tanaka   Yamashita   Anil Sharma

Sharma's wife

M.A. course in
Business Administration

Ph.D. course in
Computer Science

Neighbour
Apartment house L21

Post office L2
Restaurant L3
Hospital L9, L22
Department store L10
Bookshop L11
Road L12
Coffee shop L13, L17

☎ Phoning

Hospital L7
Bus company office L14
Taxi company L16
Prof. Kimura's home L18

紹介する
しょうかい
Introducing people

OBJECTIVES:

GRAMMAR

Ⅰ. ～です
Ⅱ. は and も〈1〉: discourse particles
Ⅲ. Question sentences
Ⅳ. の〈1〉: modifying nouns
Ⅴ. と〈1〉 *and*: connective particle

CONVERSATION

＜General Information＞
1. Formal introductions
2. Addressing people
3. Short questions and responses
4. *Aizuchi*

＜Strategies＞
S-1. How to start a conversation —1. At a party
S-2. How to introduce yourself or others
S-3. How to end a conversation —1. After a meeting

Model Conversation

Characters : Professor Kimura（木村）, Yamashita（山下）, Anil Sharma（アニル・シャルマ）

Situation : Yamashita-san meets his academic advisor Kimura-sensee at a reception. Kimura-sensee introduces Sharma-san, a student from India to him.

Flow-chart :

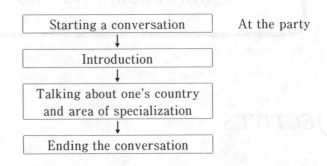

Starting a conversation	At the party

↓

Introduction

↓

Talking about one's country and area of specialization

↓

Ending the conversation

―パーティーで―

木　村：ああ、山下くん。ちょっと。
山　下：はい。
　　　　あ、先生。こんにちは。
木　村：こんにちは。

　　　　　＊　　　＊　　　＊

木　村：山下くん、こちら、インドのアニル・シャルマさん。
シャルマ：はじめまして。アニル・シャルマです。
山　下：あ、どうも。
木　村：シャルマさん、うちの研究室の山下くんです。
山　下：山下です。どうぞよろしく。
シャルマ：どうぞよろしく。

　　　　　＊　　　＊　　　＊

山　下：ええと、アニ……
シャルマ：アニル・シャルマです。
　　　　シャルマと呼んでください。
山　下：あ、じゃ、シャルマさん。あの、お国は。
シャルマ：インドです。

2

山　下　：そうですか。ご専門は。

シャルマ：コンピュータです。

山　下　：ああ、ぼくもコンピュータなんですよ。

シャルマ：そうですか。よろしくお願いします。

山　下　：こちらこそ、よろしく。

　　　　　　＊　　　＊　　　＊

山　下　：それじゃ、シャルマさん、また。

シャルマ：はい。じゃ、失礼します。

こちら、
インドの
アニル・
シャルマさん。

はじめまして。
アニル・シャルマ
です。どうぞ
よろしく。

山下です。
どうぞ
よろしく。

Report

　山下さんは松見大学の大学院の学生です。山下さんの専門はコンピュータです。シャルマさんはインドの留学生です。シャルマさんの専門もコンピュータです。山下さんとシャルマさんは木村先生の研究室の学生です。

New Words and Expressions

Words in the conversation

パーティー	paatii	*party*
ああ		*Oh*
山下くん	やましたくん	*Yamashita-kun*（addressing people）
はい		*yes*
あ		*Oh*（used when noticing something / someone）
先生	せんせい	*professor, teacher*
こちら		*this*（polite）
インド	Indo	*India*
シャルマさん	Sharuma さん	*Sharma-san*（addressing people）
です		*is/am/are*
うち		*my, our*
研究室	けんきゅうしつ	*seminar, professor's office*
じゃ		*then, in that case*
あの		*Um*（often used before addressing a stranger.）
お国	おくに	*someone else's country*（**お** is for politeness）
ご専門	ごせんもん	*someone else's field of study*（**ご** is also for politeness）
コンピュータ	konpyuuta	*computer, computer science*
ぼく		*I*（casual, used by male speaker）
また		*again*

＜*Expressions in the conversation*＞

ちょっと。　　　　　　　　　　*(Come here) for a moment.*

　ちょっと *a little* is used here as an attention getter. ⇨まとめ２ＢⅡ１.

あ、先生。　　　　　　　　　*Oh, professor.*
せんせい

　あ is a kind of interjection. ⇨まとめ１ＢⅡ３.

　先生 is used to refer to teachers, doctors, and politicians, but not normally to indicate teacher as an occupation. For that, **教師 (kyooshi)** may be used. ⇨CN2

4

Ａ：お仕事は。	*What is your job?*
Ｂ：高校の教師です。	*I'm a high school teacher.*

こんにちは。　　　　　　　　　　*Good afternoon. /Hello.*

(lit. Today (is a good day).) ⇨CN S-1

はじめまして。　　　　　　　　　*How do you do?*

Used when meeting for the first time. ⇨CN S-2

どうも。　　　　　　　　　　　　*Nice to meet you. /Thanks. /Sorry.*

/Please./etc.

A handy expression for greetings, thanks, apology, requests, etc.
⇨L3CN S-2

どうぞよろしく。　　　　　　　*Glad to meet you. (lit. Please be kind (to me.))* ⇨CN1,S-2

ええと、　　　　　　　　　　　　*Well. /Let me see,*

Used when hesitating before replying. ⇨まとめ1BⅡ3

～と呼んでください。　　　　　*Please call me～.* ⇨ CN S-2

そうですか。↘　　　　　　　　*I see. /Really? /Is that so?*

Pronounced with falling intonation. With rising intonation, it becomes a question. ⇨CN4

～（な）んですよ。　　　　　　*You see, ～/I'm telling you～*

～んです is used to emphasize that one is giving an explanation.
⇨L5GNⅤ,L7GNⅡ

よろしくお願いします。　　　*I'm glad to meet you.*

This is a polite way of saying **どうぞよろしく**. ⇨CN1,S-2

こちらこそ　　　　　　　　　　*And you.*

This is used not only for greetings but also for requests, thanks, apology, etc.

①	Ａ：どうぞよろしく。	*I'm glad to meet you.*
	Ｂ：こちらこそ、よろしく。	*I'm glad to meet YOU.*
②	Ａ：どうもありがとう。	*Thank you.*
	Ｂ：こちらこそ。	*Thank YOU.*
③	Ａ：すみません。	*I'm sorry.*
	Ｂ：いえ。こちらこそ、すみません。	*No, no. I am sorry.*

5

それじゃ、また。   *See you again.* ⇨CN S-3

    それじゃ/じゃ ⇨ まとめ2BⅡ2

失礼します。   *Please excuse me.* ⇨CN S-3
しつれい

A polite way of saying *goodbye*. This phrase is used when one leaves a meeting, ends a telephone conversation, etc.

Words in the report

松見大学	まつみだいがく	*Matsumi University*
大学院	だいがくいん	*graduate school*
学生	がくせい	*student*
留学生	りゅうがくせい	*foreign student*
木村先生	きむらせんせい	*Prof. Kimura*

Grammar Notes

I. ～です

【*Explanation*】

(I/You/He/She) am/are/is a student. is expressed in Japanese as:

学生です。

Gakusee desu.

Desu （and **da**, the plain form of **desu**）is equivalent to English *am / are / is*.
The negative form of **desu** is **ja arimasen** （or the more formal **de wa arimasen**）.

学生じゃありません。

Gakusee ja arimasen.　　　　　　　*(I/You/He/She) am/are/is not a student.*

学生ではありません。

Gakusee de wa arimasen.

To make the statement a question, add **ka** to the end of the sentence:

学生ですか。　　　　　　　　*Am / are / is (I / you / he / she) a student?*

Gakusee desu ka.

The following is a table showing the polite and plain forms of [N] **desu**.

Polite and plain forms of [N] desu				
	Non-past		Past	
	Positive	Negative	Positive	Negative
Polite	[N] desu	[N] ja arimasen [N] de wa arimasen	[N] deshita	[N] ja arimasen deshita [N] de wa arimasen deshita
Plain	[N] da	[N] ja nai [N] de wa nai	[N] datta	[N] ja nakatta [N] de wa nakatta

II. 🐟 は and も〈1〉: discourse particles

Examples

① **シャルマさんは学生です。**　　　　　　　*Sharma-san is a student.*

　　Sharuma-san wa gakusee desu.

② **木村さんは学生じゃありません。**　　　*Kimura-san isn't a student.*

　　Kimura-san wa gakusee ja arimasen.

③ **ブラウンさんも学生です。**　　　　　　　*Brown-san is also a student.*

　　Buraun-san mo gakusee desu.

【*Explanation*】

1. wa: topic particle

Attach **wa** to the word you want to talk about and put it at the beginning of the sentence, then add a comment or question. Let's call this a topic sentence. Look at the following illustration.

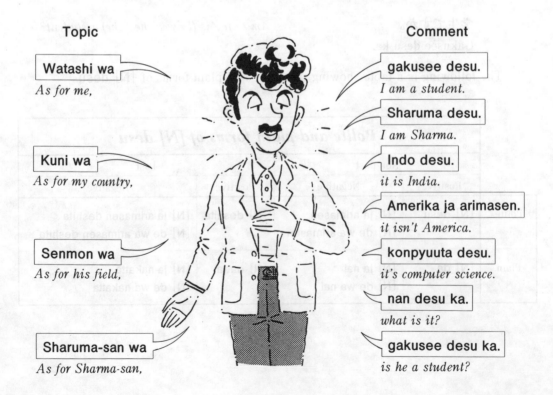

Topic		Comment
Watashi wa		**gakusee desu.**
As for me,		*I am a student.*
		Sharuma desu.
		I am Sharma.
Kuni wa		**Indo desu.**
As for my country,		*it is India.*
		Amerika ja arimasen.
		it isn't America.
Senmon wa		**konpyuuta desu.**
As for his field,		*it's computer science.*
		nan desu ka.
		what is it?
Sharuma-san wa		**gakusee desu ka.**
As for Sharma-san,		*is he a student?*

[N] **wa** is often omitted when it is understood from the situation. Topic sentences such as **Watashi wa gakusee desu** can be translated simply as *I am a student.* as long as the topic is not stressed（by intonation）. ⇨L2GNⅢ, L3GNⅢ, L4GNⅡ

2. mo: *also*

　　Mo *also, too,* can also be used to make a word a topic. All you need to do is to replace **wa** with **mo**.

1. シャルマさんは学生です。　　　　　*Sharma-san is a student.*
   Sharuma-san <u>wa</u> gakusee desu.

2. ブラウンさんも学生です。　　　　　*Brown-san is also a student.*
   Buraun-san <u>mo</u> gakusee desu.

3. シャルマさんは先生じゃありません。　*Sharuma-san isn't a teacher.*
   Sharuma-san <u>wa</u> sensee ja arimasen.

4. ブラウンさんも先生じゃありません。　*Brown-san isn't a teacher, either.*
   Buraun-san <u>mo</u> sensee ja arimasen.

Ⅲ. Question sentences

Examples

① A：シャルマさんは留学生ですか。　　*Is Sharma-san a foreign student?*
　　Sharuma-san wa ryuugakusee desu ka.

　 B：ええ、留学生です。　　　　　　　*Yes, he's a foreign student.*
　　Ee, ryuugakusee desu.

　　 いいえ、留学生じゃありません。　　*No, he isn't a foreign student.*
　　Iie, ryuugakusee ja arimasen.

② A：専門は何ですか。　　　　　　　　*What's your field of study?*
　　Senmon wa nan desu ka.

　 B：コンピュータです。　　　　　　　*It's computer science.*
　　Konpyuuta desu.

【*Explanation*】

1. Yes / No questions

① is called a Yes/No question, because it requires an answer that begins with **ee** (or the more formal **hai**) *yes* in a positive response, or **iie** (or **ie**, a short form of **iie**) *no* in a negative one. The answer is then completed with **[N] desu,** / **[N] ja arimasen.** ⇨CN3C,まとめ2AⅣ

Note that in ① **Sharuma-san wa**, the topic, is omitted in B's answer. It is usual to omit **[N] wa** when answering a question beginning with **[N] wa**, because the topic is understood from the context.　⇨CN3

Sharuma-san wa ryuugakusee desu ka.

Ee, ryuugakusee desu.

You can also simply answer **Soo desu** *That's right.* (*lit. It is so.*), or **Soo ja arimasen** (*lit. It's not so.*); in a negative response you can also use **Chigaimasu** *That's incorrect.* (*lit. It's different.*):

> **A：シャルマさんは留学生ですか。**
>
> Sharuma-san wa ryuugakusee desu ka.
>
> *Is Sharma-san a foreign student?*

> **B：ええ、そうです。**
>
> Ee, soo desu.
>
> *Yes, he is.*

> **いいえ、そうじゃありません。／いいえ、ちがいます。**
>
> Iie, soo ja arimasen. /Iie, chigaimasu.
>
> *No, he isn't.*

Avoid addressing the listener with **anata wa** *you,* which is felt to be too direct. Instead, use the name with **san** attached.

This means that the sentence **Sharuma-san wa gakusee desu ka** can have two meanings:

(1) when Sharma-san is a listener,

Sharuma-san wa gakusee desu ka.

Sharma-san, are you a student?

(1)

(2) when Sharma-san is a third person,

Sharuma-san wa gakusee desu ka.

Is Sharma-san a student?

(2)

Watashi and **watakushi** are equivalent in meaning, but the latter is more formal.

2. nan; dare/donata; doko/dochira: question words

The question word **nan** means *what?* and **dare/donata** mean *who?*, **donata** being a polite equivalent of **dare**. **Doko/dochira** mean *where?* or *which direction?*, **dochira** being a polite equivalent of **doko**.

Question words are used as follows.

A : Senmon wa <u>nan</u> desu ka. ↓ B :　　　　<u>Koogaku</u> desu.	*What's your field of study?* *(My field of study is) engineering.*
A : Sensee wa <u>donata</u> desu ka. ↓ B :　　　　<u>Kimura-sensee</u> desu.	*Who is your teacher?* *It's Kimura-sensee.*
A : Okuni wa <u>dochira</u> desu ka. ↓ B :　　　　<u>Amerika</u> desu.	*Which country are you from?* *(lit. Where is your country?)* *America. (lit. It's America.)*

Ⅳ. の〈１〉: modifying nouns

Examples

① シャルマさんはインドの学生です。

Sharuma-san wa Indo no gakusee desu.

Sharma-san is a student from India.

② 私の専門はコンピュータです。

Watashi no senmon wa konpyuuta desu.

My field of study is computer science.

【*Explanation*】

The combination [N] no [N] has a variety of meanings, which result from the relationship between the first (modifying) noun and the second (modified) noun. Witness the following examples:

```
(modifying) [N] + no + (modified) [N]
```

watashi	no	kamera	*my camera*
Sharuma-san	no	senmon	*Sharma-san's field of study*
Sharuma-san	no	kuni	*Sharma-san's country*
Indo	no	ryuugakusee	*a foreign student from India*
Indo	no	Sharuma-san	*Sharma-san from India*
Nihongo	no	sensee	*a teacher of Japanese*
daigakuin	no	gakusee	*a postgraduate student*
tomodachi	no	Buraun-san	*my friend Brown-san*

No can also join three or more nouns:

Yokohama daigaku | no | kyooiku | no | sensee

a teacher of education at Yokohama University

1. こちらはインドのシャルマさんです。

Kochira wa Indo no Sharuma-san desu.

This is Sharma-san from India.

2. シャルマさんの先生はどなたですか。

Sharuma-san no sensee wa donata desu ka.

Who is your (Sharma-san's) teacher?

V. ⊘⊘ と〈1〉 *and*: connective particle

The connective particle **to** *and* links nouns. It cannot be used to join whole sentences.

sensee to gakusee

a teacher and a student

Sharuma-san to Buraun-san to Kimura-sensee

Sharma-san, Brown-san and Kimura-sensee

シャルマさんとブラウンさんは留学生です。

Sharuma-san to Buraun-san wa ryuugakusee desu.

Sharma-san and Brown-san are foreign students.

Conversation Notes

＜*General Information*＞

1. Formal introductions

(Casual introductions ⇨L11CN2)

a. In Japanese speech, there are several levels of formality. Compare the following expressions:

> **どうぞよろしくお願いします。**
> Doozo yoroshiku onegai shimasu.
>
> *I'm very glad to meet you.* (very formal expression used to a Higher ⬆)

> **よろしくお願いします。**
> Yoroshiku onegai shimasu.
>
> (to a Higher ⬆)

> **どうぞよろしく。**
> Doozo yoroshiku.
>
> (to an Equal ➡)

> **よろしく。**
> Yoroshiku.
>
> (to a Lower ⬇)

b. お or ご can be attached to the front of some nouns as a formal way of saying *your (country)*, *your (research)*, etc. Although there are some exceptions, お is normally used with native Japanese words and ご with words of Chinese origin. See the following examples:

お国	おくに	okuni	*someone else's country*
お名前	おなまえ	onamae	*someone else's name*
お仕事	おしごと	oshigoto	*someone else's job*
ご専門	ごせんもん	gosenmon	*someone else's profession*
ご研究	ごけんきゅう	gokenkyuu	*someone else's research*

Note that お and ご cannot be used for yourself, but they can be used for third persons:

14

○ **シャルマさんのお国はインドです。**
Sharuma-san no okuni wa Indo desu.
Sharma-san's country is India.

× **私のお国はインドです。**
Watashi no okuni wa Indo desu.

○ **山田先生のご専門はコンピュータではありません。**
Yamada-sensee no gosenmon wa konpyuuta dewa arimasen.
Yamada-sensee's specialization is not computer science.

× **私のご専門はコンピュータではありません。**
Watashi no gosenmon wa konpyuuta dewa arimasen.

You may see the Kanji **御** used for both **お** and **ご**; the expressions below are examples where **御** does not mean *your* etc. but makes the word it is attached to more polite:

御手洗	おてあらい	otearai	*toilet*
御案内	ごあんない	goannai	*information*

c. Business cards called **名刺 (meeshi)** are exchanged when business people and other persons, such as administrators and university professors are introduced to each other:

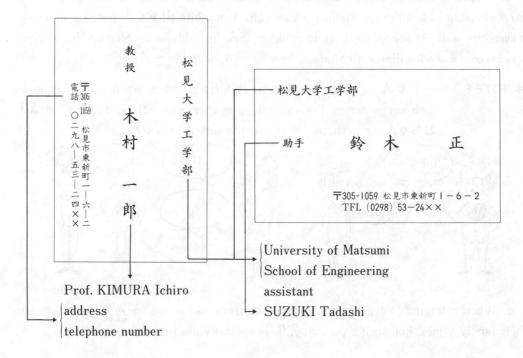

Prof. KIMURA Ichiro
address
telephone number

University of Matsumi
School of Engineering
assistant
SUZUKI Tadashi

In formal situations Japanese people bow to each other when meeting and taking leave. This bow is called **おじぎ** (**ojigi**). The best way to perfect your *ojigi* is to observe the way the Japanese do it. Recently, shaking hands is also common when Japanese meet foreigners, although you will find that bowing and shaking hands will often occur simultaneously!

2．Addressing people

a. When addressing people, **〜さん** (*Mr./Mrs./Miss etc.*) can be attached either to their family name or to their first name.

○	シャルマさん	Sharuma-san	*Mr. Sharma*
○	アニルさん	Aniru-san	*Anil*
○	田中さん	Tanaka-san	*Miss/Mrs. Tanaka*
○	みどりさん	Midori-san	*Midori*

However, you cannot attach **さん** to your own name:

> ✕　私はシャルマさんです。
>
> Watashi wa Sharuma-san desu.

b. **〜くん** is used to address men who are younger or the same age as the speaker in a relationship of familiarity. Kimura-sensee calls Yamashita **山下くん** because he knows Yamashita well. At the moment, he is using **〜さん** for addressing Sharma, but once he has become more familiar with Sharma, he may well switch to **〜くん**.

NOTE **〜ちゃん** is often attached to children's names when calling them by their given names. For example, a mother may call her son Yoshio **よしおちゃん**, or perhaps use the contraction **よっちゃん**.

c. When referring to teachers, professors, doctors and so on, **〜先生** is attached to their family names. For such a person, **先生** is normally used on its own:

① **Student**： **先生のご専門は。** ↗　*What is your specialization?*
Sensee no gosenmon wa.

Professor： **コンピュータです。**　*It's computer science.*
Konpyuuta desu.

When two professors are present, it is better to use their names to make it clear which one you are addressing:

② **Student**： **木村先生のご専門は。** ↗
Kimura-sensee no gosenmon wa.
What is your specialization, Kimura-sensee?

Professor K： **コンピュータです。**
Konpyuuta desu.
It's computer science.

Student： **田中先生のご専門は。** ↗
Tanaka-sensee no gosenmon wa.
How about you, Tanaka-sensee?

Professor T： **経済です。**
Keezai desu.
Economics.

3．Short questions and responses

a. Short questions

When asking information about someone's country, field of study and such like, a shortened form of question is often used, omitting the part in rounded brackets. This leaves just the topic, which is said with rising intonation:

お国は（どちらですか）。 ↗　*(Where is) your country?*
Okuni wa（dochira desu ka）.

ご専門は（なんですか）。 ↗　*(What is) your field of study?*
Gosenmon wa（nan desu ka）.

先生は（どなたですか）。 ↗　*(Who is) your professor?*
Sensee wa（donata desu ka）.

＊NOTE＊　question sentences/question words ⇨GNⅢ

b. When you ask different people the same question in turn, the question can be shortened as follows:

A：シャルマさんのお国は。↗   *(Where is) your country, Sharma-san?*
Sharuma-san no okuni wa.

B：インドです。   *India.*
Indo desu.

A：プラニーさんは。↗   *How about you, Puranee-san?*
Puranii-san wa.

C：タイです。   *Thailand.*
Tai desu.

A：スミスさんは。↗   *How about you, Smith-san?*
Sumisu-san wa.

D：アメリカです。   *U.S.A.*
Amerika desu.

c. Short responses

はい can be used as a short response when you are called.

① A：Bさん、ちょっと。⬇   *Excuse me, B-san.*
B-san, chotto.

B：はい。⬆   *Yes?*
Hai.

② A：ちょっと待って。⬇   *Wait a moment.*
Chotto matte.

B：はい。⬆   *Yes.*
Hai.

In the above situations, A will usually be B's Higher. Note that ええ or うん (ⓒ) cannot be used instead of はい when replying to a Higher's request or command etc.

In response to a Yes/No question, はい is used for a positive answer. In this case, you can also use ええ instead of はい. ⇨GNⅢ

③ A：お国はインドですか。⬆ ➡   *Are you from India?*
Okuni wa Indo desu ka.

B：ええ。⬇ ➡   *Yes.*
Ee.

18

④　A：ご専門は経済ですか。➡　　　*Are you specializing in economics?*
　　　Gosenmon wa keezai desu ka.

　　B：ええ。➡　　　　　　　　　　*Yes.*
　　　Ee.

4. Aizuchi

The Japanese continuously use verbal as well as non-verbal signals (so-called *aizuchi*) to indicate that they are following what is being said. Words like **はい／ええ／うん** *Yes,* **そうですか** *Really?,* **なるほど** *I see* as well as grunts or nods (or combinations of all of these) are used after almost each phrase or sentence uttered by the main speaker. If you do not use *aizuchi,* the main speaker will feel uneasy and may even stop talking because s/he will suspect that you are not listening. In the following conversation, the underlined parts are *aizuchi:*　(⇨まとめ3BⅡ2)

　　　A：きょうはさむいですね。　　　*It's cold today, isn't it?*
　　　　Kyoo wa samui desu ne.

　　　B：そうですね。↗　　　　　　　*(Yes,) it is.*
　　　　Soo desu ne.

　　　A：もう4月ですけどね。　　　　*Even though it's already April...*
　　　　Moo shigatsu desu kedo ne.

　　　B：ええ。↘　　　　　　　　　　*Yeah.*
　　　　Ee.

　　　A：けさは0どでしたよ。　　　　*It was 0 degrees Celsius this*
　　　　Kesa wa reedo deshita yo. 　　　　　　　　　　*morning.*

　　　B：そうですか。↘　　　　　　　*Really?*
　　　　Soo desu ka.

そうですね↗ (rising intonation) shows agreement, whereas **そうですか**↘ (falling intonation) signals that you had not been aware of the information but accept it without questioning it.

＊NOTE＊　　When **そうですか** is said with rising intonation, it can be a simple question, or imply disbelief.　⇨まとめ1BⅡ2

＜*Strategies*＞

S-1. How to start a conversation —1. At a party

a. When you see someone you know, you may call his/her name and start the conversation with a greeting.

A：	あ	山下さん。	こんにちは。	*Oh,*	*Yamashita-san.*	*Hello!*
	A,	Yamashita-san.	Konnichiwa.			
		先生			*Professor.*	
		sensee				

| B： | ああ、こんにちは。 | | *Oh, hello!* |
| | Aa, konnichiwa. | | |

＊NOTE＊ Other greetings： おはよう（ございます）。 *Good morning.*
Ohayoo（gozaimasu）.

こんばんは。 *Good evening.*
Konbanwa.

b. When you want to talk to people that you have not met, it is best to start with 失礼ですが *Excuse me, but,* followed by a self-introduction using 〜ともうします *My name is〜*. That will induce the other person to announce his/her name too.

A： あのう、失礼ですが。 *Excuse me.*
Anoo, shitsuree desu ga.

B： はい。 *Yes?*
Hai.

A： 私、シャルマともうします。 *My name is Sharma.*
Watakushi, Sharuma to mooshimasu.

どうぞよろしく。 *Nice to meet you.*
Doozo yoroshiku.

B： あ、どうも。 *Oh, hello.*
A, doomo.

松見大学の山下です。 *I'm Yamashita from Matsumi*
Matsumi daigaku no Yamashita desu. *University.*

こちらこそ、よろしく。　　　　　*Nice to meet you, too.*
Kochira koso, yoroshiku.

* **NOTE** *　A question like **おなまえは。** *(Your name, please.)* can be used by a
receptionist to ask for someone's name, but is not used in a social situation.

○ **good manners**　　　　× **bad manners**

c. When your professor calls out your name using **ちょっと**, you can answer with
はい,　followed by a greeting.

A： **シャルマさん、ちょっと。** ⬇　　　*Sharma-san!*
　　Sharuma-san, chotto.

B： **はい。あ、先生。こんばんは。** ⬆　　*Yes. Oh, professor.*
　　Hai. A, sensee. Konbanwa.　　　　*Good evening.*

ちょっと can only be used to call a Lower (a person of lower social status,
shown with the mark ⬇), so remember that it would be rude to call your professors,
Highers or even strangers with **ちょっと**.

○ **good manners**　　　　× **bad manners**

When you want to have a talk with your professors or Highers etc., start off with **ちょっとすみません。** *(lit. Excuse me for a moment.)*

A：先生、ちょっとすみません。 　　*Excuse me, professor.*
Sensee, chotto sumimasen.

B：あ、シャルマくん。 ⬇　　*Oh, Sharma-kun.*
A, Sharuma-kun.

S-2. How to introduce yourself or others

a. When you meet someone of higher status for the first time, you need to introduce yourself first, using the following patterns:

A：はじめまして。　　*How do you do?*
Hajimemashite.

インドのシャルマ ┃ **ともうします。**　　*I'm Sharma from India.*
Indo no Sharuma ┃ to mooshimasu.

です。
desu.

どうぞよろしく（お願いします）。　　*Nice to meet you.*
Doozo yoroshiku（onegai shimasu）.

B：東京大学の田中です。　　*I'm Tanaka from Tokyo Univ.*
Tokyoo daigaku no Tanaka desu.

よろしく。　　*Nice to meet you.*
Yoroshiku.

はじめまして。
インドのシャルマと
もうします。
どうぞよろしく。

東京大学の
田中です。
よろしく。

CN

Japanese often introduce themselves or others by giving the name of the institution or company where they study or work (university, company, department/section within an institution, etc.). Foreigners may also give the name of their country.

b. When introducing people to each other, remember to introduce the person you know better (ingroup) first. If both people are unfamiliar (outgroup), introduce the younger one to the older person first.

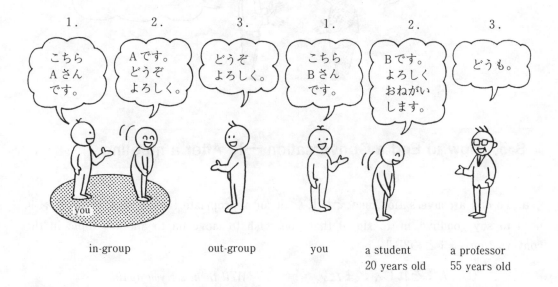

c. If you feel that your name is difficult to pronounce for a Japanese, you might consider offering a shortened version using ～と呼んでください。 *(Please call me～.).*

A：ええと、アニ……。   *Um, Ani...*
Eeto, Ani...

B：アニル・シャルマです。   *Anil Sharma.*
Aniru・Sharuma desu.

アニル Aniru	**と呼んでください。** to yonde kudasai.	*Please call me*	*Anil.* *Sharma.*
シャルマ Sharuma			

A：そうですか。↘   *I see.*
Soo desu ka.

S-3. How to End a Conversation —1. After a meeting

a. To end a conversation, use **それじゃ** at an appropriate time. **それじゃ** or **じゃ** is used to say goodbye, or to signal that you wish to move on to another topic in the conversation. ⇨まとめ2BⅡ2

① A：それじゃ、また。   *Well then, see you again.*
   Soreja, mata.

B：ええ。じゃ、また。   *O.K. See you.*
   Ee. Ja, mata.

② A：おなまえは。↗   *Your name, please.*
   Onamae wa.

CN

B：**シャルマです。**　　　　　*(My name is) Sharma.*
　　Sharuma desu.

A：**そうですか。**↘　　　　　*I see.*
　　Soo desu ka.

　　じゃ、どうぞこちらへ。　*Right, please come this way.*
　　Ja, doozo kochira e.

B：**どうも。**　　　　　　　　*Thank you.*
　　Doomo.

b. When you part from someone for some time, **さようなら** or **さよなら** is used to say goodbye. However, if you know that you will meet again soon, expressions like **じゃ、また。**（*See you again.*）, **またあとで。**（*See you later.*）, **またあした。**（*See you tomorrow.*）, etc. are used.

c. It is appropriate that you as a junior wait until your professor or senior signal the end of the conversation; however, in unavoidable circumstances you may use **すみません** to alert your senior that you must leave; etiquette requires that you then wait until your senior says goodbye first. You can then take leave using **失礼します**.
　　　　　　　　　　　　　　　　　　　　　　　　　　　　　　しつれい

① A student says goodbye to his/her professor.

Student：あの、すみません、先生。🔼　*Excuse me, professor.*
Ano, sumimasen, sensee.

それじゃ……。　*If that's it...*
Soreja,...

Professor：あ、そう。↘ 🔽　*Oh, I see.*
A, soo.

じゃ、また。　*All right then, see you.*
Ja, mata.

Student：はい。失礼します。🔼　*Please excuse me then.*
Hai. Shitsuree shimasu.

② A student says goodbye to his/her friend.

Student：じゃ、またね。➡　*Well then, see you.*
Ja, mata ne.

Friend：うん。じゃ、また。➡　*O.K. See you again.*
Un. Ja, mata.

郵便局で
ゆうびんきょく
At the post office

OBJECTIVES:

GRAMMAR

Ⅰ. Verbs in the polite form: [V (base)]-masu
Ⅱ. が〈1〉; を〈1〉; に〈1〉; へ: structure particles
Ⅲ. は and も〈2〉: discourse particles and structure particles
Ⅳ. で〈1〉 *at*; と〈2〉 *with*: structure particles
Ⅴ. なに *what?* and いくら *how much?*: question words
Ⅵ. ～まい and ～えん: counters
Ⅶ. Numbers

CONVERSATION

<General Information>

1. Post office services in Japan
2. Letters and postcards
3. Paying and receiving money

<Strategies>

S-1. How to start a conversation — 2. On the street
S-2. How to start a conversation —3. Introducing a request
S-3. How to send mail at the post office
S-4. How to buy something at the post office

Model Conversation

Characters : Tanaka（田中）, Yamashita （山下）, a post office clerk（局員）

Situation : Yamashita-san is going to the post office. On the way, he meets his friend Tanaka-san and they go together. Yamashita-san sends a letter to the U.S. and Tanaka-san buys some stamps and postcards.

Flow-chart :

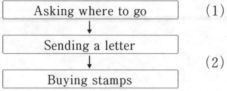

```
┌─────────────────────────┐
│   Asking where to go    │   (1) On the way（Casual style）
└─────────────────────────┘
            ↓
┌─────────────────────────┐
│    Sending a letter     │
└─────────────────────────┘   (2) At the post office
            ↓
┌─────────────────────────┐
│     Buying stamps       │
└─────────────────────────┘
```

（1）―道 で―

田 中 ：あら、山下さん。
山 下 ：あ、田中さん。おはよう。
田 中 ：おはよう。どこ行くの。
山 下 ：ちょっと郵便局まで。
田 中 ：あ、私もよ。
山 下 ：じゃ、いっしょに行く。
田 中 ：ええ。

（2）―郵便局で―

山 下 ：すみません。
局 員 ：はい。
山 下 ：これ、航空便でお願いします。
局 員 ：アメリカですね。
山 下 ：ええ。
局 員 ：ええと（weighing letter）、280円です。
山 下 ：はい。
局 員 ：はい。それじゃ、おあずかりします。
山 下 ：お願いします。

MC

＊　　　＊　　　＊

田　中　：80円切手、3まい。
局　員　：はい。
田　中　：ええと、それから、はがき5まいください。
局　員　：はい。全部で490円です。
田　中　：じゃ、これでお願いします。
局　員　：1000円ですね。
　　　　　510円のおかえしです。
田　中　：どうも。
局　員　：ありがとうございました。

Report

　山下さんは友だちの田中さんといっしょに郵便局へ行きました。山下さんは郵便局でアメリカに手紙を出しました。280円でした。

　田中さんは80円切手を3まい買いました。そして、はがきを5まい買いました。全部で490円でした。

New Words and Expressions

Words in the conversation

局員	きょくいん	*post office clerk*
道	みち	*way, road*
あら		*Oh!*（used by female ♀）
田中さん	たなかさん	*Tanaka-san*
どこ		*where?*
行く	いく	*to go*
ちょっと		*for a while, a little*
郵便局	ゆうびんきょく	*post office*
私	わたし	*I*
まで		*as far as～*
いっしょに		*together*（with～）
ええ		*Yes*
これ		*this*
航空便	こうくうびん	*air mail*
アメリカ	Amerika	*the U.S.*
～円	～えん	*～yen*
切手	きって	*postage stamp*
～まい		*counter for thin, flat objects*
それから		*and, also*
はがき		*postcard*
全部で	ぜんぶで	*in total*
おかえし		*change*

＜Expressions in the conversation＞

おはよう。

Good morning. Ⓒ（Casual）⇨L1CN S-1

どこ行くの。↗

Where are you going? Ⓒ

Casual way of asking; ～の serves to soften the question. The formal equivalent is どこへ行きますか。🔲 ⇨L5GNV

私もよ。

Me, too. Ⓒ

～よ is a final particle indicating that information is given to the listener.
⇨まとめ2BⅡ4

いっしょに行く。↗　　　　　　　　　　*Are you coming with me?* 🎧

Questions can also be marked by short rising intonation. ⇨まとめ2BⅡ3

すみません.　　　　　　　　　　　　　*Excuse me.*

This is an attention getter, which can be used to call for service in a shop or an office, etc. At natural speed, it is often pronounced **すいません。**

⇨CN S-2

お願いします。　　　　　　　　　　　*Please*（do me a favour）.
ねが

This can be used in the following situations: ⇨CN S-3

① 航空便でお願いします。　　*By airmail, please.*
　こうくうびん
② これでお願いします。　　　*I'd like to pay with this*

　　　　　　　　　　　　　　　（relatively large bill）.

③ はがき5まいお願いします。Give me 5 postcards, please.

It is also used as an attention getter. ⇨CN S-2

④ お願いします。＝すみません。　*Excuse me.*

アメリカですね。↗　　　　　　　　　*It's for America, isn't it?*

～ね with short rising intonation asks for agreement or confirmation.

⇨まとめ2BⅡ4

おあずかりします。　　　　　　　　　*(I'll) take care of it.* ⇨CN3

～（を）ください。　　　　　　　　　*(Give me)* ～*, please.* ⇨CN S-4

はがき（を）5まい｜ください。　*Give me 5 postcards, please.*
　　　　　　　　　｜お願いします。

ありがとうございました。　　　　　*Thank you very much.* 📧

This is a polite way of saying thanks. It is often used by clerks at a shop or an office in the service sector. The customer will normally reply **どうも**, or not at all. ⇨まとめ1BⅡ4

Words in the report

友だち	ともだち	*friend*
手紙	てがみ	*letter*
出します[だす]	だします	*to send*
そして		*Also* ～
買います[かう]	かいます	*to buy*

MC

Grammar Notes

I. Verbs in the polite form: [V(base)]-masu*

*[V(base)]-masu: the -masu form of verbs

【*Explanation*】

The ending **-masu** makes verbs polite; it is used in formal style conversation. Verbs are words that indicate actions or happenings; **-masu** can be used for habitual or future actions:

あした行きます。 *(I)'ll go tomorrow.*
Ashita ikimasu.

毎日行きます。 *(I) go every day.*
Mainichi ikimasu.

For the negative, use **-masen** instead of **-masu**.

行きません。 *(I) won't go.*
Ikimasen.

To make a question, simply add **ka** to the end of a sentence.

A：あした行きますか。 *Will (you) go tomorrow?*
Ashita ikimasu ka.

B：ええ、行きます。 *Yes, (I) will.*
Ee, ikimasu.

いいえ、行きません。 *No, (I) won't.*
Iie, ikimasen.

Use **-mashita** instead of **-masu** for actions that have already taken place. For the negative past, change **-mashita** to **-masen deshita**.

A：行きましたか。 *Did (you) go?*
Ikimashita ka.

B：ええ、行きました。 *Yes, (I) did.*
Ee, ikimashita.

いいえ、行きませんでした。 *No, (I) didn't.*
Iie, ikimasen deshita.

Verb forms　　[V (base)] -masu			
Non-past		Past	
Positive	Negative	Positive	Negative
-masu	-masen	-mashita	-masen deshita
ikimasu　　*to go*	ikimasen	ikimashita	ikimasen deshita
kaimasu　　*to buy*	kaimasen	kaimashita	kaimasen deshita

The following is a table showing the plain and polite forms of verbs.

Plain and polite forms of verbs				
	Non-past		Past	
	Positive	Negative	Positive	Negative
Plain	iku　　*to go*	ikanai	itta	ikanakatta
Polite	ikimasu	ikimasen	ikimashita	ikimasen deshita
Plain	kau　　*to buy*	kawanai	katta	kawanakatta
Polite	kaimasu	kaimasen	kaimashita	kaimasen deshita

Ⅱ. ◁)||┼◄ が〈1〉；を〈1〉；に〈1〉；へ: structure particles

Examples

① **切手を買います。**   *(I)'ll buy stamps.*
Kitte o kaimasu.

② **きのう郵便局へ行きました。**   *(I) went to the post office yesterday.*
Kinoo yuubinkyoku e ikimashita.

③ **友だちに手紙を出しました。**   *(I) sent a letter to a friend.*
Tomodachi ni tegami o dashimashita.

【*Explanation*】

1. Verbs and sets of structure particles

kau（plain）and **kaimasu**（polite）*to buy* are used in the sentence structure shown below; the structure particle **ga** marks the person who buys whereas **o** marks what s/he buys:

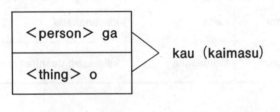

＜person＞ ga
＜thing＞ o

→ **Sharuma-san ga kitte o kau**（kaimasu）.
Sharma-san buys stamps.

Some other verbs which take the same structure are:

kiku（kikimasu）	*to hear*	miru（mimasu）	*to see*
kaku（kakimasu）	*to write*	yomu（yomimasu）	*to read*
suru（shimasu）	*to do*	benkyoo suru （benkyoo shimasu）	*to study*

→ **Buraun-san ga tegami o kaku**（kakimasu）.
Brown-san writes a letter.

34

→ **Sharuma-san ga Nihongo o benkyoo suru** (**shimasu**).
Sharma-san studies Japanese.

These verbs use **ga** to mark the person who performs the action, and **o** to mark the thing which is acted upon. **Ga** can therefore be called a subject particle, and **o** an object particle.

Iku (**ikimasu**) *to go* uses the following structure.

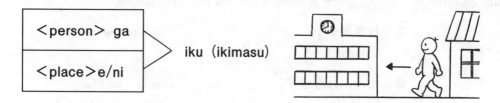

→ **Sharuma-san ga daigaku e/ni iku** (**ikimasu**).
Sharma-san goes to university.

Verbs using the same structure are:

kuru (**kimasu**)　　*to come*　　　**kaeru** (**kaerimasu**)　　*to go/come back*

→ **Buraun-san ga Nihon e kuru** (**kimasu**).
Brown-san comes to Japan.

→ **Buraun-san ga kuni ni kaeru** (**kaerimasu**).
Brown-san goes back to her country.

These verbs take the structure particles **ga** (subject particle), and **e/ni** to mark the place or goal towards which the action moves. **E/ni** can therefore be called a direction or goal particle.

Dasu (**dashimasu**) *to send, to mail,* takes the following structure.

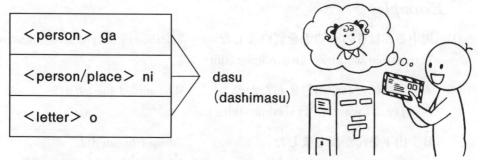

→ **Sharuma-san ga tomodachi ni tegami o dasu** (**dashimasu**).
Sharma-san sends a letter to his friend.

GN

Ga is again the subject particle, **ni** the goal particle indicating the person or place where the letter is sent, and **o** the object particle.

3. [N]＋structure particle in actual use

We saw that verbs can be used with various sets of [N] + structure particle. However, a verb isn't always accompanied by all of its [N] + structure particles; as the following conversation illustrates, generally only those [N] + structure particles that are essential to a situation are present, while the rest are omitted:

1. A：行きますか。　　　　　　　　　*Will you go?*
   Ikimasu ka.

   B：ええ、行きます。　　　　　　　　*Yes, we will.*
   Ee, ikimasu.

2. A：どこへ行きますか。　　　　　　　*Where will you go?*
   Doko e ikimasu ka.

   B：京都へ行きます。　　　　　　　　*We'll go to Kyoto.*
   Kyooto e ikimasu.

3. A：だれが行きますか。　　　　　　　*Who will go?*
   Dare ga ikimasu ka.

   B：私とシャルマさんが行きます。　　*Sharma-san and I will.*
   Watashi to Sharuma-san ga ikimasu.

Ⅲ. 🐟 は and も〈2〉: discourse particles and structure particles

Examples

① 田中さんはきのう切手を買いました。　　*Tanaka-san bought stamps yesterday.*
Tanaka-san wa kinoo kitte o kaimashita.

② A：手紙はだれが出しましたか。　　*Who mailed the letters?*
Tegami wa dare ga dashimashita ka.

B：山下さんが出しました。　　*Yamashita-san did.*
Yamashita-san ga dashimashita.

【*Explanation*】

1. Making [N]＋structure particle the topic of a sentence

Note carefully how each [N] + structure particle in the following sentence can become a topic.

Tanaka-san ga kitte o kaimashita.　　*Tanaka-san bought stamps.*

Pay close attention to the behaviour of the Topic boy.

(1)

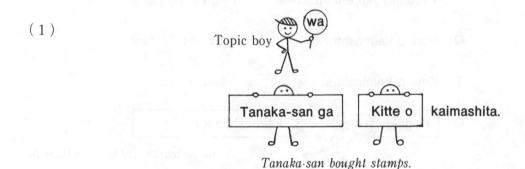

Tanaka-san bought stamps.

(2)

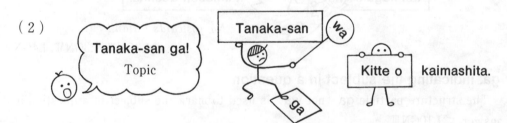

As for Tanaka-san, she bought stamps.

(3)

As for the stamps, Tanaka-san bought them.

37

Tanaka-san ga becomes the topic in sentence (2), and **kitte o** in sentence (3).

Note that the Topic boy is kicking out **ga** and **o** !! The structure particles **ga** or **o** are replaced by the discourse particles **wa** or **mo** when [N]＋ **ga/o** becomes a topic. Watch how this happens in the conversation below.

Q : Tanaka-san wa [ga] ⟩ Kinoo doko e ikimashita ka.

Tanaka-san, where did you go yesterday?

T : Yuubinkyoku e ikimashita.　　*I went to the post office.*

Q : Nani o kaimashita ka.　　*What did you buy?*

T : Kitte o kaimashita.　　*I bought stamps.*

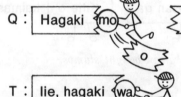

Q : Hagaki mo ⟩ kaimashita ka.

As for postcards, did you buy them too?

T : Iie, hagaki wa ⟩ kaimasen deshita.

No, postcards I didn't buy.

⇨L2GNⅢ, L3GNⅦ, L4GNⅡ

2. ga: indicating the subject in a question

The structure particle **ga** (not **wa**) is used to mark the subject in a question and its answer: ⇨L10GNⅢ

A : <u>Dare ga</u> ikimasu ka.　　*Who will go?*　　⟩ ga ikimasu ka.
　　　↓
B : <u>Sharuma-san ga</u> ikimasu.　　*Sharma-san will go.*　　⟩ ga ikimasu.

A : Kitte wa <u>dare ga</u> kaimashita ka.　　*As for the stamps, who bought them?*
　　　　　　↓
B :　　<u>Watashi ga</u> kaimashita.　　*I bought them.*

 ○ Dare ga kaimasu ka.
　　　Who will buy?
　　× Dare wa kaimasu ka.

Ⅳ. ⊲╫╫◄　で〈1〉*at*；と〈2〉*with*: structure particles

1. de:
1） particle of place of action

De indicates the place where something happens.

> 1．大学で日本語を勉強します。
>
> Daigaku de Nihongo o benkyoo shimasu.
>
> *I study Japanese at university.*

> 2．A：どこで切手を買いましたか。
>
> Doko de kitte o kaimashita ka.
>
> *Where did you buy the stamps?*

> B：郵便局で買いました。
>
> Yuubinkyoku de kaimashita.
>
> *I bought them at the post office.*

2） particle of means or method ⇨L5GNⅦ

> 3．A：これ、航空便でいくらですか。
>
> Kore, kookuubin de ikura desu ka.
>
> *How much is this by airmail?*

> B：280円です。
>
> 280-en desu.
>
> *It's 280 yen.*

2. to : companion particle

To（sometimes **to issho ni**）, meaning *with* or *together,* indicates a person with whom one does something:

> 1．シャルマさんは田中さんと図書館へ行きました。
>
> Sharuma-san wa Tanaka-san to toshokan e ikimashita.
>
> *Sharma-san went to the library with Tanaka-san.*

> 2．きのう先生といっしょにビールを飲みました。
>
> Kinoo sensee to issho ni biiru o nomimashita.
>
> *I drank beer with my teacher yesterday.*

V. なに *what?* and いくら *how much?*: question words

Nani is the basic for *what?* The variant **nan** is used when an element (particle, etc.) beginning with 'd', 't', 'n', and sometimes 'y', or any counter, is attached.

1. 何を飲みますか。
<u>Nani</u> o nomimasu ka.
What will you drink?

2. 何を買いましたか。
<u>Nani</u> o kaimashita ka.
What did you buy?

3. 専門は何ですか。
Senmon wa <u>nan</u> desu ka.
What's your field?

4. 何の本ですか。
<u>Nan</u> no hon desu ka.
What's this book about?

5. 切手は何まい買いましたか。
Kitte wa <u>nan</u>-mai kaimashita ka.
As for the stamps, how many did you buy?

Ikura means *how much?* :⇨CN S-3，まとめ1AⅢ

6. A：はがきをください。いくらですか。
Hagaki o kudasai. <u>Ikura</u> desu ka.
Can I have some postcards, please? How much are they?

B：1まい50円です。
Ichi-mai gojuu-en desu.
50 yen each.

VI. ～まい and ～えん: counters

Japanese uses a variety of counters to count objects, often on the basis of their shapes. Counters attach directly to a number. **-Mai** is used to count thin, flat things like sheets of paper, plates, etc., while **-en** is used for Japanese money. ⇨まとめ1AⅡ

To indicate how many stamps or postcards you buy, use the following structure:

（noun ＋ particle ）＋（number ＋ counter）＋ verb

1. **切手を3まい買いました。**　　　　*I bought three stamps.*
   kitte o san-mai kaimashita.

2. **はがきを1まいください。**　　　　*Give me one postcard.*
   Hagaki o ichi-mai kudasai.

3. **お金を千円払いました。**　　　　*I paid 1000 yen.*
   Okane o sen-en haraimashita.

VII. Numbers　　⇨　まとめIAI

1	いち ichi	10	じゅう juu	1000	せん sen
2	に ni	20	にじゅう nijuu	2000	にせん nisen
3	さん san	30	さんじゅう sanjuu	3000	さんぜん sanzen
4	よん／し yon/shi	40	よんじゅう yonjuu	4000	よんせん yonsen
5	ご go	⋮		⋮	
6	ろく roku	100	ひゃく hyaku	10000	いちまん ichiman
7	なな／しち nana/shichi	200	にひゃく nihyaku	20000	にまん niman
8	はち hachi	300	さんびゃく sanbyaku	30000	さんまん sanman
9	きゅう／く kyuu/ku	400	よんひゃく yonhyaku	40000	よんまん yonman
10	じゅう juu	⋮		⋮	

Conversation Notes

\<General Information\>

1. Post office services in Japan

Post offices in Japan can be identified by the postal mark 〒 and the red postbox outside. Postboxes generally have two slots; the one on the right, labelled 県内 (**kennai**)

or 都内 (**tonai**), *Within the prefecture* is for ordinary local mail. The slot on the left, labelled 他府県 (**tafuken**) *Other areas* is for out-of-prefecture mail, airmail and special delivery.

Post office services in Japan have three sections; 郵便 (**yuubin** *mail*), 送金 (**sookin** *remittances*) and 貯金 (**chokin** *banking*). Office hours are from 9 to 5, Monday to Friday. (Most are closed on Saturdays and Sundays.)

a. 郵便 (**yuubin**) *Postal service;*

In the postal service section, you can buy stamps and postcards as well as post letters and parcels.

手紙 (tegami)

はがき (hagaki)

切手 (kitte)

小包 (kozutsumi)

国内郵便	こくないゆうびん	kokunaiyuubin	*domestic mail*
外国郵便	がいこくゆうびん	gaikokuyuubin	*overseas mail*
航空便	こうくうびん	kookuubin	*air mail*
船　便	ふなびん	funabin	*sea mail*
SAL	ＳＡＬゆうびん	saru yuubin	*SAL*
速　達	そくたつ	sokutatsu	*special delivery*
書　留	かきとめ	kakitome	*registered mail*
小　包	こづつみ	kozutsumi	*parcels*

b. 送金（sookin） *Remittances;*

You can send money by money order, cash envelope（registered mail）or postal transfer.

郵便為替	ゆうびんかわせ	yuubinkawase	*postal money order*
現金書留	げんきんかきとめ	genkinkakitome	*registered mail for cash*
郵便振替	ゆうびんふりかえ	yuubinfurikae	*postal transfer*

c. 貯金（chokin） *Banking service;*

Post offices in Japan offer various types of saving accounts such as ordinary, fixed-amount and fixed-period accounts.

通常貯金	つうじょうちょきん	tsuujoochokin	*ordinary savings*
定額貯金	ていがくちょきん	teegakuchokin	*fixed savings*
定期貯金	ていきちょきん	teekichokin	*fixed period savings*

d. その他（sonota） *Other services;*

簡易保険	かんいほけん	kan'ihoken	*postal life insurance*
電　報	でんぽう	denpoo	*telegram*
自動払込	じどうはらいこみ	jidooharaikomi	*direct debit*

2. Letters and postcards

When putting addresses on envelopes and postcards, the receiver's name is written in characters larger than the address in the central area in both vertical and horizontal writing. The post code (**郵便番号 yuubinbangoo**) is written in the printed box as in the following sample:

43

\<A sample addressed envelope\>

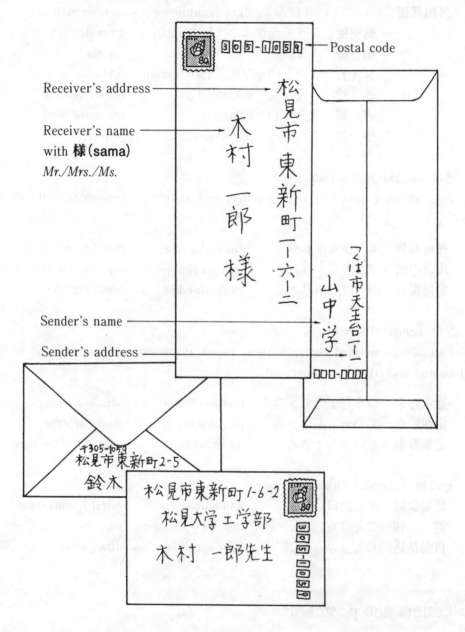

The way to read a Japanese address in Japanese is as follows, i.e. the order is consistently from the larger unit to the smaller:

（〜県）	松見市	東新町		1 – 6 – 2	
（〜-ken）	Matsumi-shi,	Higashi shin-machi	1-choome,	6-banchi,	2-goo
（prefecture）	city	town/village	street	block	house No.

44

3. Paying and receiving money

a. When paying money, you can hand over the money saying 「はい。(Hai.) *Here you are.*」. The clerk may reply 「**ありがとうございました。(Arigatoo gozaimashita.)** *Thank you very much.*」.

When you don't have small change, you can pay with a bill, saying 「**これでおねがいします。(kore de onegai shimasu.)** *Please take the amount from this.*」.

The clerk will normally confirm the amount of money handed over by saying 「**～円ですね。(～-en desu ne.)**」or「**～円おあずかりします。(～-en oazukari shimasu.)**」 *(lit. I'm taking custody of ～ yen.)*

日本の**お金** *Japanese currency* ¥＝yen

¥ 10,000　　¥ 5,000　　¥ 1,000

¥ 500　　¥ 100　　¥ 50　　¥ 10　　¥ 5

¥ 1

b. When you are given your change, you will not normally say anything, although you can say 「**どうも。(Doomo.)** *Thanks.*」

c. When you think you are given the wrong change, you can bring it to the clerk's attention by saying:

Customer：あのう、おつり、ちがってるんですけど。
Anoo, otsuri, chigatte iru n desu kedo.
Excuse me, but you gave me the wrong change.

Clerk：あ、どうもすみませんでした。
A, doomo sumimasendeshita.
Oh, I'm very sorry.

45

<Strategies>

S-1. How to start a conversation —2. On the street

a. When meeting a Japanese acquaintance on the street, you first exchange greetings; then, your acquaintance may ask you 「**どちらへ。(Dochira e.)** 🈪」 or 「**どこ行くの。 (Doko iku no.)** 🇨」 *Where are you going?* If you want to chat, you can indicate your destination using 「**ちょっと** < place > **まで。(Chotto** < place > **made.)**」 Your acquaintance may then choose to continue talking to you as in ① and ② below:

① 🈪 A：どちらへ。↗		*Where are you going?*
Dochira e.		
B：ちょっと郵便局まで。		*To the post office.*
Chotto yuubinkyoku made.		
A：あ、私もなんですよ。		*Oh, me too.*
A, watashi mo na n desu yo.		
いっしょに行きませんか。↗		*Let's go together, shall we?*
Issho ni ikimasen ka.		
B：ええ。		*O.K.*
Ee.		
② 🇨 A：どこ行くの。↗		*Where are you going?*
Doko iku no.		
B：ちょっと郵便局まで。		*To the post office.*
Chotto yuubinkyoku made.		
A：あ、	私もよ。 🧍	*Ah, so am I.*
A,	watashi mo yo.	
	ぼくもだよ。 🧍	
	boku mo da yo.	
いっしょに行く。↗		*Let's go together, shall we?*
Issho ni iku.		
B：うん。		*O.K.*
Un.		

46

b. When you do not have time to talk or don't want to say where you are going, you can answer as in ③

③ 🔊 A：**どちらへ。**↗   *Where are you going?*
Dochira e.

B：**ええ。ちょっとそこまで。**   *(Got some business) nearby.*
Ee. Chotto soko made.

A：**そうですか。じゃ、また。**   *I see. So long, then.*
Soo desu ka. Ja, mata.

B：**じゃ、失礼します。**   *Goodbye then.*
Ja, shitsuree shimasu.

The answer **ちょっとそこまで** signals to the listener that no further small talk is wanted; **どちらへ** and **ちょっとそこまで** here are more like greetings than requests for information.

S-2. How to start a conversation —3. Introducing a request

To signal that you want to make a request, you can say **すみません** or **お願いします**, handy expressions that function as attention getters.

① **Customer：すみません。**   *Excuse me.*
Sumimasen.

Clerk：はい。   *Yes.*
Hai.

Customer：航空便でお願いします。   *By airmail, please.*
Kookuubin de onegai shimasu.

② **Customer：お願いします。**   *Can you help me?*
Onegai shimasu.

Clerk：はい。   *Yes.*
Hai.

Customer：はがき5まいください。   *Five postcards, please.*
Hagaki go-mai kudasai.

47

＊NOTE＊ すみません can be used with strangers, too, to alert them that you wish to ask them a question. When you hear すみません, therefore, be prepared that someone will ask you a question, or request you to do something.（⇨L4CN S-1）In this use, すみません cannot be replaced by お願いします。

③ **A：あの、すみません。** *Excuse me.*
Ano, sumimasen.

B：はい。 *Yes.*
Hai.

A：郵便局はどこでしょうか。 *Where do I find a post office?*
Yuubinkyoku wa doko deshoo ka.

S-3. How to send mail at the post office

a. Asking to send mail

Simply put a letter, postcard or parcel, etc. on the appropriate counter and say「これ（を）お願いします。*(Please,)*」お願いします literally means *Please do me a favour* and can be used both for asking services and personal requests. In this use, it can not be replaced by すみません.

○ **これ、航空便でお願いします。** *Send this by air mail, please.*
Kore, kookuubin de onegai shimasu.

✕ **これ、航空便ですみません。**
Kore, kookuubin de sumimasen.

b. Asking about postage

When you don't know the postage, you can find out by asking「いくらですか。*(How much is it?)*」. You can indicate the destination of the mail with 〜まで and the type of mail with 〜で as follows:

＜destination＞まで ＜type of mail＞で いくらですか。

① **アメリカまで航空便でいくらですか。**
Amerika made kookuubin de ikura desu ka.
How much will it cost to the U.S. by air mail?

CN

② **インドまで船便でいくらですか。**

Indo made funabin de ikura desu ka.

How much will it cost to India by sea mail?

c. Asking how long it takes

When you want to find out how long it takes for an item to be delivered, use **どのぐらいかかりますか** *(How long will it take?)*. ⇨L11GN Ⅵ

＜destination＞まで ＜type of mail＞で　どのぐらいかかりますか。

① **アメリカまで航空便でどのぐらいかかりますか。**

Amerika made kookuubin de donogurai kakarimasu ka.

How long will it take to the U.S. by air mail?

② **インドまで船便でどのぐらいかかりますか。**

Indo made funabin de donogurai kakarimasu ka.

How long will it take to India by sea mail?

S-4. How to buy something at the post office

When you want to buy postcards or postage stamps etc., simply attach 「～をお願いします／ください」 to the item you require. In casual speech, を can be omitted.

To indicate the number of items, give the number （＋counter） after the item. Note that no particles are used after the number:

＜thing＞（を）＜number＞ | お願いします。
| ください。

① **はがき 5 まいお願いします。**

Hagaki go-mai onegai shimasu.

Five postcards, please.

② **80円切手 3 まいください。**

Hachijuu-en kitte san-mai kudasai.

Three 80 yen stamps, please.

In casual speech, you can omit お願いします or ください.

49

③ **はがき5まい。**

Hagaki go-mai.

Five postcards.

④ **エアログラム4まい。**

Earoguramu yon-mai.

Four aerograms.

A domestic letter (25g or less) costs 80 yen and a postcard costs 50 yen. Make a trip to the post office to check current prices for postal services.

レストランで

At a restaurant

OBJECTIVES:

GRAMMAR

Ⅰ. に〈2〉 *from/to*: structure particle
Ⅱ. です substituting for a verb
Ⅲ. ～にします and ～になります: する verbs and
　　　　　　　　　　　　　　　　　　　　　なる verbs 〈1〉
Ⅳ. いつ *when?*: question word
Ⅴ. ～ましょう and ～ませんか
Ⅵ. ひとつ，ふたつ，……: counter for things
　　ひとり，ふたり，……: counter for people
Ⅶ. は and も〈3〉: more about discourse particles

CONVERSATION

＜General Information＞

1. At a restaurant
2. Expressions used in restaurants and shops
3. Fast food shops

＜Strategies＞

S-1. How to ask for something you need
S-2. How to give and receive something
S-3. How to order
S-4. How to deal with problems in a restaurant
S-5. How to pay the cashier

Model Conversation

Characters ： a waitress（ウェートレス）, Yamashita（山下）, Tanaka（田中）, a cashier（会計）

Situation ： Yamashita-san and Tanaka-san have lunch together in a restaurant.

Flow-chart ：

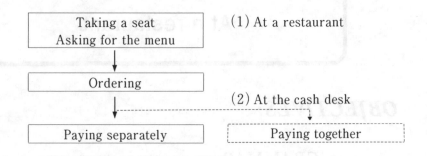

```
┌─────────────────────────┐
│    Taking a seat         │   (1) At a restaurant
│  Asking for the menu     │
└─────────────────────────┘
           │
           ▼
┌─────────────────────────┐
│       Ordering           │
└─────────────────────────┘       (2) At the cash desk
           │ ┄┄┄┄┄┄┄┄┄┄┄┄┄┄┄┄┄┄┄┄┄┄┄┄┄
           ▼                        ▼
┌─────────────────────────┐   ┌─────────────────────────┐
│   Paying separately      │   │   Paying together        │
└─────────────────────────┘   └─────────────────────────┘
```

（1）―レストランで―

ウェートレス：いらっしゃいませ。何名さまですか。
山　下　　：2人です。
ウェートレス：こちらへどうぞ。

　　　　　　　＊　　　＊　　　＊

田　中　　：すみません。
ウェートレス：はい。
田　中　　：あの、メニューありますか。
ウェートレス：はい、メニューでございますね。
　　　　　　　少々お待ちください。

　　　　　　　＊　　　＊　　　＊

ウェートレス：はい、どうぞ。
田　中　　：あ、どうも。

　　　　　　　＊　　　＊　　　＊

山　下　　：すみません。
ウェートレス：はい。ご注文は。
山　下　　：ええと、ぼくは天ぷら定食。
ウェートレス：はい。

田　中　　　：私はビーフカレーとコーヒー。
ウェートレス：はい。
山　下　　　：あ、ぼくもあとでコーヒーもらおうかな。
ウェートレス：はい。天ぷら定食がおひとつ、ビーフカレーがおひとつ、コーヒーお
　　　　　　　ふたつですね。
山　下　　　：ええ。

＊　　　＊　　　＊

ウェートレス：コーヒーはアイスになさいますか、ホットになさいますか。
田　中　　　：私、ホット。
山　下　　　：じゃ、ホットふたつね。
ウェートレス：はい、かしこまりました。

（2）―会計で―

山　下：お願いします。
会　計：はい。ごいっしょですか。
山　下：あ、いや、べつべつにしてください。
田　中：私、ビーフカレーとコーヒー。
会　計：ええと、ちょうど1000円になります。
田　中：はい。
山　下：天ぷら定食とコーヒー。
会　計：1150円いただきます。
山　下：はい。
会　計：2000円おあずかりします。
　　　　850円のおつりです。ありがとうございました。
山　下：どうも。

Report

　山下さんと田中さんはレストランへ行きました。レストランで山下さんは天
ぷら定食、田中さんはビーフカレーを注文しました。それから、2人はホット
コーヒーを飲みました。山下さんは1150円、田中さんは1000円でした。山下さ
んは2000円はらいました。そして、おつりをもらいました。

New Words and Expressions

Words in the conversation

ウェートレス	weetoresu	*waitress*
会計	かいけい	*cashier, cash desk*
レストラン	resutoran	*restaurant*
何名さま	なんめいさま	*how many people?*
2人	ふたり	*two people*
メニュー	menyuu	*a menu*
あります [ある]		*to have*
ご注文	ごちゅうもん	*your order*
天ぷら定食	てんぷらていしょく	*set tempura meal*
ビーフカレー	biifukaree	*beef curry*
コーヒー	koohii	*coffee*
あとで		*later*
もらいます [もらう]		*to receive*
ひとつ		*one*
ふたつ		*two*
アイス	aisu	*iced (coffee)*
ホット	hotto	*hot (coffee)*
いや		*No.* 🚹 ＝いいえ、いえ
べつべつ		*separately*
ちょうど		*just, exactly*
あずかります [あずかる]		*to receive, to keep*
おつり		*change*＝おかえし

<Expressions in the conversation>

いらっしゃいませ。	*Welcome (to this shop).* ⇨CN2
こちらへどうぞ。	*This way, please.* ⇨CN2
～でございますね。	*It is ～, isn't it?*
	でございます is a very formal equivalent of です. ⇨CN2
少々お待ちください。 しょうしょう　ま	*Please wait a moment.*
少々　　しょうしょう	*a little*
待ちます [まつ] まちます	*to wait*

54

　　　　cf. ＝ちょっと待ってください。⇨CN S-4

どうぞ。　　　　　　　　　　　　　*Here you are.* ⇨CN S-2

どうも。　　　　　　　　　　　　　*Thank you.* ⇨CN S-2
　　　　cf. ＝どうもありがとうございます。🈁⇨まとめ1B

ほくもあとでコーヒーもらおうかな。　*I'll also have some coffee later.* ⇨CN S-3
　　もらおう *is the* **-(y)oo** *-form of*　もらいます［もらう］　*to get, to have.*
　　　⇨L16GNI
　　～かな makes an implied request less direct.⇨まとめ2BⅡ4

アイスになさいますか、ホットになさいますか。*Which do you prefer, iced or hot?*
　　　　　　　　　　　　　　　　　⇨CN S-3
　　　～になさいます［なさる］＝します［する］　*to have, to decide.* ⇨GNⅢ

かしこまりました。　　　　　　　　*Very well. (lit. I've understood.)* ⇨CN2

お願いします。　　　　　　　　　　*(The bill), please.* ⇨CN S-3
　ねが

ごいっしょですか。　　　　　　　　*Are you paying together?* ⇨CN S-5

べつべつにしてください。　　　　　*Please add it up separately.* ⇨CN S-5
　　～にします　　　　　　　　　　⇨GNⅢ

1000円になります。　　　　　　　　*That will be 1000 yen.*
　えん
　　～になります　　　　　　　　　*to become, to be* ⇨GNⅢ2

1150円いただきます。　　　　　　　*1150 yen, please.* ⇨CN2

　　　いただきます［いただく］　　*to get, to receive*

2000円おあずかりします。　　　　　*(lit. I've received 2000 yen.)* ⇨CN2
　　　あずかります［あずかる］　　*to receive, to keep* ⇨CN2

Words in the report

注文します［する］	ちゅうもんします	to order
飲みます［のむ］	のみます	to drink
はらいます［はらう］		to pay

Grammar Notes

Examples

① **田中さんはウェートレスにおつりをもらいました。**

Tanaka-san wa ueetoresu ni otsuri o moraimashita.

Tanaka-san received the change from the waitress.

② **山下さんにケーキをあげました。**

Yamashita-san ni keeki o agemashita.

I gave the cake to Yamashita-san.

③ **だれにケーキをもらいましたか。**

Dare ni keeki o moraimashita ka.

From whom did you get the cake?

【*Explanation*】

Morau (**moraimasu**) *to receive* uses **ga** to mark the receiver, **o** to mark the object that changes hands, and **ni** to mark the giver.

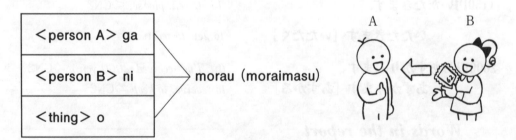

→ **Sharuma-san ga Tanaka-san ni kitte o morau** (**moraimasu**).

Sharma-san receives stamps from Tanaka-san.

Other verbs using the same structure include:

kariru (**karimasu**)   *to borrow*   **narau** (**naraimasu**)   *to learn*

56

→ **Sharuma-san ga Tanaka-san ni hon o kariru (karimasu).**
Sharma-san borrows a book from Tanaka-san.

→ **Gakusee ga sensee ni Nihongo o narau (naraimasu).**
The students learn Japanese from the teacher.

In Lesson 2, we saw the structure particle **ni**, indicating a goal. Compare ① with the following sentence.

GN

1. 田中さんはウェートレスにお金をはらいました。

Tanaka-san wa ueetoresu <u>ni</u> okane o haraimashita.
Tanaka-san paid money to the waitress.

Ni *from* in ① and **ni** *to* in the above sentence seem to have opposite meanings, but in fact we are dealing with the same structure particle. **Ni** basically indicates a point, and it is the verb with which it is used that specifies whether the direction is towards the subject, or away from it.

2. （私は）田中さんにあげました。

（Watashi wa） Tanaka-san <u>ni</u> agemashita.
I gave it to Tanakan-san.

3. （私は）田中さんにもらいました。

（Watashi wa） Tanaka-san <u>ni</u> moraimashita.
I received it from Tanaka-san.

Kara *from* can be used instead of **ni**.

4. シャルマさんは田中さんから切手をもらいました。

Sharuma-san wa Tanaka-san <u>kara</u> kitte o moraimashita.
Sharma-san received stamps from Tanaka-san.

Ⅱ. です substituting for a verb

Examples

① A：どこへ行きますか。 *Where will you go?*
   Doko e ikimasu ka.

   B：大学です。 *To the university.*
   Daigaku desu.

② W：何になさいますか。 *What will you have (to eat)?*
   Nan ni nasaimasu ka.

   A：私はポークです。 *I'll have pork. (lit. As for me, pork.)*
   Watashi wa pooku desu.

   B：私はチキン。 *I'll have chicken.*
   Watashi wa chikin.

【*Explanation*】

In reply to a question containing a question word, you can substitute structure particle ＋ verb with **desu**. ⇨まとめ2AⅢ

A：Doko de kaimashita ka. *Where did you buy it?*
B：Oosaka de kaimashita. *I bought it in Osaka.*
            ↓
   Oosaka   desu

A：Dare ga ikimasu ka. *Who will go?*
B：Tanaka-san ga ikimasu. *Tanaka-san will go.*
            ↓
   Tanaka-san   desu

In colloquial language, substitutions of the type seen in ② are commonplace. A and B are at a restaurant, and the waitress (W) is taking the order. A's order **Watashi wa pooku desu** literally means *I am (a) pork*, but the situation makes it clear that he is <u>ordering</u> a pork dish. The same applies to B. Sentences which use **desu** this way have the structure **[N] wa [N] desu**, though **desu** can be omitted as in ②B.

GN

Ⅲ．〜にします and 〜になります：する verbs and なる verbs〈1〉

【*Explanation*】

The difference between **suru (shimasu)** *to make, to do* and **naru (narimasu)** *to become,* is very important in Japanese. ⇨L9GNIV

Both **suru (shimasu)** and **naru (narimasu)** have a wide range of meanings, which include the following:

1．[N] ni shimasu

1. 鈴　木：何にしますか。
   Suzuki：Nan ni shimasu ka.
   What shall we have?

   田　中：コーヒーにしましょう。
   Tanaka：Koohii ni shimashoo.
   Let's have coffee.

2. ウェートレス：ごいっしょですか。
   Waitress：Goissho desu ka.
   Are you paying together?

   鈴　木：いえ、べつべつにしてください。
   Suzuki：Ie, betsubetsu ni shite kudasai.
   No, please make separate bills.

   ええ、いっしょにしてください。
   Ee, issho ni shite kudasai.
   Yes, together.

2．[N] ni narimasu

田 中：いくらですか。
Tanaka：Ikura desu ka.
How much?

ウェートレス：全部で1500円になります。
Waitress：Zenbu de 1500-en ni narimasu.
It comes to 1500 yen.

Ⅳ．いつ *when?*: question word

1．A：いつ日本へ来ましたか。 　　*When did you come to Japan?*
　　　Itsu Nihon e kimashita ka.

　　B：先月来ました。 　　　　　*I came last month.*
　　　Sengetsu kimashita.

2．A：いつ国へ帰りますか。 　　*When will you return to your country?*
　　　Itsu kuni e kaerimasu ka.

　　B：あした帰ります。 　　　*I'll return tomorrow.*
　　　Ashita kaerimasu.

Ⅴ．〜ましょう and 〜ませんか

1．-mashoo

-mashoo, expresses the following:

1）suggesting a course of action:

1．いっしょに行きましょう。 　　*Let's go together.*
　　Issho ni ikimashoo.

2．A：帰りましょうか。 　　　*Shall we go home?*
　　　Kaerimashoo ka.

　　B：ええ、帰りましょう。 　　*Yes, let's go home.*
　　　Ee, kaerimashoo.

２）the speaker's proposed intention:

　　　　　3．A：だれが行きますか。　　　　*Who will go?*
　　　　　　　　Dare ga ikimasu ka.

　　　　　　　B：わたしが行きましょう。　　*I propose to go.*
　　　　　　　　Watashi ga ikimashoo.

２．-masen ka

　　　-masen ka, which takes the form of a negative question, is used for making an invitation:

　　　　　1．A：いっしょに行きませんか。　　*Won't you come with us?*
　　　　　　　　Issho ni ikimasen ka.

　　　　　　　B：ええ、行きましょう。　　　　*Yes, let's go.*
　　　　　　　　Ee, ikimashoo.

　　　　　2．A：私のうちへ来ませんか。　　*Won't you come to my home?*
　　　　　　　　Watashi no uchi e kimasen ka.

　　　　　　　B：ありがとうございます。　　*Thank you very much.*
　　　　　　　　Arigatoo gozaimasu.

Ⅵ．ひとつ，ふたつ，……: counter for things
**　　ひとり，ふたり，……: counter for people**

１．Things

　　　Use the following counting system for things in general.

ひとつ(1),	ふたつ(2),	みっつ(3),	よっつ(4),	いつつ(5),
hitotsu	futatsu	mittsu	yottsu	itsutsu
むっつ(6),	ななつ(7),	やっつ(8),	ここのつ(9),	とお(10),
muttsu	nanatsu	yattsu	kokonotsu	too
じゅういち(11),	じゅうに(12),	…………	にじゅう(20)	
juuichi	juuni		nijuu	

いくつ *how many?*
ikutsu

　　　　　1．コーヒーをふたつください。
　　　　　　　Koohii o <u>futatsu</u> kudasai.
　　　　　　　We'd like two coffees.

GN

2．A：漢字はいくつ勉強しましたか。

Kanji wa <u>ikutsu</u> benkyoo shimashita ka.

How many Kanji did you study?

B：さんじゅう勉強しました。

<u>Sanjuu</u> benkyoo shimashita.

I studied 30 Kanji.

2．People

Use the following counting system for people.

ひとり（1），ふたり（2），さんにん（3），よにん（4），ごにん（5），…じゅうにん（10）
hitori　　　futari　　　san-nin　　　yo-nin　　　go-nin　　　　juu-nin

なんにん　*how many (people)?*
nan-nin

A：学生は何人来ましたか。

Gakusee wa <u>nan-nin</u> kimashita ka.

How many students came?

B：ふたり来ました。

<u>Futari</u> kimashita.

Two came.

VII. は and も〈3〉: more about discourse particles

In Lesson 2, we saw how to replace the structure particles **ga/o** with the discourse particles **wa/mo** to make [**N**] + structure particles **ga/o** the topic of a sentence. With other structure particles (**ni, e, de, to** etc.), **wa/mo** are added on:

(1)

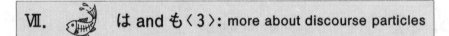

Sharma-san went to Tokyo with Brown-san yesterday.

(2)

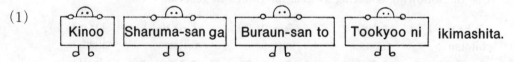

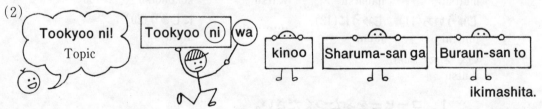

ikimashita.

*As for (going) to Tokyo, Sharma-san went
there with Brown-san yesterday.*

(3)

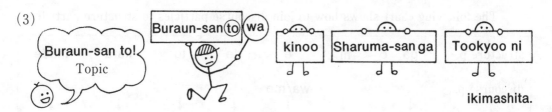

ikimashita.

*As for (going) with Brown-san, Sharma-san went
to Tokyo with her yesterday.*

GN

(4)

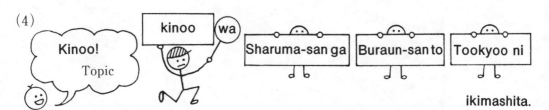

ikimashita.

*As for yesterday, Sharma-san went to
Tokyo with Brown-san.*

Note how [N] + ni/e/de/to etc. become topics in the conversation below:

Q :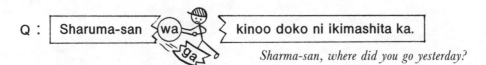

Sharma-san, where did you go yesterday?

S : Kyooto ni ikimashita.　　　*I went to Kyoto.*

Q : 　dare to ikimashita ka.

As for (going) to Kyoto, with whom did you go?

S : Buraun-san to ikimashita.　　*I went with Brown-san.*

Q :

What did you see in Kyoto?

S : Kinkakuji o mimashita.　　*We saw Kinkakuji temple.*

The following chart shows how to join discourse particles to structure particles.

structure p.	ga	o	ni*	e	de	to	kara	made
				+				
discourse p.				wa/mo				
	↓	↓	↓	↓	↓	↓	↓	↓
	wa	wa	ni wa	e wa	de wa	to wa	kara wa	made wa
	mo	mo	ni mo	e mo	de mo	to mo	kara mo	made mo

* **Ni** is also occasionally replaced by **wa/mo**. ⇨ L1GN Ⅱ, L2GN Ⅱ, L4GN Ⅱ, L14GN Ⅰ

Conversation Notes

<General Information>

1. At a restaurant

a. The menu

Restaurants in Japan often display plastic replicas of the food they serve in a glass case outside. Other restaurants will have a printed menu with photographs of their dishes as in the example below.

Many restaurants serve set lunches between 11 : 30 a.m. and 2 p.m.; coffee shops often have set breakfast menus called モーニングサービス（**mooningu saabisu**, *Morning Service*）until about 11 a.m..

Set meals at Japanese-style restaurants are called 定食（**teeshoku**）whereas at Western-style restaurants they are called セット（**setto**).

b. Payment

In Japan, one usually pays at the cash desk rather than at the table. Some restaurants require customers to buy tickets called 食券（**shokken**）for each item of food and drink at the entrance. This is indicated by a sign 「食券をお求めください （**Shokken o omotome kudasai.** *Please buy a ticket.*）」at the cash desk.

At most restaurants, you pay when you leave. Sometimes you will see a sign at the cash desk saying 「お会計はお帰りにどうぞ（**Okaikee wa okaeri ni doozo.** *Please pay when leaving.*）」

Some restaurants add サービス料（**saabisuryoo** *service charge*）to your bill; 消費税（**shoohizee** *consumption tax*）is sometimes included in the price, and sometimes added on.

2. Expressions used in restaurants and shops

Waiters or waitresses in restaurants and clerks in shops use super-polite expressions when speaking to customers.（Some fixed expressions used in department stores are introduced in L10. ⇨L10 CN2）

a. Expressions used by waiters and waitresses

When you enter a restaurant, the waiter will greet you with 「いらっしゃいませ。 （**Irasshaimase.** *Welcome*）」Then, he will often ask 「何名さまですか。（**Nanmee-sama desu ka.** *How many of you?*）」and guide you to a seat. Counter for people ⇨GNVI

Look at the following examples:

① こちらへどうぞ。　　　　　*This way, please.*
　Kochira e doozo.　　　　　（indicating the direction by gesture）

　どうぞこちらへ。
　Doozo kochira e.

In some restaurants, you can seat yourself.

The waiter or waitress will often confirm your order using the polite expression like ～でございますね，おひとつ，etc. as follows:

② **Customer**：メニューありますか。   *Do you have a menu?*
Menyuu arimasu ka.

   Waitress：メニューでございますね。   *The menu, (very well).*
Menyuu de gozaimasu ne.

③ **Customer**：コーヒー、ひとつ。   *Coffee, one.*
Koohii, hitotsu.

   Waitress：コーヒー、おひとつ。
Koohii, ohitotu.

④ **Waitress**：少々お待ちください。   *Please wait for a moment.*
Shooshoo omachi kudasai.

⑤ **Waitress**：何になさいますか。   *What is your order?*
Nan ni nasaimasu ka.

⑥ **Waitress**：かしこまりました。   *Very well.*
Kashikomarimashita.

b. Expressions used by the cashier (⇨CN S-5)

The cashier will indicate how much the check is with the following expressions.

① **1150円** | いただきます。   *1150 yen, please.*
itadakimasu.

になります。
ni narimasu.

でございます。／です。
de gozaimasu.   desu.

If you pay with a bill that exceeds the amount required, the cashier will first confirm the amount, then give you your change as follows:

② **Customer**：はい。   *Here you are.*
Hai.

   Cashier：**2000円** | おあずかりします。   *2000 yen.*
oazukari shimasu.

のおあずかりです。
no oazukari desu.

Cashier：850円 のおかえしになります。　　*That's 850 yen change.*

no okaeshi ni narimasu.

のおかえしです。

no okaeshi desu.

のおつりです。

no otsuri desu.

3. Fast food shops

In fast food shops like McDonald's and Kentucky Fried Chicken, the young sales personnel speak in accordance with the sales manual (a prescribed set of phrases). Such fixed expressions include the following:

① **いらっしゃいませ。**　　　　　　*Welcome to our shop.*

Irasshaimase.

② **ご注文は。**　　　　　　　*What do you order?*

Gochuumon wa.

③ **お飲み物はいかがですか。**　　*Would you like a drink?*

Onomimono wa ikaga desu ka.

④ **こちらでめしあがりますか、お持ち帰りですか。**

Kochira de meshiagarimasu ka, omochikaeri desu ka.

Will you eat here, or take it out?

<Strategies>

S-1. How to ask for something you need

In some situations, you can use ありますか↗, with slightly rising intonation to ask for something you want.

<thing>（が）ありますか。　　　*Do you have* ～ ?

See the examples for different situations below:

① （At a restaurant, wanting to see the menu.）
メニュー、ありますか。↗
Menyuu, arimasu ka.

② （At a restaurant, when you want to order what is not written on the menu.）
アイスクリーム、ありますか。↗
Aisukuriimu, arimasu ka.

③ （At the stationer's, wanting to buy something you can't see on the shelves.）
航空便のふうとう、ありますか。↗
Kookuubin no fuutoo, arimasu ka.

④ （Wanting to borrow something.）
ボールペン、ありますか。↗
Boorupen, arimasu ka.

⑤ （Wanting to receive something.）
パンフレット（a pamphlet）、ありますか。↗
Panfuretto, arimasu ka.

⑥ （Wanting to know the time.）
時計、ありますか。↗
Tokee, arimasu ka.

時計
ありますか。

ええ。
いま９時ですよ。

CN

S-2. How to give and receive something

When the waiter/waitress brings you something you have asked for, you can acknowledge it by using どうも.

① **Waitress**：どうぞ。   *Here you are.*
             Doozo.

      Customer：どうも。   *Thank you.*
             Doomo.

どうも can also be used to accept an offer:

② **A**：どうぞ。（offering sweets）   *Please take one.*
        Doozo.

      B：あ、どうも。   *Oh, thank you.*
        A, doomo.

③ **A**：どうぞ。（offering a seat）   *Please have a seat.*
        Doozo.

      B：どうもすみません。   *Thank you very much.*
        Doomo sumimasen.

④ **A**：どうぞ。（offering the way）   *After you.*
        Doozo.

      B：あ、どうも。   *Thanks.*
        A, doomo.

S-3. How to order

a. The waiter or waitress may ask for your order as follows:

何になさいますか。   *What would you like?*
Nani ni nasaimasu ka.

ご注文は。↗   *What's your order?*
Gochuumon wa.

おきまりですか。 *Have you decided?*

Okimari desu ka.

You can order as follows:

コーヒー	**（を）お願いします。**	*A coffee, please.* ⇨L2CN S-4
Koohii	（o）onegai shimasu.	
	（を）ください。	
	（o）kudasai.	
	（を）もらおうかな。	*I'll have a coffee, I think.*
	（o）moraoo kana.	
	にします。	
	ni shimasu.	
	ひとつ。	*One coffee.*
	hitotsu.	

b. Making a choice

When there is a choice, the waiter/waitress may ask you:

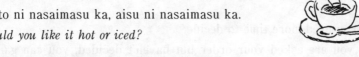

ホットになさいますか、アイスになさいますか。

Hotto ni nasaimasu ka, aisu ni nasaimasu ka.

Would you like it hot or iced?

ホットにしますか、アイスにしますか。

Hotto ni shimasu ka, aisu ni shimasu ka.

ホットですか、アイスですか。

Hotto desu ka, aisu desu ka.

You can then make your choice by using one of the following expressions:

ホット	**（を）お願いします。**	*I'd like it hot.*
Hotto	（o）onegai shimasu.	
	（を）ください。	
	（o）kudasai.	
	にします。	
	ni shimasu.	
	です。	
	desu.	

71

c. Summing up

After each of you ordered different things, one of you can summarize the order with じゃ. ⇨まとめ2BⅡ2

① A：私、ホット。   *For me, hot coffee.*
    Watashi, hotto.

B：じゃ、ホットふたつね。   *Two hot coffees, then.*
    Ja, hotto futatsu ne.

② A：ぼく、コーヒー。   *I'll have coffee.*
    Boku, koohii.

B：私、紅茶。   *I'll have tea.*
    Watashi, koocha.

C：じゃ、コーヒーふたつ、紅茶ひとつ、ください。
    Ja, koohii futatsu, koocha hitotsu kudasai.
    Two coffees and one tea, then, please.

S-4. How to deal with problems in a restaurant

a. When you need more time to decide

When you are asked your order but haven't decided, you can gain time by using the following expressions:

Customer：あ、もう	少し	待ってください。 📖 ⇨L5GNIV
A, moo	sukoshi	matte kudasai.
	ちょっと	待って。 🇨
	chotto	matte.

Oh, can you give me a little more time.

Waitress：じゃ、お決まりになりましたら、お呼びください。
Ja, okimari ni narimashitara, oyobi kudasai.
Please call me when you have decided.

b. When the food you ordered doesn't come

When your order is slow in coming, you can prompt the waiter with 「まだですか。 *Not yet?* 」 as follows:

Customer : **すみません。**　　　　*Excuse me.*
Sumimasen.

Waitress : **はい。**　　　　*Yes?*
Hai.

Customer : **あの、コーヒー、まだ** | **でしょうか。**
Ano, koohii, mada | deshoo ka.

| **ですか。**
| desu ka.

What's happened to my coffee?

Waitress : **申しわけございません。もう少々お待ちください。**
Mooshiwake gozaimasen. Moo shooshoo omachi kudasai.
We are very sorry. It won't be much longer.

c. When the waiter or waitress brings the wrong dish

If you are served something you didn't order, you can tell the waiter as follows:

Waitress : **お待たせいたしました。どうぞ。**
Omatase itashimashita. Doozo.
I'm sorry to have kept you waiting. Here it is.

Customer : **あの、これ、ちがっているんですけど。**
Ano, kore, chigatte iru n desu kedo.
Um, this is not what I ordered.

Waitress : **え↗、そうですか。どうも申しわけありません。**
E, soo desu ka. Doomo mooshiwake arimasen.
Oh, really? I am terribly sorry.

d. When you cannot read the menu

When you can't work out an item on the menu, you can ask information using 「**これ、何ですか。**（Kore, nan desu ka.）*What is this?*」or 「**何が入っているんですか。**（Nani ga haitte iru n desu ka.）*What is in it?*」

If there are foods or ingredients you can't eat, you can check with the waiter/waitress if they are used in a dish you want to order.

これ、＜item＞ が入っていますか。

Customer：あの、これ、ぶた肉が入っていますか。

Ano, kore, butaniku ga haitte imasu ka.

Excuse me. Is there any pork in this?

Waitress：ぶた肉ですか。いえ、入っていませんよ。

Butaniku desu ka. Ie, haitte imasen yo.

Pork? No, there isn't.

S-5. How to pay the cashier

a. Paying the bill

When two or more people have had a meal together, the cashier may ask if you wish to pay together or separately. If you pay together, just answer **はい** (①); to pay separately, answer as shown in ②.

Customer：お願いします。

Onegaishimasu.

Cashier：はい。ごいっしょですか。　*Will you pay together?*

Hai. Goissho desu ka.

① **Customer**：はい。

Hai.

② **Customer**：いえ、べつべつにしてください。

Ie, betsubetsu ni shite kudasai.

No, please add it up separately.

b. Receiving one's change

After paying or receiving your change, you can say **どうも** or **ごちそうさまでした** (*Thank you for the meal.*).

＊NOTE＊　Japanese people usually say **いただきます** (*Thank you I'll have it.*) before eating and **ごちそうさまでした** after eating. ⇨L19CN S-3

場所を聞く
ばしょ
Asking the whereabouts

OBJECTIVES:

GRAMMAR

Ⅰ. The こ/そ/あ/ど system ⟨1⟩
Ⅱ. Expressions of existence
Ⅲ. ～から⟨1⟩ *because*～: connective particle
Ⅳ. ～なら⟨1⟩ *if you mean* ～
Ⅴ. や and とか *and*: connective particles

CONVERSATION

＜General Information＞

1. Location

＜Strategies＞

S-1. How to start a conversation ―4. Introducing a question
S-2. How to ask the whereabouts of things/people
S-3. How to get something you didn't catch repeated
S-4. How to confirm information ―1.
S-5. How to gain time to collect your thoughts
S-6. How to end a conversation ―2. After asking a question

Model Conversation

(1)

Characters ：Lisa Brown（リサ・ブラウン）, a female student（女子学生）

Situation ：Brown-san is looking for a washing machine in her dormitory.

Flow-chart ：

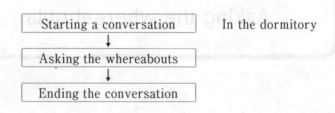

```
┌──────────────────────────┐
│ Starting a conversation  │        In the dormitory
└──────────────────────────┘
            ↓
┌──────────────────────────┐
│ Asking the whereabouts   │
└──────────────────────────┘
            ↓
┌──────────────────────────┐
│ Ending the conversation  │
└──────────────────────────┘
```

―宿舎で―

ブラウン：あの、すみません。

女子学生：はい。

＊　　　＊　　　＊

ブラウン：あの、せんたく機はどこでしょうか。

女子学生：せんたく機。

ブラウン：ええ。
　　　　　場所、わかりますか。

女子学生：せんたく機なら、4階のあっち側にありますよ。

ブラウン：4階ですか。

女子学生：ええ。
　　　　　そっちに階段がありますから。

ブラウン：はい。

＊　　　＊　　　＊

ブラウン：どうもありがとうございました。

女子学生：どういたしまして。

（2）

Characters ：Anil Sharma（アニル・シャルマ）, Tanaka（田中）

Situation ：Sharma-san is looking for a telephone on campus.

Flow-chart ：

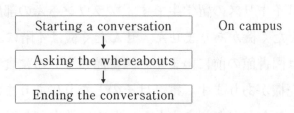

Starting a conversation	On campus

↓

Asking the whereabouts

↓

Ending the conversation

MC

―キャンパスで―

シャルマ：あの、すみません。
田　中：はい。

　　　　　　　＊　　　　＊　　　　＊

シャルマ：このへんに、電話ありますか。
田　中：電話ね。
シャルマ：ええ。
田　中：ああ、食堂の自動販売機のとなりにありますよ。
シャルマ：じどう……。
田　中：自動販売機。
　　　　ほら、あのコーラとかジュースとかの。
シャルマ：ああ、わかりました。
　　　　そのとなりですね。
田　中：そう。

　　　　　　　＊　　　　＊　　　　＊

シャルマ：どうもすみませんでした。
田　中：いいえ。

77

Report

　ブラウンさんはイギリスの留学生です。ブラウンさんの部屋は宿舎の2階です。2階にはせんたく機がありません。せんたく機は4階にあります。

　シャルマさんは図書館の前にいます。図書館のうしろに食堂があります。食堂の中に自動販売機があります。電話はそのとなりにあります。自動販売機にはコーラやジュースなどがありますから、近くに学生がたくさんいます。

New Words and Expressions

Words in the conversation

宿舎	しゅくしゃ	*dormitory, student accomodation*
女子学生	じょしがくせい	*female student*
せんたく機	せんたくき	*washing machine*
場所	ばしょ	*place, location*
わかります［わかる］		*to know, to understand*
～階	～かい	*counter for floors*
あっち側	あっちがわ	*the other side, far side*
あります［ある］		*to be, to exist*
そっち		*over there*
階段	かいだん	*stairs*
キャンパス	kyanpasu	*campus*
このへん		*around here*
電話	でんわ	*telephone*
食堂	しょくどう	*restaurant, cafeteria*
自動販売機	じどうはんばいき	*vending machine*
となり		*next to*
コーラ	koora	*cola*
ジュース	juusu	*juice, soft drink*

＜Expressions in the conversation＞

せんたく機はどこでしょうか。↘　　　*Could you tell me where the washing machine is?*

　　～でしょうか↘ forms a polite question. ⇨CN S-2, L19GNⅠ

場所、わかります。↗　　　*Do you know the place?*
ばしょ

　　This works as a question only with short rising intonation. ⇨まとめ1BⅡ2

せんたく機なら、　　　*(If it's) the washing machine,*
き
　　～なら ⇨GNⅣ

そっちに階段がありますから。　　　*The stairs are right there.*
かいだん
　　そっち ⇨GNⅠ，**～に～があります** ⇨GNⅡ，**～から** ⇨GNⅢ

どういたしまして。　　　*You're welcome* ⇨まとめ1BⅡ4

ほら、あのコーラとかジュースとかの。	*You know, that machine selling things like cola and soft drinks.*

　　　ほら、あの〜 indicates that you are reminding someone of something obvious.

　　　〜とか〜とか indicates that samples are being given. ⇨GN Ⅴ

ああ、わかりました。	*Oh, I see.*
そのとなりですね。↗	*It's next to that (vending machine), isn't it?*
そう。↘	*Right.* 🄖➡⬇
どうもすみませんでした。	*Thank you very much.* ⇨まとめ1BⅡ4
いいえ。	*Not at all.* ⇨まとめ1BⅡ4

Words in the report

イギリス	Igirisu	U.K., England
部屋	へや	room
図書館	としょかん	library
前	まえ	before, in front of
うしろ		behind
中	なか	inside
近く	ちかく	nearby
たくさん		many, much
います［いる］		to be, to exist

<*Expressions in the report*>

コーラやジュースなどがありますから、　　　*As there are cola and soft drinks, etc.,*

　　　〜や〜など lists representative examples; it is used in formal speech. ⇨GN Ⅴ

　　　〜から indicates a reason. ⇨GN Ⅲ

Grammar Notes

I. The こ／そ／あ／ど system ⟨1⟩

Examples

① A：どの本を読みましたか。 *Which book did you read?*
  Dono hon o yomimashita ka.

  B：この本を読みました。 *I read this book.*
  Kono hon o yomimashita.

② A：どの本を読みましたか。 *Which book did you read?*
  Dono hon o yomimashita ka.

  B：これを読みました。 *I read this.*
  Kore o yomimashita.

③ A：あれはだれの本ですか。 *Whose book is that?*
  Are wa dare no hon desu ka.

  A：私の（本）です。 *(It's) mine.*
  Watashi no（hon）desu.

【Explanation】

The choice of **ko/so/a** depends on the spatial relationship between speaker, listener and item referred to: the **ko**-series refers to items nearer to the speaker, the **so**-series to items nearer to the listener, and the **a**-series to items that are at a distance from both speaker and listener. The **do**-series consists of question words.

1. kono/sono/ano/dono ＋ [N]

(1) **Kono hon** refers to a book which is nearer the speaker.
(2) **Sono hon** refers to a book which is nearer the listener.
(3) **Ano hon** refers to a book which is at a distance from both speaker and listener.
(4) **Dono hon** is used to find out which book is being referred to.

Kono, sono, ano and dono cannot be used on their own; they must precede a noun (or a noun phrase).

2. kore/sore/are/dore

Kore, sore, are and dore are, grammatically speaking, nouns. They can be used in place of kono/sono/ano/dono ＋ [N], and are used when the items indicated are so obvious that there is no need to mention them by name. In ②, for instance, B uses kore *this* rather than kono hon *this book,* because A's question clearly refers to a book B read.

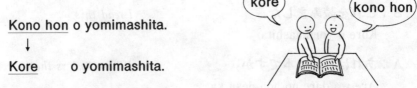

Kono hon o yomimashita.
     ↓
Kore   o yomimashita.

The chart below illustrates this distinction between words beginning with ko/so/a/do.

	The ko/so/a/do system			
S＝speaker	**ko**-series	**so**-series	**a**-series	**do**-series
L＝listener	nearer S	nearer L	away from S/L	Question word
thing	kono [N]	sono [N]	ano [N]	dono [N]
	kore	sore	are	dore
area	kono hen	sono hen	ano hen	dono hen
place	koko	soko	asoko	doko
direction <Formal>	kochira	sochira	achira	dochira
<Casual>	kotchi	sotchi	atchi	dotchi

1. <u>あの</u>ビルは図書館です。　*That building over there is a library.*

   <u>Ano</u> biru wa toshokan desu.

2. 鈴木さんは<u>あちら</u>へ行きました。*Suzuki-san went in that direction.*

   Suzuki-san wa <u>achira</u> e ikimashita.

3. <u>ここ</u>はどこですか。　*Where am I? (lit. Where is this place?)*

   <u>Koko</u> wa doko desu ka.

➪L19GNⅦ, L21GNⅡ

Ⅱ. Expressions of existence

Examples

① **A：このへんに電話がありますか。**

   Kono hen ni denwa ga arimasu ka.

   Is there a telephone around here?

B：ええ、あります。

   Ee, arimasu.

   Yes, there is.

いいえ、(このへんには) ありません。

   Iie,(kono hen ni wa) arimasen.

   No, there isn't (at least around here).

② **この大学には留学生がたくさんいます。**

   Kono daigaku ni wa ryuugakusee ga takusan imasu.

   There are many foreign students in this university.

③ **留学生はこの大学にたくさんいますか。**

   Ryuugakusee wa kono daigaku ni takusan imasu ka.

   Are there many foreign students in this university?

④ **A：電話はどこにありますか。**

   Denwa wa doko ni arimasu ka.

   Where is the telephone?

B：つくえの上にあります。

   Tsukue no ue ni arimasu.

   It's on the desk.

⑤ A：田中さんはどこにいますか。

Tanaka-san wa doko ni imasu ka.

Where is Tanaka-san?

B：（田中さんは）あそこにいます。

（Tanaka-san wa）asoko ni imasu.

(She's) over there.

【*Explanation*】

1. aru（arimasu）and iru（imasu）: verbs of existence

1）The distinction between **aru** and **iru** is that **aru（arimasu）** is used for non-animate/non-moving objects, whereas **iru（imasu）** is used with animate or living things, including people. Below are the structures of the two verbs:

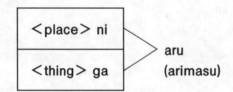

→ Asoko ni denwa ga aru.
There is a telephone over there.

→ Asoko ni onna no hito ga iru.
There is a woman over there.

2）🐟 ni 〈3〉: location particle

The structure particle **ni** can indicate location, or place of existence.

3）＜place＞ ni ～ ga arimasu/imasu: *there is*

This structure indicates that a thing or person can be found at the place mentioned. Therefore, in a question like ① above, A's main concern is to find out if there is a telephone. Answer **Ee/Hai, arimasu** if the answer is *yes*, or **Iie, arimasen** if it is *no*. Here are some more examples:

1. 教室にコンピュータがあります。　　*There is a computer in the classroom.*

Kyooshitsu ni konpyuuta ga arimasu.

2. 2階に事務室があります。　　*There's an office on the 2nd floor.*

Ni-kai ni jimushitsu ga arimasu.

3. A：**教室に学生がいますか。**　　　*Is there a student in the classroom?*
　　Kyooshitsu ni gakusee ga imasu ka.

　B：**はい、います。**　　　　　　　*Yes, there is.*
　　Hai, imasu.

　　いいえ、いません。　　　　　*No, there isn't.*
　　Iie, imasen.

2. 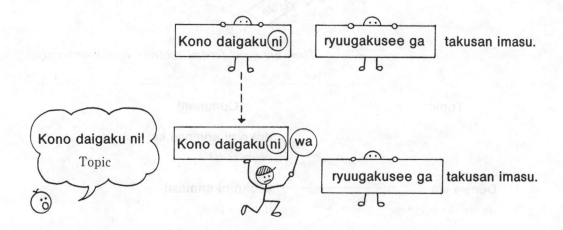 wa in expressions of existence

1) **<place> ni wa ~ ga arimasu/imasu:** what's in a place

　In ②, **<place> ni** is followed by **wa** making it the topic:

In this university, there are many foreign students.

Having established **<place> ni wa** as topic, you can now have a conversation（or a series of comments）about a place:

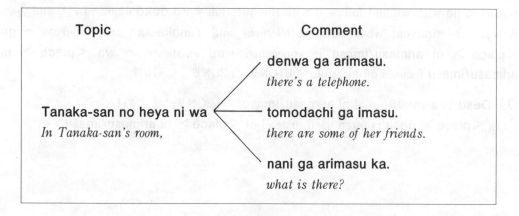

Topic	Comment
	denwa ga arimasu. *there's a telephone.*
Tanaka-san no heya ni wa *In Tanaka-san's room,*	**tomodachi ga imasu.** *there are some of her friends.*
	nani ga arimasu ka. *what is there?*

85

2） **~ wa <place> ni arimasu/imasu:** the whereabouts of things/persons

In ③, **~ ga** is made into a topic by replacing it with **~ wa.**

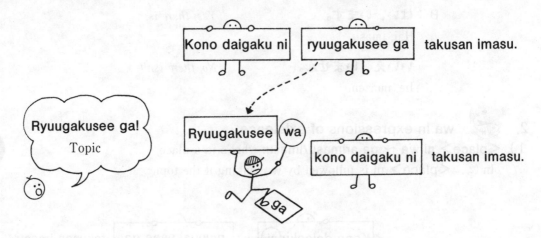

There are many foreign students at this university.

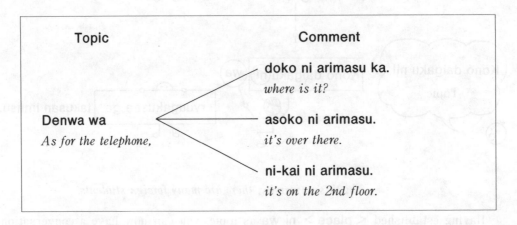

To ask the whereabouts of a thing or person, change **~ ga** into a topic by replacing **ga** with **wa** and follow it with the question word **doko** *where?*. In ④ and ⑤, A wants to find out where **denwa** *telephone* and **Tanaka-san** are. Whereas **~ ga <place >** **ni arimasu/imasu** is concerned with existence, **~ wa <place >** **ni arimasu/imasu** focuses on location. ⇨L1GN Ⅱ, L2GN Ⅲ, L3GN Ⅶ

3） **Desu** as a substitute of **ni arimasu/imasu.** ⇨L3GN Ⅱ, まとめ1A

　 <place> desu is often used instead of **<place>** **ni arimasu/imasu.**

A : Denwa wa <u>doko ni arimasu</u> ka.

　　　　　　↓

　Denwa wa <u>doko desu</u> ka.

B : <u>Asoko ni arimasu.</u>

　　　　↓

　<u>Asoko desu.</u>

Where is the telephone?

(It)'s over there.

Be careful about **ni** !

○　**Denwa wa asoko ni arimasu.**　　*The telephone is over there.*

○　**Denwa wa asoko desu.**

✕　**Denwa wa asoko ni desu.**

3. Expressions of relative location

Tsukue no ue in ④ indicates whereabouts in relation to a desk, i.e. whether a thing or person is on, under, behind a desk etc. The most common Japanese expressions of relative location are the following:

～ no mae	*in front of ～*	～ no ushiro	*behind ～*
～ no ue	*on ～*	～ no shita	*under ～*
～ no naka	*in ～*	～ no soto	*outside ～*
～ no migi	*to the right of ～*	～ no hidari	*to the left of ～*
～ no tonari	*next to ～*		
～ no chikaku	*near ～*		

1. **つくえの下にねこがいます。**

   <u>Tsukue no shita ni</u> neko ga imasu.

   There's a cat under the desk.

2. **大学の近くに銀行があります。**

   <u>Daigaku no chikaku ni</u> ginkoo ga arimasu.

   There's a bank near the university.

3. **ポストは郵便局の前にあります。**

   Posuto wa <u>yuubinkyoku no mae ni</u> arimasu.

   The mailbox is in front of the post office.

4. **パスポートはかばんの中にあります。**

   Pasupooto wa <u>kaban no naka ni</u> arimasu.

   The passport is in the bag.

87

Note that when the subject of the sentence is presented as the topic (familiar information marked by **wa**), English uses *the*, whereas when the subject is marked by **ga** (indicating new information), English uses *a* (⇨まとめ1A).

Ⅲ. 〜から〈1〉*because* 〜: connective particle

Examples

① **田中さんが来ましたから、いっしょに昼ごはんを食べました。**
Tanaka-san ga kimashita kara, issho ni hirugohan o tabemashita.
Because Tanaka-san came, (I) had lunch with her.

② **あしたは日本語の授業がありませんから、東京へいきます。**
Ashita wa Nihongo no jugyoo ga arimasen kara, Tookyoo e ikimasu.
As there is no Japanese class tomorrow, I'll go to Tokyo.

③ **ちょっと待ってください。鈴木さんに電話しますから。**
Chotto matte kudasai. Suzuki-san ni denwa shimasu kara.
Please wait a moment, as I'm going to call Suzuki-san.

④ **A：すみません。このへんに電話がありますか。**
　 Sumimasen. Kono hen ni denwa ga arimasu ka.
　 Excuse me. Is there a telephone around here?

　 B：ええ、2階にあります。エレベーターのすぐ前ですから。
　 Ee, ni-kai ni arimasu. Erebeetaa no sugu mae desu kara.
　 Yes, there is one on the 2nd floor. It's right in front of the lift.

【*Explanation*】

In {Sentence 1} kara {Sentence 2}, {S₁} expresses the reason for {S₂}, as illustrated by ① and ②. However, the order of {S₁} and {S₂} is often changed, as in ③, so that the main point is given first, and the reason is added on after it.

{S₁} (reason/cause) から	+	{S₂} (result)

田中さんが来ましたから、いっしょに昼ごはんを食べました。
Because Tanaka-san came, (I) had lunch with her.

88

When used at the end of a sentence (without {S₂}), ～ **kara.** indicates that the speaker is saying something s/he thinks should be obvious to the listener, as in ④.

GN

> ## Ⅳ. ～なら〈1〉: *if you mean ～*

Examples

① **A：あした、いっしょに東京に行きませんか。**
　　　Ashita, issho ni Tookyoo ni ikimasen ka.
　　　Won't you come to Tokyo with me tomorrow?

B：あしたならいいです。あしたは授業がありませんから。
　　　Ashita nara ii desu. Ashita wa jugyoo ga arimasen kara.
　　　If you're talking about tomorrow, it's OK, because there is no class tomorrow.

② **A：ペン、ありますか。**
　　　Pen, arimasu ka.
　　　Do you have a pen?

B：いいえ、えんぴつならあります。
　　　Iie, enpitsu nara arimasu.
　　　No, but if you want a pencil, I've got one.

【*Explanation*】

Nara attaches directly after a noun and indicates that noun is taken up for further comment in the sense of *if you mean* **[N]**:

A：せんたく機はどこにありますか。
　　　Sentakuki wa doko ni arimasu ka.
　　　Where is the washing machine?

B：<u>せんたく機なら</u>4階にありますよ。
　　　<u>Sentakuki nara</u> yon-kai ni arimasu yo.
　　　If it's the washing machine you want, it's on the 4th floor.

V.  や and とか *and*: connective particles

Ya and **toka** are used for citing samples, without being exhaustive.

1. **ペンや本があります。**

   Pen ya hon ga arimasu.

   ペンとか本（とか）があります。

   Pen toka hon（toka）ga arimasu.

   There is a pen, a book and such like.

2. **田中さんや鈴木さんといっしょに図書館へ行きます。**

   Tanaka-san ya Suzuki-san to issho ni toshokan e ikimasu.

   田中さんとか鈴木さん（とか）といっしょに図書館へ行きます。

   Tanaka-san toka Suzuki-san（toka）to issho ni toshokan e ikimasu.

   (I)'ll go to the library with Tanaka-san and Suzuki-san, among others.

Nado can be added to the last noun in order to reinforce the idea of *etcetera:*

3. **肉ややさいなどを買いました。**

   Niku ya yasai nado o kaimashita.

   肉とかやさいなどを買いました。

   Niku toka yasai nado o kaimashita.

   I bought meat and vegetables etcetera.

Look at the difference between [N] **to** [N] and [N] **ya/toka** [N] in the examples below:

4. **肉とやさいを買いました。**

   Niku to yasai o kaimashita.

   I bought meat and vegetables (and nothing else).

5. **肉 や／とか やさいを買いました。**

   Niku ya /toka yasai o kaimashita.

   I bought meat and vegetables (and some other things).

When making an order in a restaurant, you wouldn't normally use [N] **ya/toka** [N], because that would imply that you want the waiter to bring other dishes as he sees fit! Use [N] **to** [N] instead. ⇨L1GN V

Conversation Notes

1. Location

Basic words of location are illustrated as follows:

上（うえ ue）　　下（した shita）

前（まえ mae）　　後ろ（うしろ ushiro）

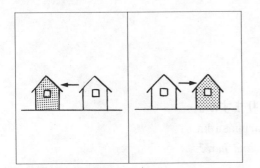

左（ひだり hidari）右（みぎ migi）

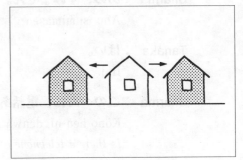

となり（tonari）

中（なか naka）

近く（ちかく chikaku）

91

<Strategies>

S-1.　How to start a conversation —4.　Introducing a question

Before asking a question, you can attract the listener's attention as follows:
⇨L5CN S-1

> **あの、ちょっとすみません。**⬆️➡️　　　　*Excuse me.*
> Ano, chotto sumimasen.

> **あの、すみません。**⬆️➡️
> Ano, sumimasen.

> **あの。**
> Ano.

> **あの、ちょっと。**➡️⬇️
> Ano, chotto.

> **Sharma**　：**あの、すみません。**
> 　　　　　　Ano, sumimasen.

> **Tanaka**　：**はい。**
> 　　　　　　Hai.

> **Sharma**　：**このへんに、電話ありますか。**
> 　　　　　　Kono hen ni, denwa arimasu ka.
> 　　　　　　*Is there a telephone around here?*

You can make it more polite: ⇨L7CN S-4

> **あの、ちょっとうかがいますが。**⬆️
> Ano, chotto ukagaimasu ga.
> *Excuse me, but may I ask you something?*

S-2. How to ask the whereabouts of things/people

a. You can ask directly with **どこ** as follows: ⇨GN I, L1GN Ⅲ

〜（は） 〜(wa)	どこ。↗ 🄒➡⬇ *Where is 〜?* doko.
	どこですか。↗ 📱 doko desu ka.
	どこにありますか。↗ 📱 doko ni arimasu ka.

In this pattern, **は** is often omitted even in formal speech. Recall it is also possible to use **〜は**↗ as a short casual question. ⇨L1CN3

To ask politely, use **でしょうか**↘. ⇨L19GN I

> **〜（は）どこでしょうか。↘ 📱**
> 〜(wa) doko deshoo ka.

① **Brown：あの、せんたく機はどこでしょうか。↘**
　　　　 Ano, sentakuki wa doko deshoo ka.
　　　　 Could you tell me where the washing machine is?

You can make your question even more polite by using **どちら** instead of **どこ**.

| 〜（は）
〜(wa) | どちらですか。↗ 📱
dochira desu ka. |
| | どちらでしょうか。↘ 📱
dochira deshoo ka. |

To find out if something you are looking for is available in the vicinity, ask with **このへんに**.

| このへんに、〜
kono hen ni, 〜 | ありますか。↗ 📱   *Is there 〜 around here?*
arimasu ka. |
| | ありませんか。↗ 📱
arimasen ka. |

② **Sharma：このへんに、電話ありますか。↗**
　　　　 Kono hen ni, denwa arimasu ka.

b. When you are looking for a person, you can ask as above, but do not forget to use います instead of あります. ⇨GNⅡ

① （Asking a senior student where your classmate is）

山下さん、 　　どこですか。↗ 🔲
Yamashita-san, 　doko ni imasu ka.

　　　　　　　　どこにいますか。↗ 🔲
　　　　　　　　doko desu ka.

② （Asking your adviser where his assistant is）
鈴木さんはどこでしょうか。↘ 🔲
Suzuki-san wa doko deshoo ka.

When the person you are looking for is a Higher, use どちら and/or いらっしゃいます. ⇨L9GNⅥ

③ （Asking Prof. Kimura's assistant where Prof. Kimura is）
木村先生は　　　　どちらでしょうか。↘ 🔲
Kimura-sensee wa 　dochira deshoo ka.

　　　　　　　　どちらにいらっしゃいますか。↗ 🔲
　　　　　　　　dochira ni irasshaimasu ka.

S-3. How to get something you didn't catch repeated

a. When you didn't catch or understand what someone said, you can make a polite request to have it repeated:

すみません、もういちどお願いします。
Sumimasen, moo ichido onegai shimasu.
Excuse me but could you say it again, please?

すみません、ゆっくりお願いします。
Sumimasen, yukkuri onegai shimasu.
Excuse me but could you speak more slowly, please?

b. When you could understand only part of a key word or phrase, you can repeat it hesitantly; this also a signal to the speaker that you would like it repeated.

① A：**自動販売機のとなりにありますよ。**

　　Jidoohanbaiki no tonari ni arimasu yo.

　　It's beside the vending machine.

　 B：**じどう……。**

　　Jidoo......

　 A：**じどうはんばいき。**

　　Jidoohanbaiki.

② A：**自動販売機のとなりにありますよ。**

　　Jidoohanbaiki no tonari ni arimasu yo.

　 B：**自動販売機の……。**

　　Jidoohanbaiki no......

　 A：**となり。**

　　Tonari.

c. Saying **え**↗ or **はあ**↗ is another way of getting the speaker to repeat something; however, these aren't very polite. ⇨まとめ2BⅡ3

　 A：**自動販売機のとなりにありますよ。**　　*It's beside the vending machine.*

　　Jidoohanbaiki no tonari ni arimasu yo.

　 B：**え。**↗　　　　　　　　　　　　　　*Hey?/ Say again?*

　　E.

　 A：**自動販売機のとなり。**　　　　　　　*Beside the vending machine.*

　　Jidoohanbaiki no tonari.

　 B：**ああ、わかりました。**　　　　　　　*Oh, I see.*

　　Aa, wakarimashita.

S-4. How to confirm information —1.

a. To confirm information you have been given, simply repeat it with short falling intonation.

～。↘ ☺
～ですか。↘ 👤
～desu ka.

If the information surprises you, you can show this by using short rising intonation.

～。↗ ☺
～ですか。↗ 👤
～desu ka.

female student：4階のあっち側にありますよ。
　　　　　　　　Yon-kai no atchigawa ni arimasu yo.
　　　　　　　　It's on the other side of the 4th floor.

Brown：4階ですか。↗
　　　　Yon-kai desu ka.
　　　　The 4th floor?

female student：ええ。
　　　　　　　　Ee.

b. To indicate that you are convinced or satisfied with the information given, repeat or paraphrase using **ね↗**.　⇨まとめ2BⅡ4

～ね。↗ ☺➡⬇
～ne.
～ですね。↗ 👤
～desu ne.

Tanaka：ほら、あのコーラとかジュースとかの……。
　　　　Hora, ano koora toka juusu toka no......
　　　　You know, that (machine selling) cola and soft drinks etc.

Sharma：ああ、わかりました。そのとなりですね。↗
　　　　Aa, wakarimashita. Sono tonari desu ne.
　　　　Oh, right! It's next to that, isn't it?

Tanaka：そう。
　　　　Soo.
　　　　Yes.

S-5. How to gain time to collect your thoughts

a. When you can't answer a question straight away, you can repeat the key word to gain time, as we saw in S-4.

> **Brown：あの、せんたく機はどこでしょうか。**
> Ano, sentakuki wa doko deshoo ka.
>
> **female student：せんたく機。↘／↗**
> Sentakuki.
>
> **Brown：ええ。**
> Ee.

b. With this strategy, you can add **ね**↘ to the key word in casual speech. ⇨まとめ 2BⅡ4（In formal speech, you need to add **ですか**↘.）

> **Sharma：このへんに、電話ありますか。**
> Kono hen ni, denwa arimasu ka.
>
> **Tanaka：電話ね。↘**
> Denwa ne.
>
> **Sharma：ええ。**
> Ee.

c. ええと can also be used for this purpose. ⇨まとめ1BⅡ3

S-6. How to end a conversation —2. After asking a question

a. Once you have the information required, you can end the conversation politely with an expression of thanks such as **どうもありがとうございました** or **どうもすみませんでした**.

> ①　　**Brown：どうもありがとうございました。**
> Doomo arigatoo gozaimashita.
>
> **female student：どういたしまして。**
> Doo itashimashite.

② **Sharma**：どうもすみませんでした。
Doomo sumimasen deshita.

Tanaka：いいえ。
Iie.

b. If the listener can't answer your question, you can end the conversation politely with **あ、そうですか** and **どうもすみませんでした**. ⇨L5CN S-4

A：ちょっと……わからないんですけど。
Chotto...... Wakaranai n desu kedo.
I'm afraid...... I don't know.

B：あ、そうですか。↘ どうもすみませんでした。
A, soo desu ka. Doomo sumimasen deshita.
I see. Thank you anyway.

A：いいえ。
Iie.

c. If you can't understand what you are being told, you will also want to bring the conversation to an end politely; you can do this by saying **あの、すみません** followed by an expression of thanks:

A：× × ×……

B：あの、すみません。
Ano, sumimasen.

A：？

B：どうもありがとうございました。
Doomo arigatoo gozaimashita.

まとめ 1

A. GRAMMAR

Ⅰ. Numbers
Ⅱ. Counters
Ⅲ. Summary of question words
Ⅳ. Structure particls
Ⅴ. が and は : basic differences between が and は

B. CONVERSATION

Ⅰ. Summary of Conversational Strategies

Ⅱ. Additional Information
1. Personal pronouns for the 1st and 2nd person
2. Types of intonation
3. Interjections あ/あの/ええと
4. Expressions of thanks

A. Grammar

Ⅰ. Numbers

1	いち	10	じゅう	100	ひゃく	1,000	せん
2	に	20	にじゅう	200	にひゃく	2,000	にせん
3	さん	30	さんじゅう	300	さんびゃく	3,000	さんぜん
4	よん／し	40	よんじゅう	400	よんひゃく	4,000	よんせん
5	ご	50	ごじゅう	500	ごひゃく	5,000	ごせん
6	ろく	60	ろくじゅう	600	ろっぴゃく	6,000	ろくせん
7	なな／しち	70	ななじゅう	700	ななひゃく	7,000	ななせん
8	はち	80	はちじゅう	800	はっぴゃく	8,000	はっせん
9	きゅう／く	90	きゅうじゅう	900	きゅうひゃく	9,000	きゅうせん

10,000	いちまん
20,000	にまん
30,000	さんまん
40,000	よんまん
50,000	ごまん
60,000	ろくまん
70,000	ななまん
80,000	はちまん
90,000	きゅうまん
100,000	じゅうまん
1000,000	ひゃくまん

808	（はっぴゃくはち）	1,500	（せんごひゃく）
3,650	（さんぜんろっぴゃくごじゅう）	4,190	（よんせんひゃくきゅうじゅう）
170,000	（じゅうななまん）	2,250,000	（にひゃくにじゅうごまん）

Ⅱ. Counters

1	いちまい	いちだい	いっかい	いっぽん	いっぱい
2	にまい	にだい	にかい	にほん	にはい
3	さんまい	さんだい	さんがい	さんぼん	さんばい
4	よんまい	よんだい	よんかい	よんほん	よんはい
5	ごまい	ごだい	ごかい	ごほん	ごはい
6	ろくまい	ろくだい	ろっかい	ろっぽん	ろっぱい
7	ななまい	ななだい	ななかい	ななほん	ななはい
8	はちまい	はちだい	はちかい	はちほん	はちはい
			はっかい	はっぽん	はっぱい
9	きゅうまい	きゅうだい	きゅうかい	きゅうほん	きゅうはい
10	じゅうまい	じゅうだい	じっかい	じっぽん	じっぱい
			じゅっかい	じゅっぽん	じゅっぱい
?	なんまい	なんだい	なんがい	なんぼん	なんばい

100

III．Summary of question words

1．A：ご専門は何ですか。
　　　せんもん　なん

　　B：医学です。
　　　い がく

2．A：シャルマさんの先生はどなたですか。
　　　　　　　　　　せんせい

　　B：木村先生です。
　　　き むら

3．A：だれのカメラですか。

　　B：タンさんのカメラです。

4．A：大学はどちらですか。
　　　だいがく

　　B：千葉大学です。
　　　ち ば

5．A：京都へは何で行きましたか。
　　　きょうと　　い

　　B：バスで行きました。

6．A：何を買いましたか。
　　　なに　か

　　B：カメラを買いました。

7．A：はがきをください。いくらですか。

　　B：1まい50円です。
　　　　　えん

8．A：日本へは、いつ来ましたか。
　　　にほん　　　　き

　　B：先月来ました。
　　　せんげつ

9．A：留学生が何人いますか。
　　　りゅうがくせい　なんにん

　　B：300人います。

10．A：たまごはいくつ買いましたか。
　　　　　　　　　　か

　　B：とお買いました。

11．A：シャルマさんは（お）いくつですか。

　　B：27です。

What's your field?

My field is medical science.

Who is Sharma-san's teacher?

Kimura-sensee (is).

Whose camera is this?

It's Tan-san's camera.

Which university are you from?

Chiba University.

How did you go to Kyoto?

I went by bus.

What did you buy?

I bought a camera.

I'd like a postcard. How much is it?

50 yen per card.

When did you come to Japan?

I came last month.

How many foreign students are there?

There are three hundred.

How many eggs did you buy?

I bought ten.

How old is Sharma-san?

He is 27 (years old).

まとめ

Ⅳ. Structure particles

Tell how many structure particles 買います, 行きます, あげます and もらいます
か　　　い
take.

subject particle

| <person>が |

買います

object particle

| <thing>を |

行きます

point(goal/source) particle

| <person>に |

direction/particle

| <place>へ |

あげます

place of action particle

| <place>で |

もらいます

means particle

| <means>で |

companion particle

| <person>と |

V. 🐟 🐟 が and は: basic differences between が and は

1. が is used when a situation or happening (underlined) is noticed for the first time. Look at the following illustrations.

コーヒーを飲みました。
We had a cup of coffee.

お金を払いましょう。
Let's pay.

あ、お金がありません。
Oops, I haven't got any money.

A-san had a cup of coffee at the restaurant. When he was about to pay, he discovered that there was no money in his wallet. Note that he uses が in お金がありません because he realizes for the first time that he has no money on him.

バスが来ません。
The bus doesn't come.

バスが来ましたよ。
The bus has come!

I was waiting for the bus, but I realized that it didn't come. After a while a child saw the bus come and informed me. The child uses が in バスが来ましたよ because it realizes that the bus is coming.

103

2. **は** is used when both speaker and listener share a commom topic.

スパゲッティ、ありますか。
Do you have spaghetti?

すみません、スパゲッティはありません。
Sorry. We don't have spaghetti.

A-san asked the waitress whether spaghetti was on the menu. This establishes 'spaghetti' as a common topic for these two.

ビール（を）飲みますか。
Do you drink beer?

いいえ、ビールは飲みません。
No. I don't drink beer.

B-san asks whether A-san drinks beer. 'Beer' is thus established as a common topic between the two.

In this way, **は** is usually used when a speaker refers to something that has already been mentioned, or with which both speaker and listener are familiar.

B. Conversation

＜Summary of Conversational Strategies

Check the strategies and tick the square on the left（YC＝Your Check）if you are confident that you have mastered the strategy. If you feel that you cannot use a strategy, return to the relevant section(s) and practise more.

（The square on the right is for your teacher's use: TC＝Teacher's Check）

1. Factual information

Yc Tc
□ □ Introductions   ⇨L1S-2b   ：インドのシャルマです。
                                        専門はコンピュータです。

□ □ Short questions and responses   ：はい/いいえ
              ⇨L1GI-3

     How to send mail at the post office

□ □ (a)Asking the postage   ⇨L2S-3b   ：アメリカまで航空便でいくらですか。

□ □ (b)Asking how long it takes   ：アメリカまで航空便でどのくらいかか
              ⇨L2S-3/4   りますか。

□ □ How to ask the whereabouts of   ：～（は）どこに｜ありますか。
     things/people   ⇨L4S-2   ｜いますか。
                                        ～（は）どこでしょうか。

□ □ How to get something you didn't   ：すみません。もう一度お願いします。
     catch repeated   ⇨L4S-3   ゆっくりお願いします。

□ □ How to confirm information ⇨L4S-4 ：4階ですか。↘／↗
                                        4階ですね。↘

2. Judgement

3. Emotions

4. Actions

□ □ Saying what you want to be called   ：アニルとよんでください。
              ⇨L1S-2c

□ □ How to send mail at the post office ：これ、～でお願いします。
              ⇨L2S-3a

□ □ How to buy something   ⇨L2S-4   ：～（を）〈number〉お願いします。
                                        ～ください。

□ □ How to ask for something ⇨L3S-1   ：～（が）ありますか。

105

□ □ How to order　　　　　⇨L3S-3　　：〜（を）お願いします。
　　　　　　　　　　　　　　　　　　　　　〜（を）ください。
　　　　　　　　　　　　　　　　　　　　　〜にします。

□ □ How to deal with problems in a　：あの、〜まだでしょうか。
　　　 restaurant　　　　⇨L3S-4

□ □ How to pay the cashier ⇨L3S-5　：お願いします。
　　　　　　　　　　　　　　　　　　　　　べつべつにしてください。

5. Social formulas

□ □ How to introduce yourself⇨L1S-2a　：はじめまして。
　　　　　　　　　　　　　　　　　　　　　アニル・シャルマ｜です。
　　　　　　　　　　　　　　　　　　　　　　　　　　　　｜ともうします。
　　　　　　　　　　　　　　　　　　　　　ーどうぞよろしく。
　　　　　　　　　　　　　　　　　　　　　ーこちらこそ。

□ □ Greeting　　　　　　　⇨L1S-1a　：こんにちは。／こんばんは。

□ □ How to give/receive something　：どうぞ。ーどうも。
　　　　　　　　　　　　　⇨L3S-2

□ □ Thanks　　　　　⇨まとめ1BⅡ4　：どうもありがとう。
　　　　　　　　　　　　　　　　　　　　　ーどういたしまして。

6. Communication strategies

　　　How to start a conversation:

□ □ 1. At a party　　　　　⇨L1S-1a　：あ、先生。こんにちは。

□ □ 2. On the street　　　　⇨L2S-1　：どこ行くの。
　　　　　　　　　　　　　　　　　　　　　ーちょっと郵便局まで。

□ □ 3. Introducing a request　⇨L2S-2　：すみません。／お願いします。

□ □ 4. Introducing a question ⇨L4S-1　：あの、ちょっとすみません。

　　　How to end a conversation:

□ □ 1. Taking leave　　　　⇨L1S-3　：それじゃ、また。
　　　　　　　　　　　　　　　　　　　　　はい。じゃ、失礼します。

□ □ 2. After asking a question ⇨L4S-6　：どうもありがとうございました。
　　　　　　　　　　　　　　　　　　　　　どうもすみませんでした。

　　　How to help the flow of the conversation

□ □ 1. Getting attention ⇨まとめ1BⅡ3　：あ／あのう

□ □ 2. Gaining time to think　⇨L4S-5　：ええと

□ □ 3. *Aizuchi*　　　　　⇨L1GI-4　：はい／いいえ

II. *Additional Information*

1. Personal pronouns for the 1st and 2nd person

Several personal pronouns are used for the 1st *I* and 2nd person *you* :

	Formal 🔲	Casual 😊
1st person	わたし（わたくし） watashi (watakushi)	あたし🚹／ぼく🚹／おれ🚹 atashi / boku / ore
2nd person	あなた／先生／etc. anata / sensee	あなた🚹／きみ🚹／おまえ🚹 anata / kimi / omae

However, personal pronouns are usually omitted in conversation. In very formal speech, **わたくし** is often used, whereas in casual speech, a male speaker may use **ぼく**, **おれ** and a female speaker **あたし** for emphasis or clarification. Personal pronouns are avoided when speaking to a senior. In formal speech, **あなた** is rarely used for *you*, because it has connotations that make it unacceptable as a *neutral* term; instead, **〜さん**, **〜先生** or certain kinship terms are used.

In casual speech, **あなた** is often used by females towards their husbands or lovers. **きみ／おまえ** or a name without **さん** may be used in casual speech by a male speaker to address someone close of equal status, or someone of lower status.

2. Types of intonation

Japanese conversation features several types of intonation that occur at the end of an utterance:

a. [↘] : Short falling

To say something with confidence, or to make a short reply use short falling intonation, the basic pattern of intonation in Japanese:

① **Sharma**：はじめまして。↘　アニル・シャルマです。↘
　　　　　　　Hajimemashite. Aniru Sharuma desu.

　　Yamashita：あ、どうも。↘
　　　　　　　　A, doomo.　　　　　　　　　　　　　　　　　〈L1 MC〉

② **Tanaka**：ええと、それから、はがき5まいください。↘
　　　　　　　Eeto, sorekara, hagaki go-mai kudasai.

　　　Clerk：はい。↘
　　　　　　　Hai.　　　　　　　　　　　　　　　　　　〈L2 MC〉

This type of intonation can also be used for:

③ **Waitress**：ええと、てんぷら定食がおひとつ、↘
　　　　　　　Eeto, tenpura teeshoku ga ohitotsu,

　　　　　　　：ビーフカレーがおひとつ、↘……
　　　　　　　Biifukaree ga ohitotsu,......　　　　　　　〈L3 MC〉

b. [↗] : Short rising

　　To elicit a response to your question, or request confirmation, short rising intonation is usual:

① **Waitress**：何名さまですか。↗
　　　　　　　Nanmee-sama desu ka.

　　Yamashita：ふたりです。
　　　　　　　　Futari desu.　　　　　　　　　　　　　　〈L3 MC〉

② **Clerk**：アメリカですね。↗
　　　　　　　Amerika desu ne.

　　Yamashita：はい。
　　　　　　　　Hai.　　　　　　　　　　　　　　　　　〈L2 MC〉

でしょうか↘ is an exception; although it is a polite question, it is usually said with short falling intonation.

③ **Brown**：あの、せんたく機　どこでしょうか。↘
　　　　　　　Ano, sentakuki wa doko deshoo ka.

c. [↘] : Long falling

To show that you are not sure about something, use long falling intonation.

① **Sharma**：このへんに、電話ありますか。

　　　Kono hen ni, denwa arimasu ka.

　　Tanaka：電話ね。↘

　　　Denwa ne.

② **Yamashita**：ううん↘　困ったな。↘　ちょっとわかんないな。↘

　　　Uun, komatta na, Chotto wakannai na.

You can also use this type to indicate that you are impressed:

③ **Sharma**：わあ、ずいぶん大きいですね。↘

　　　Waa, zuibun ookii desu ne.

d. [↗] : Long rising

In reaction to some unexpected information, this intonation can be used to show surprise or doubt:

⚠ This intonation must be used with care as in some situations it can indicate doubt about the validity of what the other person has said.

① **Clerk**：じゃ、この荷物。

　　　Ja, kono nimotsu.

　　Sharma：わあ、↗　ずいぶん大きいですね。

　　　Waa, zuibun ookii desu ne.　　　　　　　　　　　　〈L6 MC〉

② **A**：ちょうど5000円になります。

　　　Choodo gosen-en ni narimasu.

　　B：ええ。↗　5000円ですか。↗

　　　Ee. Gosen-en desu ka.

3. Interjections あ/あの/ええと

Before you speak, you can give out a signal to indicate that you are about to say something, useful for smoother communication. There are these expressions with slightly different meanings:

a. あ（ああ）／あら🚹

あ is often used to introduce the mention of some person or thing you have just noticed. ⇨L6CN3 Women tend to use **あら** instead. ⇨まとめ2BⅡ3

> **Tanaka：あら、山下さん。**
> Ara, Yamashita-san.
>
> **Yamashita：あ、田中さん。おはよう。**
> A, Tanaka-san. ohayoo. 〈L2 MC〉

b. あの（あのう）

This is useful for getting the listener's attention at the beginning of a conversation or when changing the topic of conversation. It is also a polite way of showing hesitation.

> ① **Brown：あの、すみません。**
> Ano, sumimasen.
>
> **Student：はい。**
> Hai. 〈L4 MC〉
>
> ② **Sharma：シャルマと呼んでください。**
> Sharuma to yonde kudasai.
>
> **Yamashita：あ、じゃ、シャルマさん。あの、お国は。**
> A, ja, Sharuma-san. Ano, okuni wa.
>
> **Sharma：インドです。**
> Indo desu. 〈L1 MC〉

c. ええと

ええと signals that you need some more time to collect your thoughts; it is similar to English *Let me see* or *Um*.

> ① **Clerk：ええと、**（weighing a parcel）**280円です。**
> Eeto, nihyaku hachijuu-en desu.
>
> **Yamashita：はい。**
> Hai. 〈L2 MC〉
>
> ② **Waitress：ご注文は。**
> Gochuumon wa.
>
> **Yamashita：ええと、ぼくはてんぷら定食。**
> Eeto, boku wa tenpura teeshoku. 〈L3 MC〉

110

4. Expressions of thanks

a. You can say thanks with varying degrees of formality:

> ありがとうございます。🈁
> ありがとう。🈂➡⬇
> どうも。🈂

You can add **どうも**:

> どうもありがとうございます。🈁
> どうもありがとう。🈂➡⬇

In reply to the above, you can use the following: ⇨まとめ2BⅡ3

> いいえ、どういたしまして。🈁　　　　*You're welcome./Not at all.*
> どういたしまして。🈁
> いいえ。(いえ)🈁／🈂
> ううん。⤴🈂➡⬇
> いや（いやいや）。🈂➡⬇🈯

Note that **ううん**⤴ pronounced with rising and falling intonation like **うう↗ん**↘, is different from **ううん**↘. ⇨まとめ2BⅡ3

はい or **うん** can also be used as a response; it is not very polite, though.

Look at the examples below, dealing with a variety of situations.

① （At a party, B brings a glass to A. They do not know each other.）
> **A：ありがとうございます。**⬆
> Arigatoo gozaimasu.

> **B：いいえ、どういたしまして。**⬆
> Iie, doo itashimashite.

② （B offers to lend A book. B is A's teacher.）
> **A：どうもありがとうございます。**⬆
> Doomo arigatoo gozaimasu.

> **B：はい。**⬇
> Hai.

まとめ

③ （B brings A a tape recorder. B is A's assistant.）

A：どうもありがとう。⬇

Doomo arigatoo.

B：いいえ。⬆

Iie.

④ （B gives A a present. They are good friends.）

A：ありがとう。➡

Arigatoo.

B：ううん。⤻ ➡

Uun.

c. すみません can be used not only for apologizing but for thanks as well, especially when you feel that the person you are thanking is taking trouble on your behalf:

（B offers to fix A's bicycle. B is A's senior.）

A：どうもすみません。⬆

Doomo sumimasen.

B：いや。⬇👤

Iya.

d. When saying thanks for something that has already been done for you, use **ありがとうございました** or **すみませんでした** in formal speech; in casual speech, however, **ありがとう** can be used.

① （B showed A the way to the station. B is a passer-by.）

A：どうもありがとうございました。⬆

Doomo arigatoo gozaimashita.

B：いいえ。⬆

Iie.

② （B fixed A's bicycle. B is A's senior.）

A：どうもすみませんでした。⬆

Doomo sumimasen deshita.

B：いやいや。⬆👤

Iya iya.

第 5 課

わからないことばを聞く
Asking about unknown words

OBJECTIVES:

GRAMMAR

Ⅰ. The -(r)u form of verbs: [V-(r)u]
Ⅱ. The -te form of verbs: [V-te]
Ⅲ. The -ta form of verbs: [V-ta]
Ⅳ. ～てください: expression of request
Ⅴ. ～んです〈1〉: explanatory ending
Ⅵ. どうして *why* ?: question word
Ⅶ. で〈2〉: uses of the structure particle
Ⅷ. Days of the week

CONVERSATION

＜General Information＞

1. Katakana words

＜Strategies＞

S-1. How to introduce a main topic —1.
S-2. How to ask for information about a word
S-3. How to make sure you have understood
S-4. How to end a conversation —3. When the listener does not give the required explanation

Model Conversation

(1)

Characters : Anil Sharma（アニル・シャルマ）, a female student（女子学生）

Situation : Sharma-san gets a message from the notice board, but can't understand it.

Flow-chart :

Starting a conversation
↓
Asking the meaning
↓
Asking how to read it and its meaning in English
↓
Ending the conversation

In front of a notice board

―掲示板の前で―

シャルマ：あの、ちょっとすみません。
女子学生：はい。
シャルマ：掲示板にこれがはってあったんですけど……。
女子学生：ええ。

＊　　　＊　　　＊

シャルマ：何て書いてあるんですか。
女子学生：ええと、けさあなたに荷物が来たから、
シャルマ：ええ。
女子学生：事務室へ取りに来てくださいって。
シャルマ：事務室って、宿舎の事務室ですか。
女子学生：ええ、そう。あそこですよ。

＊　　　＊　　　＊

シャルマ：あ、それから、この字、何て読むんでしょうか。
女子学生：ええと、あ、これね。宅急便。

＊　　　＊　　　＊

シャルマ：たっきゅうびん。
女子学生：ええ。ううん……荷物をとどけるサービス。
シャルマ：あの、すみません。英語で何ていうんですか。
女子学生：ええと、delivery service かな。
シャルマ：ああ、わかりました。どうもありがとう。

（2）

Characters ：Lisa Brown（リサ・ブラウン）, Yamashita（山下）

Situation ：Brown-san finds some information about a party on the notice board, but can't understand a word of it.

Flow-chart ：

Asking the meaning
↓
Asking the reason
↓
Finishing the conversation

In front of a notice board

MC

─ 掲示板の前で ─

ブラウン：あの、すみません。
山　下　：はい。
ブラウン：（Pointing at poster）このコンパって何ですか。
山　下　：ええと、先生や友だちとパーティーをするんですよ。
ブラウン：ああ、そうですか。
山　下　：ええ。

　　　　　＊　　　＊　　　＊

ブラウン：コンパって、英語で何ていうんですか。
山　下　：ううん……、コンパニーかな。
ブラウン：どうしてコンパニーがコンパなんですか。
山　下　：ううん、困ったな。ちょっとわからないな。

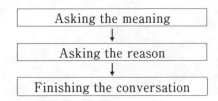

　　　　　＊　　　＊　　　＊

ブラウン：あ、じゃ、いいです。どうもすみませんでした。
山　下　：いいえ。
ブラウン：ありがとうございました。

115

Report

　掲示板にメモがありました。でも、シャルマさんは、メモの漢字がわかりませんでした。そこで、近くの学生に聞きました。学生は、「けさ、荷物が来たから、事務室に取りにきてくださいって。」と言いました。シャルマさんは、宿舎の事務室に行きました。

New Words and Expressions

Words in the conversation

掲示板	けいじばん	notice board
はります [はる]		to put
書きます [かく]	かきます	to write
けさ		this morning
あなた		you
荷物	にもつ	parcel
来ます [くる]	きます	to come
事務室	じむしつ	office
あそこ		over there
字	じ	letter, character
読みます [よむ]	よみます	to read
宅急便	たっきゅうびん	delivery service ⇨L6CN1
とどけます [とどける]		to deliver
英語	えいご	English
わかります [わかる]		to understand
コンパ	konpa	party with teachers and students（only used in the universities）
します [する]		to do
コンパニー	konpanii	company
どうして		why?
困ります [こまる]	こまります	to be at a loss

MC

＜Expressions in the conversation＞

掲示板にこれがはってあったんですけど…
けい じ ばん

This was posted on the notice board, but...
⇨CN S-1

はってあった here means *It was posted*. 〜てある indicates a state resulting from the action（of posting it）. This structure will be dealt with later.
⇨L15GNⅢ

何て書いてあるんですか。
なん か

What's written on it?

117

ええと、   *Let me see.*

ええと is used to gain thinking time without giving up one's turn to speak. ⇨ CNまとめ1BⅡ3

取りに来てください**って**。   *That says to please come and collect it.*

〜**って** is used for quoting. ⇨CN S-3

［V（base）］**に来る** indicates the purpose of coming. ⇨L14GNⅢ

事務室って、宿舎の事務室ですか。   *"Office" is the dormitory office, I take it ?*
                                       ⇨CN S-3

荷物をとどけるサービス   *(It is) a parcel delivery service.* ⇨ L13GNⅢ

〜かな。   *I wonder if...*

かな indicates uncertainty on the part of the speaker; Women tend to use **かしら** in place of **かな**. ⇨まとめ2BⅡ4

どうして、コンパニーがコンパなんですか。 *Why is it that company becomes KONPA ?*
                                       ⇨CNS-2

どうして ⇨GNⅥ   〜**んです** ⇨GNⅤ

ううん、困ったな。ちょっとわからないな。 *Hmm, I don't know the answer to that, I'm afraid.*

ううん is a hesitation marker, giving the speaker time to think of the right word or phrase. There are several other words and phrases used for this purpose, such as **ええと** and **あのう**. ⇨まとめ1BⅡ3

わからない is a plain negative form of **わかりません**. ⇨L8GNⅠ

At natural speed, it is often pronounced **わかんない**.

じゃ、いいです。   *It's all right, then.* ⇨CN S-4

Words in the report

メモ	memo	*memorandum*
でも		*however, but*
そこで		*so, accordingly*
近く	ちかく	*nearby*

<*Expressions in the report*>

〜は「……」と言いました。   *〜 said "......"* ⇨L9GNⅡ

Grammar Notes

I. The -(r)u form of verbs: [V-(r)u]

【*Explanation*】

1. Plain and polite forms

So far you have learned verbs in their polite forms: **tabemasu**, **tabemasen**, **tabemashita**, **tabemasen deshita**. They have corresponding plain forms, **taberu**, **tabenai**, **tabeta**, **tabenakatta**. ⇨ Pre-session, L2 GN I

The plain non-past positive form of a verb ends in either **-ru** or **-u**, which is the same as the form you see listed in a dictionary. Therefore, you need to be familiar with this form to be able to look up verbs in a dictionary. This form is also needed because a number of sentence endings, such as ～んです (⇨GN V) are attached directly to it.

2. Verb inflection patterns

Japanese verbs have three inflection patterns, Group I, Group II and Group III. **[V-(r)u]** (the dictionary form) of Group I verbs ends in **-u** (ex. **nom-u, ka-u, ik-u**) while Group II verbs end in **-eru** or **-iru** (ex. **tab-eru, m-iru**).

Some Group I verbs, like **kaer-u** *to return* or **kir-u** *to cut,* look like Group II verbs, but if you look at their **-masu** forms, **kaer-imasu** and **kir-imasu**, it becomes clear that **er / ir** is not part of the ending. On the other hand, **kae-ru** *to change* and **ki-ru** *to wear* are Group II verbs; this can be tested by looking at their **-masu** forms, **kae-masu** and **ki-masu**, which are formed without the **ru**.

Group I	**kaeru** *to return*	**kiru** *to cut*
	kaer-u	**kir-u**
	↓	↓
	kaer-imasu → **kaerimasu**	**kir-imasu** → **kirimasu**
Group II	**kaeru** *to change*	**kiru** *to wear*
	kae-ru	**ki-ru**
	↓	↓
	kae-masu → **kaemasu**	**ki-masu** → **kimasu**

Group Ⅲ has only two verbs, **kuru** *to come* and **suru** *to do*. Their inflection patterns do not fit into Group Ⅰ or Ⅱ, so we treat them as irregular verbs. Refer to the tables:

Verb forms	[V-(r)u] & [V(base)]	
Verb groups & formation	[V-(r)u]	[V(base)] -masu
Group Ⅰ: **-u** ending	**kiku** *to hear, to ask* **iku** *to go* **isogu** *to hurry* **nomu** *to drink* **yobu** *to call* **shinu** *to die* **hanasu** *to talk* **kau** *to buy* **kaeru** *to go back* **matsu** *to wait*	**kikimasu** **ikimasu** **isogimasu** **nomimasu** **yobimasu** **shinimasu** **hanashimasu** **kaimasu** **kaerimasu** **machimasu**
Group Ⅱ: **-ru** ending	**taberu** *to eat* **miru** *to see*	**tabemasu** **mimasu**

Group Ⅲ: irregular	**kuru** *to come*
	suru *to do*
	benkyoo suru
	  to study
		kimasu
		shimasu
		  benkyoo shimasu

II. The -te form of verbs: [V-te]

【Explanation】

A verb ending in **-te** or **-de** can be represented as [V-te]; let us call this the **-te** form. The **-te** form is tenseless; it is used to string together sequences of verbs. In this lesson, let's take a look at the structure [V-te]ください, which expresses a request.

Refer to III below for the formation of [V-te], as it is formed in a way similar to [V-ta].

III. The -ta form of verbs: [V-ta]

【Explanation】

[V-ta] is the **-ta** form of a verb, which is plain-past-positive. The **-ta** form of **taberu** *to eat* is **tabeta** *ate* (you already know the polite equivalent of **tabeta**, **tabemashita**).

[V-te] and [V-ta] are derived from **-(r)u** form as illustrated in the table. You will see that the only difference (in form) between [V-te] and [V-ta] is the final vowel.

Verb forms		[V-te] & [V-ta]	
	[V-(r)u]	[V-te]	[V-ta]
	-ku, -gu	-ite, -ide	-ita, -ida
	kiku　*to hear*	kiite	kiita
	iku　*to go*	itte*	itta*
	isogu　*to hurry*	isoide	isoida
Group I			
	-mu, -bu, -nu	-nde	-nda
	nomu　*to drink*	nonde	nonda
	yobu　*to call*	yonde	yonda
	shinu　*to die*	shinde	shinda

Group I	-ru, -tsu, -u		-tte		-tta	
	kaeru	*to return*	kaette		kaetta	
	matsu	*to wait*	matte		matta	
	kau	*to buy*	katte		katta	
	-su		-shite		-shita	
	hanasu	*to talk*	hanashite		hanashita	
Group II	-ru		-te		-ta	
	taberu	*to eat*	tabete		tabeta	
	miru	*to see*	mite		mita	
Group III	kuru	*to come*	kite		kita	
	suru	*to do*	shite		shita	
	benkyoo suru		benkyoo shite		benkyoo shita	
		to study				

*iku → itte, itta: this formation is irregular.

Ⅳ. ～てください: expressions of request

Examples

① もういちど読んでください。　　*Read it once more, please.*

② どうぞ食べてください。　　*Please eat.*

③ ちょっと待って。　　*Wait a moment.*

【*Explanation*】

Adding ください to ［V-te］ enables you to ask a favour of someone, like *Please*

～ in English. **どうぞ** in ② can be used to reinforce the meaning of *please (go ahead)*. In casual speech, **ください** is omitted and the sentence ends with the **-te** form as in ③. Recall that **ください** can also be used to request a thing (⇨L3CN S-4). Compare the sentences:

水をください。
みず
Water, please.

ちょっと待ってください。
ま
Wait a moment, please.

| ＜thing＞をください | ～［V-te］ください |

水をください。
Water, please.

待ってください。
Please wait.

手紙をください。
てがみ
Please give me the letter.

話してください。
はな
Please talk.

これをください。
Please give me this one.

あした来てください。
き
Please come tomorrow.

Ｖ．～んです〈1〉: explanatory ending

Examples

① Ａ：この漢字何て読むんですか。
　　かんじなん　よ
　　How do you read this kanji?

　Ｂ：宅急便。
　　たっきゅうびん
　　Takkyuubin.

② A：郵便局へ行くんですか。
　　　You're going to the post office?

　 B：ええ、友だちに手紙を出すんです。
　　　Yes, I'm going to post a letter to my friend.

【*Explanation*】

Sentences ending in 〜んです are commonly used for giving or requesting an explanation or reason. In ①, for instance, A is asking to have some kanji explained, while in ② A assumes that B is going to the post office, and asks for confirmation or details. B then explains why she is going to the post office, also with 〜んです. Now, compare the following dialogues:

(1) 郵便局へ行くんですか。　ええ、友だちに手紙を出すんです。

(2) 郵便局へ行きますか。　ええ、行きます。or いいえ、行きません。

（1）He assumes that she is going to the post office, and wants her to confirm it.
（2）He wants to know if she is going to the post office or not.

んです is attached directly to the plain form of [V] and [A]. With [N] or [NA], you need to add な before んです：

[N]　na n desu → 英語なんです　*It's (in) English.*

[NA]　na n desu → 有名なんです　*It's famous.*

Look at the chart:

Verb plain form ＋ ～んです			
Non-past		Past	
Positive	Negative	Positive	Negative
[V-(r)u]	[V-nai]	[V-ta]	[V-nakatta]
taberu n desu	tabenai n desu	tabeta n desu	tabenakatta n desu

! なん of なんです is different from 何 *what?*:

1. 英語で何ていうんですか。　　　　*How do you say it in English?*
   えいご　なん

2. 英語なんですか。　　　　*Is it (in) English?*

3. コンパって何ですか。　　　　*What is konpa?*

4. どうしてコンパなんですか。　　　　*Why does it become konpa?*

⇨S-2, L7GN Ⅱ, L8CN S-3, L9CN S-1 for more about ～んです
⇨L5GN Ⅰ, for [V-(r)u] and [V-ta]
⇨L8GN Ⅰ, for negative verb forms [V-nai] and [V-nakatta]

Ⅵ. どうして *why?*: question word

Examples

① A：どうして日本語を勉強するんですか。
　　　　　　にほんご　　べんきょう
Why do you study Japanese?

B：日本の大学で勉強するんです。
　　にほん　だいがく
Because I am going to study at a Japanese university.

② A：どうしてかたかななんですか。
Why is it in katakana?

B：英語ですから。
Because it's an English word.

【*Explanation*】

　　どうして *why?* asks a reason; as shown in the examples, どうして sentences frequently use the 〜んです ending, implying that an explanation is being asked for. The answer to such a question will also be given with 〜んです.　⇨CN S-2

Ⅶ.　◁╫╪◀　で〈2〉: uses of the structure particle

【*Explanation*】

　　The Structure particle で indicates

　　1）location/place of action　　　　⇨L2GNⅣ, L6GNⅥ
　　2）method/means/transportation　　⇨L2CNⅣ, L2CN S-3
　　3）extent　　　　　　　　　　　　⇨L11GNⅤ

1）The location or place of an action

　　　　図書館で勉強しました。
　　　　と しょかん　べんきょう
　　　　(I) studied in the library.

2）The method/means by which someone performs an action:

　　　1．航空便でお願いします。
　　　　こうくうびん　　ねが
　　　　Please (send this) by air mail.

　　　2．日本語で手紙を書きました。
　　　　に ほん ご　て がみ　か
　　　　(I) wrote a letter in Japanese.

　　　3．日本人ははしでごはんを食べます。
　　　　に ほんじん　　　　　　　　　た
　　　　The Japanese eat (their) meals with chopsticks.

　　　4．自転車で行きました。
　　　　じ てんしゃ　い
　　　　(I) went (there) by bicycle.

　　　5．ペンで書いてください。
　　　　Please write (it) with a pen.

3） Extent（after expressions of quantity）:

1. **全部で391円です。**
   ぜんぶ　　　えん
   They cost 391 yen altogether.

2. **このりんごは３つで300円です。**
   These apples are three for 300 yen.

3. **おふたりで3000円になります。**
   It costs 3000 yen for two.

Ⅷ. Days of the week

1. A：**きょうは何曜日ですか。**
   　　　　　　なんようび
   What day (of the week) is it today?

   B：**水曜日です。**
   　　すいようび
   It's Wednesday.

2. **土曜日に行きます。**
   どようび い
   I'll go on Saturday.

3. **あした行きます。**
   I'll go tomorrow.

When the days of the week（⇨まとめ2AⅠ）indicate a point of time (as 2. above), they usually require the structure particle**に**. By contrast, relative expressions of time like **きのう** *yesterday,* **きょう** *today* and **あした** *tomorrow* don't take **に**.（as 3. above）

Conversation Notes

＜General Information＞

1. Katakana words

コンパ is a truncated (shortened) form of コンパニー, an English word, and in Japanese it means 'a certain kind of party', which is somewhat different from the meaning of its original. Foreign words, when borrowed in Japanese, often have some changes in their forms or meanings, as well as in their pronunciations or writings.
⇨ Introduction Ⅲ

a. Change of meaning

Many loanwords have narrower meanings than in the original language. For example, ライス is generally used only for boiled rice served with Western food. In other cases, a loanword is used in a broader sense than the original (eg. ボーイフレンド boy friend: male friend in general), or has developed a meaning that is not found with the original (eg. スマート smart: *slender, elegant, sophisticated.*)

b. Change of form

In principle, loan-adjectives belong to the class of **na** adjectives (eg. ハンサムな *handsome,* シックな *chic*), while verbs become 〜する *to do* verbs (eg. チェックする *to check,* テストする *to test*). Compound words can also be formed from loanword elements, sometimes even in combination with Japanese or Chinese-derived elements.

When a word is perceived to be too long, it is often truncated, another reason why learners find it difficult to understand the Katakana-go. As we saw earlier, Katakana words tend to end up being quite long, acquiring many additional moras in the course of the sound assimilation to Japanese. However, the average length of a Japanese word is quite short, being only three to four moras, which accounts for the tendency to shorten most loanwords that would exceed that length. Below are some common examples of truncated loanwords.

テレビ	**televi**sion
デパート	**depart**ment store
パソコン	**perso**nal **com**puter
エアコン	**air con**ditioner

128

<Strategies>

S-1. How to introduce a main topic —1.

掲示板にこれがはってあったんですけど。
This was posted on the notice board, but......

せんたく機の場所、わからないんですけど。
I don't know where the washing machine is, but......

The above type of unfinished sentence ending in **けど** is an introductory remark leading into the main part of the conversation that follows. It is a useful way of implying that one wants to ask a question or make a request. Leaving unsaid the actual request or question, which is obvious to the listener anyway from the situation, is considered more polite. ⇨L7GNⅢ

CN

① 掲示板にこれがはってあったんですけど、（何ですか）。

② せんたく機の場所、わからないんですけど、（教えてください）。

Even when you do spell out your question or request, an introductory remark is necessary. Recall how Sharuma-san starts the dialogue in L.5:

Step 1 : Starting a conversation

シャルマ：あのう、ちょっとすみません。

学　生　：はい。

Step 2 : Introductory remark

シャルマ：掲示板にこれがはってあったんですけど。

学　生　：ええ。

Step 3 : Bringing up the main topic

シャルマ：この字、なんて読むんですか。

Sharuma-san here takes two steps before the main topic is introduced. Politeness in Japanese is not only a matter of using polite expressions; it is also necessary to follow the right steps in a conversation.

To open a conversation with a stranger, **あの、すみません。** is commonly used, with several variations being available:

> **あの/あのう。**
> **すみません/すいません。**
> **あの、ちょっとすみません。**

As a general rule, the length of the sentence indicates the degree of politeness; however, the above examples are about equal in politeness. **あの、ちょっと** or **あのう、ちょっと** are often used, in a hesitant way. c.f. Use of ちょっと ⇨ まとめ2BⅡ1

S-2. How to ask for information about a word

a. Finding out how to read it.

> **A：これ何て読むんですか。**
> **B：＜Reading＞ ですよ。**

When you want to double-check the reading, you can proceed as follows:

> **A：これ何て読むんですか。**
>
> **B：がっこうですよ。**
>
> **A：「がっこう」ですか、「がこう」ですか。**
> **小さい「つ」がありますか。**
> *lit. Is there a small 'tsu' sound?*

b. Finding out the meaning.

There are several expressions that can be used to ask the meaning of a word:

> ① **これ、どんな意味なんですか。**
> *What does this mean?*
>
> ② **教室。↗ 😊**
>
> **教室って。↗ 😊**
>
> **教室って何ですか。↗ 🔲**

Example ① is used to find out the meaning of an unknown word. The examples in ② achieves the same by repeating the word with slightly raised intonation. More politely, you can add 「**何ですか。 ↗**」(rising intonation)

c. Finding out an English or a Japanese equivalent.

＜word＞は、＜language＞で何ていうんですか。

How do you say ‹word› in ‹language›?

① 　**A：Physics は、日本語で何ていうんですか。**

　　B：物理っていうんですよ。

d. Requesting an explanation.

The combination 「**どうして…んですか**」 is used when requesting an explanation. Note that explanations concerning personal matters should not be sought from a superior (this is considered impolite). However, such a restriction does not apply when requesting factual information. ⇨GNⅤ，GNⅥ

CN

S-3. How to make sure you have understood

You have been told to go to the office, but you are unsure which of the many offices in the university is being referred to. In such a situation, you can check as follows:

① **事務室って、宿舎の事務室ですか。**
Office? You mean the dormitory office?

② **山下さんって、学生の山下さんですか。**
Yamashita-san? You mean Yamashita the student?

c.f. Use of って ⇨ まとめ2BⅡ5

S-4. How to end a conversation —3. When the listener does not give the required explanation.

学　生：ううん、困ったな。よくわかんないな。 ↘ 😊➡⬇
Hmm... Sorry. I'm not sure.

シャルマ：じゃ、いいです。➡
It's all right, then.

There are some short signals that indicate that the person you asked the question can't help you and feels embarrassed:

ううん.... ↘　　　*hmm*
さあ.... ↘　　　*I wonder*

ううん and さあ are pronounced with a dangling intonation, and indicate that the person asked doesn't know the answer to your question. You are expected to pick up these signals and finish the conversation with じゃ、いいです.

* Note the difference in intonation between ううん *no,* and ううん *hmm.* The negative ううん (⤻) has an intonation which first rises, then falls. ⇨ まとめ2BⅡ3

Recall that ええと is used when looking for the right word, whereas ううん ....'and さあ indicate that the answer is not known.

Compare the examples below:

① You can't understand the difference between the particles **wa** and **ga**, so you ask a teacher to explain it to you in English.

A：すみません。
B：はい。
A：英語で説明してください。
B：ううん....。

② You can't understand the meaning of a word. You ask a teacher.

A：すみません。
B：はい。
A：これは，英語で何ですか。
B：ええと....。
A：ええ。
B：**Difference** ですよ。

第6課

事務室で
じ む しつ
At the office

OBJECTIVES:

GRAMMAR

Ⅰ. Adjective sentences
Ⅱ. 非常に 大変 すごく とても あまり
ひじょう たいへん
ずいぶん: adverbs of degree
Ⅲ. どう *how?*: question word
Ⅳ. 〜て〈1〉: listing successive actions or events
Ⅴ. 〜でいい: 〜 *is all right,* 〜 *will do*
Ⅵ. に〈3〉 and で〈3〉: structure particles

CONVERSATION

＜General Information＞
1. Office instructions
2. Delivery service

＜Strategies＞
S-1. How to introduce a main topic —2.
S-2. How to ask for instructions
S-3. How to correct others' mistakes
S-4. How to ask for advice implicitly
S-5. How to give an alternative

Model Conversation

Characters ： Anil Sharma（アニル・シャルマ）, a clerk（事務員）

Situation ： Sharma-san comes to the dormitory office to collect his parcel.

Flow-chart ：

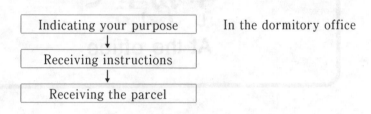

| Indicating your purpose | In the dormitory office |
| Receiving instructions |
| Receiving the parcel |

― 宿舎の事務室で ―

シャルマ：こんにちは。

事 務 員：はい。こんにちは。

シャルマ：あの、掲示板にこれがあったんですけど。（Showing the note）

事 務 員：ああ、宅急便ですね。 たっきゅうびん

シャルマ：ええ。

事 務 員：ええと、お名前は。

シャルマ：はい。シャルマです。

事 務 員：ええと、インドのアニル・シャルマさんですね。

シャルマ：はい、そうです。 aniru

※ ※ ※

事 務 員：じゃ、ここに名前書いて、はんこ押してください。

シャルマ：ここですか。（Pointing to the wrong spot）

事 務 員：いや。そこじゃなくて、こっち。（Pointing to the right spot）

シャルマ：え。

事 務 員：ここですよ。（Pointing to the right spot again）

シャルマ：ああ、わかりました。

　　　　　（Filling in the form）

事 務 員：そうそう。

　　　　　それから、はんこね。

シャルマ：ええと、はんこは持ってないんですけど。

事 務 員：じゃ、サインでいいですよ。 sign

シャルマ：ああ、そうですか。

134

シャルマ：（Signing his name）
　　　　　これでいいですか。（Showing the form）
事 務 員：はい、けっこうです。

＊　　　　＊　　　　＊

事 務 員：じゃ、この荷物。
シャルマ：わあ、ずいぶん大きいですね。
事 務 員：重いですよ。
シャルマ：あ、ほんとうだ。（Picking up the parcel）
事 務 員：ひとりでだいじょうぶかな。
シャルマ：ええ、だいじょうぶです。
　　　　　どうも。
事 務 員：じゃ、気をつけて。
シャルマ：はい。どうもありがとうございました。

Report

　シャルマさんは宿舎の事務室に行って，宅急便のメモを見せました。事務室の人は「名前を書いてはんこを押してください。」と言いました。シャルマさんははんこがありませんでしたから、サインをして荷物を受けとりました。とても重かったです。

135

New Words and Expressions

Words in the conversation

事務員	じむいん	clerk
名前	なまえ	name
書く	かく	to write
はんこ		*seal*; the Japanese stamp used for official documents instead of a signature
押す	おす	to push, to stamp
ここ		here
そこ		there
こっち		here, this way, this one
持つ	もつ	to have
サイン	sain	signature
いい		good, all right
けっこう		good, all right
ずいぶん		quite, very
大きい	おおきい	big, large
重い	おもい	heavy
ほんとう		indeed, really
ひとりで		alone, by oneself
だいじょうぶ		all right, safe
気をつける	きをつける	to take care, to be careful

＜Expressions in the conversation＞

掲示板にこれがあったんですけど。　　　　*I found this (message) on the notice board.*
けいじばん　　　　　　　　　　　　　　⇨CN S-1, L5CN S-1

名前書いて、はんこ押してください。　　*Write your name and put your seal on it.*
なまえか　　　　　お　　　Recall that 〜て、〜 links a series of actions. ⇨GN Ⅳ

そこじゃなくて、こっち。　　　　　　　*Not there; here.* 🄒
　　〜じゃなくて、〜 is used to make a correction. ⇨CN S-3

え。↗　　　　　　　　　　　　　　　　*Eh? Say again.* 🄒 ⇨CN S-3, まとめ2BⅡ3

そうそう。　　　　　　　　　　　　　　*That's right.* 🄒

136

はんこね。↗　　　　　　　　　　　　　　*Now seal it.* 🅲

　　ね↗ can be added to give a friendly tone to a request in casual speech.
　　⇨まとめ2BⅡ4

はんこは持ってないんですけど。　　　　　*I don't have a seal.* ⇨CN S-4

　　　　～んです ⇨L5GNⅥ, L7GN Ⅱ, **～けど** ⇨L11CN S-1
　　　　～てない is the shortened form of **～ていない** ⇨L8GNⅥ

サインでいいですよ。↘　　　　　　　　　*It's all right if you sign.*

　　　　～でいい means *will do.* ⇨GNⅤ
　　　　よ↘ is often added to an obvious comment. ⇨まとめ2BⅡ4

これでいいですか。↗　　　　　　　　　　*Will this do?*

けっこうです。　　　　　　　　　　　　　*That's fine.*

　　This is often said in a businesslike manner. It can also mean *No, thank you.*
　　⇨まとめ3BⅡ

わあ、↗　**ずいぶん大きいですね。**↘　　　*Wow, it's quite big, isn't it!*

　　わあ↗ shows surprise and **ね**↘ here shows the speaker's emotion. ⇨まと
　　め2BⅡ4

ほんとうだ。　　　　　　　　　　　　　　*You are right!* 🅲

　　In casual speech, **ほんとう** is often shortened to **ほんと**.

だいじょうぶかな。↘　　　　　　　　　　*Is it all right, I wonder?* 🅲

　　かな↘ shows uncertainty. ⇨まとめ2BⅡ4

気をつけて。　　　　　　　　　　　　　　*Take care!, Be careful!* 🅲　　⇨L5GNⅣ

Words in the report

見せる	みせる	*to show*
～の人	～のひと	*person in/of/at/from ～*
受けとる	うけとる	*to receive*
とても		*very much*

＜Expressions in the report＞

～と言いました。　　　　　　　　　　　*(He) said that ～.* ⇨L9GNⅡ

はんこがありませんでしたから、　　　　*As (Sharma-san) didn't have a seal, ～*

137

Grammar Notes

Ⅰ. Adjective sentences

Examples

① この荷物は重いです。   *This parcel is heavy.*

② これは安くありません。   *This isn't cheap.*

③ 私のカメラは高くありませんでした。   *My camera wasn't expensive.*

④ あの人はとても親切です。   *That person is very kind.*

【*Explanation*】

1. Plain and polite forms

Adjective sentences (sentences with an adjective as the predicate) can be plain or polite. (⇨ Pre-session) In this lesson we will look at polite adjective sentences which end in **desu**, **deshita** or **arimasen**, **arimasen deshita**, as illustrated in the examples above.

The basic structure of an adjective sentence is:

> < subject > が —— adjective

→ この荷物が重い。   *This parcel is heavy.*

1. この荷物は重いです。   *This parcel is heavy.*

2. あの人は親切です。   *That person is kind.*

2. [A] : -i adjective
[NA] : na adjective

Japanese adjectives can be assigned to one of the two groups, **-i** adjectives and **na** adjectives.

(1) [A] : やすい *cheap*, たかい *expensive, high*, おもい *heavy*

(2) [NA] : しんせつ *kind*, しずか *quiet*, べんり *convenient*

An [A] ends in い, whereas a [NA] doesn't. A [NA] uses な only when it precedes (or modifies) a noun (⇨L10GN I), as follows:

(1) [A-i] [N] : 重い荷物 *a heavy parcel,* 安いカメラ *a cheap camera*
(2) [NA] na [N] : 親切な人 *a kind person,* 静かな部屋 *a quiet room,* 便利なところ *a convenient place*

3. Inflection of adjectives

[A] is similar to a verb in that its forms are [A-i], [A-ku] nai, [A-katta], [A-ku] nakatta, [A-kute]. In contrast, the forms of [NA] are like those of a noun: [NA] da, [NA] ja nai, [NA] datta, [NA] ja nakatta, [NA] de, etc. ⇨ the tables of [A], [NA] and [N] forms on the next page.

The polite negative form of [A] is [A-ku] arimasen / [A-ku] nai desu for non-past, and [A-ku] arimasen deshita / [A-ku] nakatta desu for past. The plain form of [A] combines with desu to make up the polite form.

ja is a contraction of de wa; both ja or de wa are used.

いい *good* is irregular: いい derives from よい *good,* and its inflection is largely based on よい:

Plain form: ii *is good,* yoku nai *isn't good,* yokatta *was good,* yoku nakatta *wasn't good*

Polite form: ii desu *is good,* yoku arimasen *isn't good,* yokatta desu *was good,* yoku arimasen deshita *wasn't good*

きれい *pretty, beautiful,* きらい *dislike* and ゆうめい *famous* are [NA], even though they seem to end in い when written in kana.

GN

Polite and plain forms of adjectives and nouns

	Non-past		Past	
[A]	Positive	Negative	Positive	Negative
Polite	yasui desu	yasuku arimasen yasuku nai desu	yasukatta desu	yasuku arimasen deshita yasuku nakatta desu
Plain	yasui *to be cheap*	yasuku nai	yasukatta	yasuku nakatta
[NA]				
Polite	benri desu	benri ja arimasen benri ja nai desu	benri deshita	benri ja arimasen deshita benri ja nakatta desu
Plain	benri da *to be convenient*	benri ja nai	benri datta	benri ja nakatta
[N]				
Polite	hon desu	hon ja arimasen hon ja nai desu	hon deshita	hon ja arimasen deshita hon ja nakatta desu
Plain	hon da *to be a book*	hon ja nai	hon datta	hon ja nakatta

Ⅱ. 非常に　大変　すごく
とても　あまり　ずいぶん : adverbs of degree

Examples

① 非常に小さいです。　　　　　*(It)'s very small.*

② 大変有名です。　　　　　　　*(It)'s very famous.*

③ すごく安いです。　　　　　　*(It)'s so cheap.*

④ とても親切です。　　　　　　*(He)'s very nice.*

⑤ あまり親切じゃありません。　*(He)'s not so nice.*

⑥ ずいぶん重いですね。　　　　*(It)'s quite heavy.*

140

【*Explanation*】

adverbs	＜degree＞
非常に／大変／とても／すごく	*very*
あまり ＋ negative	*not very/not so*
ずいぶん	*quite*

あまり is always used in negative sentences. 非常に and 大変 are typically used in the formal style, とても and すごく in the casual style. ずいぶん shows that the degree is far greater than expected. 大変 is also used as a ［NA］ meaning *hard, difficult* ex. 大変ですね。 *It's hard, isn't it?*

Ⅲ. どう *how?*: question word

Examples

① A：宿題はどうですか。 　　　　　*How's the homework?*

B：大変です。 　　　　　　　　　*It's hard.*

② A：日本の料理はどうですか。 　*What do you think of Japanese food?*
　　　　　　　　　　　　　　　　(lit. How is Japanese food?)

B：とてもおいしいです。 　　　　*It's very delicious.*

【*Explanation*】

どう *how?* is used to ask how the listener feels or what s/he thinks about something: ＜something＞はどうですか. It can be used to ask about things, persons, matters, etc.

Ⅳ. ～て〈1〉: listing successive actions or events

Examples

① これから食堂に行ってごはんを食べて、郵便局に行きます。
Now (I') ll go to the cafeteria, eat lunch and (then) go to the post office.

② きのう東京に行って、友だちに会って、映画に行きました。
Yesterday (I) went to Tokyo, met my friend, and went to a movie.

③ ここに名前を書いてはんこを押してください。
Please write your name and put your seal here.

【Explanation】

1. The main function of ［V-te］

［V-te］ is used to connect two or more verbs. ［V-te］ is used after all but the last sentence in a sequence. By connecting sentences with ［V-te］ you can:

1） list successive actions or events,

食堂に行ってごはんを食べます。
(I)'ll go to the cafeteria and (then) eat lunch.

2） list simultaneous actions, where the first action indicates the means of accomplishing the second:

1. 漢字を書いて覚えます。
(I) memorize Kanji by writing them.

2. バスに乗って行きます。
(I) will go by bus.

3. ラジオを聞いて日本語を勉強しました。
I studied Japanese by listening to the radio.

142

3）give a reason or explanation. ⇨L21GN I

おそくなって、すみません。
I'm sorry I'm late.

[**A-kute**] and [**NA**] **de** (the **-te** form of adjectives) are also used in this way.
⇨L9GN I

2. Style, tense and mood

The style of the sentence (formal or casual), and its tense and mood are expressed only by the final verb of the series, not by [**V-te**]. For instance, ① is in the formal style and its tense is non-past, as expressed by the final verb 行きます. Likewise, 行きました in ② indicates the past tense, formal style. The mood of ③ is a request, indicated by the final ください. The actions requested are (1) *Write your name.* and (2) *Put your seal.*

Look at the illustration below: actions A, B, and C occur one after another. The verbs for A and B are in the [**V-te**] form, whereas the verb for C ends in ～ます. The subject (performer) of actions A, B and C are assumed to be the same (unless a change of subject is clearly indicated).

GN

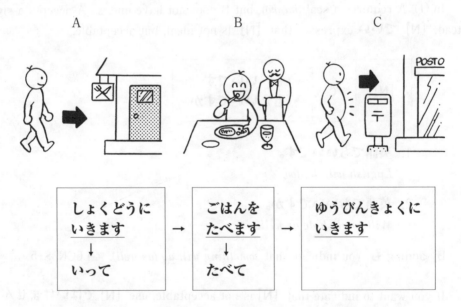

A	B	C

しょくどうに いきます ↓ いって	ごはんを たべます ↓ たべて	ゆうびんきょくに いきます

私は食堂に行って、ごはんを食べて、郵便局に行きます。
I'll go to the cafeteria, eat lunch, and then go to the post office.

V. 〜でいい: *〜 is all right, 〜 will do*

Examples

① A：はんこを押してください。   *Please put your seal here.*

B：はんこはないんですけど。   *I haven't got a seal. (What shall I do?)*

A：じゃ、サインでいいです。   *In that case, your signature will do.*

② A：日本語で書いてください。   *Please write in Japanese.*

B：日本語はわからないんですけど。   *I don't know Japanese.*

A：じゃ、英語でいいです。   *In that case, it's OK in English.*

【*Explanation*】

In ①, A requires a seal (*hanko*), but B does not have one, so A accepts a signature instead. [N] でいい expresses that [N] is not ideal, but acceptable.

[N]	で	（も）いいです （も）いいですか

1. 英語でもいいです。
English will do, too.

2. 英語でもいいですか。
Will English do as well?

By adding も, you indicate that *something will do (as well).* ⇨L6CN S-5

If you want to indicate that [N] is not acceptable, use [N] ではいけません。

英語ではいけません。
English won't do.

Ⅵ. 〈⊷⊶◀ に〈3〉and で〈3〉: structure particles

Let's see how ＜place＞に and ＜place＞で differ.

京都で手紙を書きます。
きょうと　　てがみ　か

京都に手紙を書きます。

ここで書いてください。

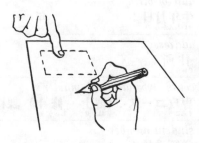

ここに書いてください。

駅で電話をかけます。
えき　でんわ

駅に電話をかけます。

で indicates the place where the action is performed.

に indicates the place which is reached or affected by the action.

Conversation Notes

<General Information>

1. Office instructions

a. When you fill in a form, the office clerk may instruct you as follows:

これ｜に〜（を）書いてください。　　*Please write 〜.*
ここ

A form to be filled in at a university:

name 名前 なまえ	*sex (male/female)* 性別：（男・女） せいべつ　だん　じょ	*nationality* 国籍： こくせき
date of birth 生年月日：　　　　年　　　月　　　日 せいねんがっぴ　　　ねん　　がつ　　にち		*age* 年齢：　満　　　才 ねんれい　まん　　さい
address　　　　　　　　**Tel.** (　　　　　　) 住所： じゅうしょ		
course type (doctoral/master's) 専攻コース：（博士・修士）課程 せんこう　　　はかせ　しゅうし　かてい		*postgraduate course* 研究科 けんきゅうか
student number 学籍番号： がくせきばんごう	*academic adviser* 指導教官： しどうきょうかん	

b. You may be given further instructions such as the following:

サインしてください。　　　　　　*Please sign.*

はんこ｜（を）押してください。　　*Please put your seal on it.*
印鑑　　　　　お
いんかん

写真（を）はってください。　　　*Please paste your photo on it.*
しゃしん

学生証（を）見せてください。　　*Please show your student card.*
がくせいしょう　　　み

指導教官のサイン（を）もらってください。
しどうきょうかん

　　　　　　　　　　　　　　　　Please get your adviser's signature.

受講届け｜（を）出してください。　*Please submit your course*
じゅこうとど　　　　　だ　　　　*registration form.*

受講票
じゅこうひょう

146

2. Delivery service

Takkyuubin（宅急便）is a proper noun（*express delivery service*）used by one of the largest delivery service companies, so it has come to be used alongside the general term **takuhaibin**（宅配便 *home delivery service*）.

This service enables you to send parcels, luggage etc. to all areas in Japan for next-day delivery; it is available not only at airports and stations, but also home and many shops.

All you need to do is to fill out a form and pay the（reasonable）fee.

<*Strategies*>

S-1. How to introduce a main topic —2.

CN

a. When you show something that explains the purpose of your visit, you can indicate how you got it with **んですけど** or **んですが**: ⇨L5CN S-1

① シャルマ：あの、掲示板にこれがあったんですけど。
Excuse me. I found this on the notice board.

事務員：ああ、宅急便ですね。
Oh, it's a delivery item, isn't it?

Or you might take an article that was forgotten（わすれもの）to the office and tell them where you found it:

② A：あの、教室にこれがあったんですけど。
Excuse me. I found this in the classroom.

B：ああ、わすれものですね。どうも。
It's been forgotten, hasn't it? Thank you.

A：いいえ。
Not at all.

b. When you have come to claim something, you can simply show your note and say お願いします.

① あの、これ、お願いします。

You can also specify what you are claiming:

② あの、宅急便お願いします。

たっきゅうびん　ねが

Alternatively, you can simply give your name and identity, such as your room number, followed by けど.

③ あの、402号室のシャルマですけど。

ごうしつ

S-2. How to ask for instructions

a. You can ask how to do something as follows:

| 〜 | がわからないんですけど。 | *I'm not sure how to 〜.* |
| | を教えてください。 | *Can you show me how to 〜.* |

おし

① (You don't know how to fill in a form.)
すみません、書き方がわからないんですけど。

か　かた

② (You don't know how to use a dictionary.)
すみません、使い方を教えてください。

つか　かた

③ (You don't know how to play a game.)
あの、やり方がわからないんですけど。

かた

You can also ask in a more general way as follows:

④ すみません、ちょっと | わからないんですけど。

| 教えてください。

b. When you have done something according to instructions, you can then check if it is OK by asking これでいいですか. If it is, the response will be けっこうです.

シャルマ：これでいいですか。(Showing the form)

事務員：はい、けっこうです。

じ　む　いん

S-3. How to correct others' mistakes

To correct a mistake, you can use **いいえ/いえ, いや** or **ううん**へ:

① A：アリさんですね。

B：いいえ、シャルマです。

② 会　計：ごいっしょですか。
かい けい

山　下：あ、いや、べつべつにしてください。
やま した

If you want to emphasize your correction, you can use **じゃなくて**.

③ A：アリさんですね。

B：いえ、アリじゃなくてシャルマです。
No, not Ali but Sharma.

④ A：ここですか。

B：ううん。そこじゃなくて、こっち。

S-4. How to ask for advice implicitly

When you can't comply with a request, you can ask for advice implicitly by explaining your circumstances, using **んですけど** or **んですが**.

① 事　務　員：それから、はんこね。
じ む いん
Then, a seal, please.

シャルマ：ええと、はんこは持ってないんですけど。
も
Er..., I don't have a seal.

事　務　員：じゃ、サインでいいですよ。
You can sign instead, then.

② 山　下：きょうやってますか。
やま した
Are you open today?

149

受 付：いいえ。火曜の午後は 休診なんですが。
Sorry, we are closed on Tuesday afternoon.

山 下：あ、そうですか。

S-5. How to give an alternative

a. じゃ can be used to suggest, or give permission for, an alternative course of action:
⇨まとめ2BⅡ2

> じゃ、〜で（も）｜いい。🅒➡️⬇️
> いいです。🅕
> けっこうです。🅕⬆️

Adding **よ** makes for a friendly tone: ⇨まとめ2BⅡ4

① シャルマ：ええと、はんこは持ってないんですけど。

事 務 員：じゃ、サインでいいですよ。

You can use **じゃ** to suggest an alternative.

> じゃ、〜は。🅕／🅒
> じゃ、〜は｜どう。↗ 🅒➡️⬇️
> ｜どうですか。↗ 🅕

② 受 付：火曜の午後は 休診なんですが。

山 下：あ、そうですか。じゃ、あしたの午後は。
How about tomorrow afternoon, then?

b. When you are unable to comply with a request, you can ask permission for an alternative, often introduced hesitantly with **あの**. ⇨L6V, L8CN S-3, まとめ1BⅡ3

> あの、〜で（も）｜いい。↗ 🅒➡️⬇️
> ｜いいですか。↗ 🅕

（B is given an instruction.）
A：ここに、はんこ押してください。

B：あの、サインでもいいですか。↗
Excuse me, is it all right if I sign instead?

電話をかける (1) 病院
でん わ　　　　　　びょういん

Phoning (1): A hospital

OBJECTIVES:

GRAMMAR

Ⅰ. ～たい: *want to* ～

Ⅱ. ～んです〈2〉: explanatory ending

Ⅲ. ～ { が〈2〉 / けれど / けど } : ～ *but*

Ⅳ. に〈4〉 *at*
    から〈2〉 *from* : structure particles
    まで *until*

Ⅴ. ごろ: *about, approximately* (of time)

Ⅵ. ～時～分 and ～月～日: time and date
    じ　ふん　　　　がつ　にち

CONVERSATION

<General Information>

1. Telephones
2. Telephone numbers

<Strategies>

S-1. How to ask for a telephone number
S-2. How to make a telephone call
S-3. How to deal with a wrong number
S-4. How to introduce a question politely
S-5. How to ask about office hours
S-6. How to make an appointment

Model Conversation

（1）

Characters : Yamashita(山下), Suzuki(鈴木), a research assistant in the department

Situation : Yamashita-san asks Suzuki-san the telephone number of the hospital.

Flow-chart :

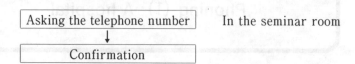

| Asking the telephone number | In the seminar room |

↓

Confirmation

―研究室で―

山　下：鈴木さん、井上医院の電話、わかりますか。
鈴　木：ええと、たしか……５２の３１８１だよ。
山　下：５２の３８１８。
鈴　木：いや、３１８１。
山　下：あ、３１８１ですね。どうもすみません。
鈴　木：どうした。
山　下：ええ。ちょっと、かぜひいたらしいんです。

（2）

Characters : Yamashita（山下）, a hospital receptionist（受付）

Situation : Yamashita-san rings to ask office hours and make an appointment.

Flow-chart :

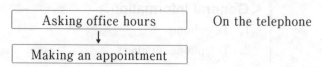

| Asking office hours | On the telephone |

↓

Making an appointment

―電話で―

受　付：井上医院です。
山　下：あの、ちょっと、おたずねしたいんですが。
受　付：はい。
山　下：きょうの午後、やってますか。

受　付：いいえ、火曜の午後は休診なんですが。

山　下：あ、そうですか。

　　　　じゃ、あしたの午後は。

受　付：はい、やっています。

山　下：何時から何時までですか。

受　付：午後は、2時から5時半までです。

　　　　　　＊　　　＊　　　＊

山　下：じゃ、あしたの午後、お願いしたいんですが。

受　付：はい。

　　　　どうなさいました。

山　下：かぜひいたらしいんです。

受　付：そうですか。

　　　　ええと、お名前は。

山　下：山下です。

受　付：山下さんですね。

山　下：はい。

受　付：それじゃ、4時15分に来てください。

山　下：4時15分ですね。

受　付：はい。

山　下：どうも。

受　付：いいえ。お大事に。

井上医院
診療：9:00〜12:00
　　　14:00〜17:30
休診：火・土の午後
　　　日・祭日

Report

　山下さんはかぜをひいたので、鈴木さんに井上医院の電話番号を聞いて、電話をかけました。井上医院は日曜日が休みです。ほかの日は朝9時から夕方5時半までやっていますが、火曜日と土曜日は昼の12時までです。きょうは火曜日で午後は休みですから、あしたの午後にしました。

New Words and Expressions

Words in the conversation

井上医院	いのうえいいん	Inoue Clinic
たしか		if I'm not mistaken
かぜ		cold
（かぜを）ひく		to catch a cold
たずねる		to ask (a question)
午後	ごご	afternoon
やる		to do, to open
休診	きゅうしん	closed (hospital)
何時	なんじ	what time?
2時	にじ	2 : 00
5時半	ごじはん	5 : 30
願う	ねがう	to request
4時15分	よじじゅうごふん	4 : 15

＜Expressions in the conversation＞

たしか……５２の３１８１だよ。   *It's 52-3181, if I remember correctly.* 🗣♦

たしか〜 indicates lack of confidence that one's memory is correct. In casual speech, men use **だよ** where women would use **よ**. ⇨まとめ2BⅡ4

どうした。↗   *What's the matter?* 🗣♦

In casual speech, you can also say **どうしたの**↗（**どうしたんですか**↗ in formal speech）.

かぜひいたらしいんです。   *It seems I've caught a cold.*

In conversation, the particle **を** is often omitted. **〜らしい** shows the speaker's guess. ⇨L22GNⅡ

ちょっと、おたずねしたいんですが。   *May I ask you a question?*

おたずねする is a humble form of **たずねる**. ⇨L18GNⅠ

きょうの午後、やってますか。   *Are you open this afternoon?*

やっている usually means *to be open*. ⇨CN S-5

休診なんですが   *Sorry, we are closed.*

〜んですが ⇨L6CN S-4

154

何時から何時までですか。
なんじ

lit. From what time to what time? ⇨ L7 GNⅣ

あしたの午後お願いしたいんですが。
ご　ご　ねが

Can I have an appointment tomorrow afternoon?

The basic meaning of **お願いしたいんですが** is *May I ask you a favour?* **お願いする** is a humble form of **願う**. ⇨L18GNⅠ

どうなさいました。↗

What's the problem?

This is often used to enquire about a patient's symptoms.

お大事に。
だい じ

Take care.

A stock phrase said to patients/people feeling unwell instead of good bye.

Words in the report

（電話を）かける		*to make (a telephone call)*
ほかの〜		*other 〜*
日	ひ	*day*
朝	あさ	*morning*
9時	くじ	*9 : 00*
夕方	ゆうがた	*evening*

MC

<Expressions in the report>

〜が、〜	*〜, but, however 〜* ⇨GNⅢ
〜ので、〜	*as 〜, 〜* ⇨L9GNⅢ

ので can be used to offer a personal reason politely.

155

Grammar Notes

Ⅰ. 〜たい: *want to* 〜

Examples

① コーヒーが飲みたいです。　　*I want to drink coffee.*

② コーヒーは飲みたくありません。　*I don't want to drink coffee.*

③ お茶が飲みたかったです。　　*I wanted to drink tea.*

【*Explanation*】

1. [V(base)]-tai

　　[V(base)] (the verb-base) is the part that remains if you detach **-masu,** eg. **nomi** is the verb-base of **nomi-masu.** Adding **-tai** to [V(base)] indicates what you want to do.

nomitai	*I want to drink.*
tabetai	*I want to eat.*
ikitai	*I want to go.*

2. Inflection of -tai

　　-tai inflects in the same way as [**A**] (**-i** adjectives):

nomimasu → nomitai	*I want to drink.*
nomitaku nai	*I don't want to drink.*
nomitakatta	*I wanted to drink.*
nomitaku nakatta	*I didn't want to drink.*

	[V (base)]-tai			
	Non-past		Past	
	Positive	Negative	Positive	Negative
Polite	-tai desu	-taku arimasen -taku nai desu	-takatta desu	-taku arimasen deshita -taku nakatta desu
Plain	-tai	-taku nai	-takatta	-taku nakatta

3. Subject of the sentence

The subject of 〜たいです statement is always *I* or *we*, whereas when used in a question 〜たいですか it is always *you*. As the subject is obvious, it is usually omitted:

1. 飲みたいです。
   の
   I want to drink.

2. 飲みたいですか。
   Do you want to drink?

The wishes of a third person are indicated by adding expressions like *it seems that ~*, *I hear/understand that~*, *he said that ~* etc.

3. 鈴木さんは飲みたいそうです。　　⇨L19GNⅢ
   すずき
   (I understand that) Suzuki-san wants to drink.

4. 鈴木さんは飲みたいと言いました。　⇨L9GNⅡ
   い
   Suzuki-san (said that he) wants to drink.

Note that while in English it is possible to say *Suzuki-san wants to drink*, the direct equivalent to such a sentence in Japanese is incorrect:

✕　鈴木さんは飲みたいです。

4. ⟨∎∥∥∥≪ が as object particle

An object is normally marked by を, as in コーヒーを飲みます. However, with たい sentences が is sometimes preferred: コーヒーが飲みたいです, although some speakers use を（コーヒーを飲みたいです）.

Particles other than を remain the same, as shown below:

1. 友だちに会いたいです。
   とも　あ
   I want to meet my friend.

2. 京都へ行きたいです。
   きょうと　い
   I want to go to Kyoto.

3. 船便で出したいです。
   ふなびん　だ
   I want to send (it) by sea mail.

GN

157

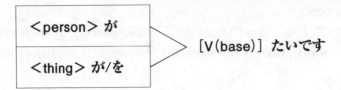

→ 私がコーヒーが/を飲みたい（飲みたいです）。

I want to drink coffee.

4. コーヒーが飲みたいです。 *I want to drink coffee.*

5. コーヒーが飲みたいですか。 *Do you want to drink coffee?*

6. コーヒーは飲みたくないです。 *I don't want to drink coffee.*

Expression of one's wishes too directly is generally avoided in Japan, especially by junior people in front of seniors; instead, less direct expressions such as 〜たいんですが and 〜たいと思います are used. ⇨L11GNⅡ, ⇨L8CN S-3

Ⅱ. 〜んです〈2〉: explanatory ending

Examples

① A：どうしたんですか。 *What's the matter?*

B：お金がないんです。 *I haven't got any money.*

② doctor：かぜですよ。 *You've got a cold.*

patient：かぜなんですか。 *So it is a cold?*

③ A：あしたひまですか。 *Are you free tomorrow?*

B：いいえ、日本語の試験なんです。 *No, I have a Japanese test.*

【*Explanation*】

1. Explanation asked for and given

The general meaning of んです was explained in L5; the above are some further examples. In ①, A is aware that B has a problem and uses んです to ask him to explain it. B then explains, using んです. ⇨L5GNⅤ

2. Uses of んです:

1) As **んです** can be used to explain the reason for a situation without indicating it explicitly, (① and ③), it is a handy expression for making an excuse.

2) Expressing confirmation for one's suspicions: ②. After the doctor has confirmed what the patient had been suspecting, the patient reacts using **んです**.

3) Showing surprise or irritation.

GN

3. [N] なんです: かぜなんです
[NA] なんです: 元気なんです

You may have noticed the **な** before **んです** in ② and ③, (**かぜなんです** and **試験なんです**). After [V] and [A], **んです** is attached to the plain form but after [N] and [NA], **な** is inserted before **んです** as indicated by '**＊**' in the following table.
⇨L5GN V

～ んです		
	Plain form	
[V]	taberu　　　*to eat* tabeta tabenai tabenakatta	んです＊＊
[A]	akai　　　*red* akakatta akaku nai akaku nakatta	
[NA]	shizuka na＊　*quiet* shizuka datta shizuka ja nai shizuka ja nakatta	
[N]	shiken na＊　*test* shiken datta shiken ja nai shiken ja nakatta	

＊ **Na** is used instead of **da**.
＊＊ Instead of **んです**, **のです** is used in written sentences.

160

Ⅲ.

$$\sim \begin{Bmatrix} が〈2〉 \\ けれど \\ けど \end{Bmatrix} : \sim but$$

Examples

① **これは小さいですが、重いです。**
　　This is small but heavy.

② **勉強しましたけれど、わかりません。**
　　I have studied it, but I don't understand it.

③ **あした筑波山へ行くんですけど。**
　　Tomorrow I'll go to Mt. Tsukuba... (Would you like to come with me?)

【*Explanation*】

1. ～が／～けれど

To express the idea of {S₁} but {S₂}, the connective particles **が**, **けれど** or **けど**, are used as in ① and ②.

$$\{S_1\} \begin{Bmatrix} が \\ けれど \\ けど \end{Bmatrix} \{S_2\}$$

❗ This **が** is not a subject particle.

が is more formal than **けれど**. **けど** is short for **けれど** and is the most casual of the three.

が＞　　けれど＞けど
formal ←　　→ casual

In spoken Japanese, 〜が usually follows the polite rather than the plain form. けれど/けど, however, can be attached to either the plain or polite form.

○ 勉強しましたが、わかりません。
× 勉強したが、わかりません。
○ 勉強したけど、わかりません。
○ 勉強しましたけど、わかりません。

2. 〜んですが/〜んですけど

Conversations are often started with 〜んですけど/〜んですが as in ③ to foreshadow that the speaker is about to make an offer, request, etc. (けど/が in this use doesn't mean *but*). The speaker will often pause before the second half of the sentence (or leave it unsaid), thus preparing the listener for the request, a clever strategy to secure the listener's sympathy. ⇨L5CN S-1, L7CN S-6, L8CN S-2,3

1. ちょっと頭が痛いんですけど。(授業を休んでもいいですか。)
   I've got a headache... (May I be absent from the class?)

2. あした休診なんですが。(ほかの日に来てください。)
   We are closed tomorrow... (Please come on a different day.)

The sentence in (　　) is obvious from the situation and therefore often omitted.

Ⅳ. 　に〈4〉*at*

　　　から〈2〉*from*: structure particles

　　　まで *untill*

【*Explanation*】

After expressions of time, に means *at*.

から means *from*; after expressions of time, it indicates the starting time. After nouns of place, it indicates the starting point.

まで means *until, up to* and is attached to expressions of time or place.
⇨L12CN S-3

① 9時に来ます。
We come at 9 o'clock.

② 9時から勉強します。
We study from 9 o'clock.

③ 3時半まで勉強します。
We study until 3:30.

④ 3時半に帰ります。
We go home at 3:30.

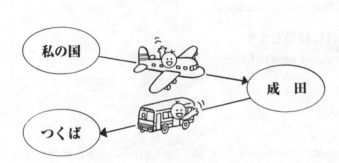

私の国から成田まで飛行機で来ました。

From my country to Narita, I came by airplane.

GN

成田からつくばまでバスで来ました。

From Narita to Tsukuba, I came by bus.

V. ごろ: *about, approximately* (of time)

To express an approximate time, add **ごろ** after the time, eg. **6時ごろ (に)** *(at) about 6 o'clock.* **に** is optional after **ごろ**, but **から** and **まで** cannot be omitted after **ごろ**.

○ 6時ごろ/6時ごろに	✕ 6時にごろ
○ 9時ごろから	✕ 9時からごろ
○ 3時半ごろまで	✕ 3時半までごろ

1. 私は毎日6時ごろ (に) 起きます。　*I wake up at about 6 o'clock everyday.*

2. 3時半ごろまで勉強します。　*We study until 3:30 or so.*

163

Ⅵ. 〜時〜分，and 〜月〜日: time and date　　⇨まとめ2AⅠ

Examples

① A：いま何時ですか。
　　What time is it now?

　 B：4時5分です。
　　It's five past four.

　 A：電車は4時7分に来るんですね。
　　The train will arrive at 4:07, I take it.

　 B：ええ。
　　Yes.

② A：結婚式は何月ですか。
　　When (which month) will you get married?

　 B：4月です。 4月10日に結婚します。
　　In April.　I'll get married on April 10.

【Explanation】

Combinations of number/counter indicating date and time are often irregular: it is best to memorize the time expressions listed in まとめ2AⅠ.

To ask the time, add 何(なん) before the appropriate counter: 何時 for the hours, 何分 for the minutes, 何月 for the month, 何日 for the day of the month, and 何曜日 for the day of the week.

Time expressions like 〜曜日, 〜月〜日 and 〜時〜分 require the structure particle に as shown below. Recall that expressions of relative time such as きょう, あした, etc. never take に.　⇨L5GNⅧ

1. 金曜日に会いましょう。　　　　*Let's meet on Friday.*

2. 6月23日に来てください。　　　*Please come on June 23.*

3. クラスは3時半に終わります。　*Our class will finish at 3:30.*

4. あしたやります。　　　　　　　*I'll do it tomorrow.*

Conversation Notes

<General Information>

1. Telephones

Calls from public telephones, **公衆電話 (こうしゅうでんわ)**, can be made using ¥10/¥100 coins or a telephone card. No change is given for unused coins. The charge depends on the length and destination of the call.

You will find several types of public telephones in use. The red telephone with a dial is the oldest type. The red and yellow ones on station platforms and similar places are also coin-operated, whereas the green telephone with push-buttons is a new type that can be used with a telephone card or coins.

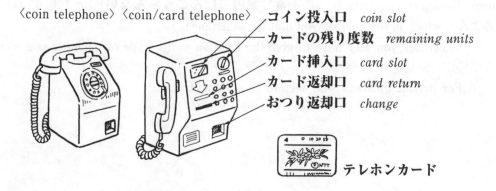

〈coin telephone〉〈coin/card telephone〉

コイン投入口　*coin slot*
カードの残り度数　*remaining units*
カード挿入口　*card slot*
カード返却口　*card return*
おつり返却口　*change*

テレホンカード

2. Telephone numbers

a. How to read a number

In Japan, a telephone number consists of the following three parts:

(0 2 9 8) 5 2 − 3 1 8 1

The first part (0 2 9 8) is the area code, the second and last part (5 2 − 3 1 8 1) the user's number. It's possible to read each number separately, linking the parts with **の**. Alternatively, the second part is often read as indicated in the parentheses overleaf.

ゼロ・にい・きゅう・はち　の
ごう・にい（ごじゅうに）　の　さん・いち・はち・いち

When reading the numbers one by one, they are read as follows:

1：いち　2：にい　3：さん　4：よん　　5：ごう
6：ろく　7：なな　8：はち　9：きゅう　0：ゼロ（れい/まる）

In phone numbers, 2 is read as **にい** and 5 as **ごう**. 0 can also be read as **まる** when it is placed between numbers or at the end.

（内） or **（内線）** indicates an extension:
（0298）52−3181　（内線）105
「**（内線）105**」is read as follows:
ないせん　の　いち・まる・ごう

b. How to find a number

You can get a telephone number through directory enquiries or from the telephone book. Directory enquiries is called **番号案内（ばんごうあんない）** or **104（いちまるよん）**, which is the number you dial for assistance.

Sometimes you may have to give the location or the type of business you wish to call. ⇨CN S-1

For private numbers, you need to give the address.

＜Strategies＞

S-1. How to ask for a telephone number

a. You can ask if someone knows a telephone number as follows:

～の電話（番号）	わかる。↗ 🄒➡️⬇️	*Do you know ～ ?*
	わかりますか。↗ 🄒	
	ごぞんじですか。↗ 🄒⬆️	

when you are certain that the listener knows the answer, you can use the verb 教える.

～の電話（番号）	教えて。↗ 🄒➡️⬇️	*Tell me～.*
	教えてください。↘ 🄒	
	教えていただけませんか。↗ 🄒⬆️	

① 山　下：鈴木さん、井上医院の電話、わかりますか。

鈴　木：ええと、たしか……５２の３１８１だよ。
　　　　Let me see... it is 52-3181, if I'm not mistaken.

② （At an office in the university）

　A：木村先生の研究室の電話番号、教えていただけませんか。

　B：ええと……ちょっと待ってください。

b. When asking directory enquiries for a telephone number, you can use お願いします（電話番号 is not necessary）.

～	（の電話番号）、お願いします。
＜Location＞の ～	
～ っていう＜type of business＞	

You may need give other details, such as the address or type of business.

① 緑町の井上医院、お願いします。
Inoue clinic in Midori-choo, please.

② 緑町３丁目の「ノア」っていう喫茶店、お願いします。
The coffee shop called "NOA" in Midori-choo 3-choome, please.

CN

S-2. How to make a telephone call

When connected, the caller normally says **もしもし**, whereas the person taking the call will say **はい** in response.

① A：もしもし。 *Hello!*

B：はい、井上医院です。 *Hello. this is Inoue hospital.*

To confirm that you've got the right number, use **あの** as follows:

② A：もしもし。

B：はい。

A：あの、井上医院ですか。

B：はい、そうです。

Use **ですが** or **ですけど** to give your name or identity:

③ A：はい、留学生課（*Department of foreign students*）です。

B：あの、インドのシャルマですが。

S-3. How to deal with a wrong number

When you have misdialled, apologize by saying 「**すみません、まちがえました。**」; when someone else calls you by mistake, it is usual to say 「**いいえ、ちがいます。**」.

① A：もしもし。井上医院ですか。

B：いいえ、ちがいます。うちは山田ですけど。
No. You have called the wrong number. This is Yamada.

A：あ、どうもすみません。まちがえました。
I'm sorry (I have misdialled).

〜じゃありませんか↗ can be used to double-check on the number:

② A：もしもし。井上医院ですか。

B：いいえ、ちがいます。

A：あ、すみません。

　　あの、５２の３１８１じゃありませんか。

B：いいえ、うちは５３の３１８１ですよ。

A：あ、どうもすみませんでした。

S-4. How to introduce a question politely

When you want to ask a question politely. start the conversation with the
following expressions.

| あの、ちょっと | うかがいますが。
おたずねしますが。 | *Excuse me but may I ask*
you a question? |

You can ask more politely by using 〜たいんですが.

| あの、ちょっと | うかがいたいんですが。
おたずねしたいんですが。 | |

山　下：あの、ちょっと、おたずねしたいんですが。
やま　した

受　付：はい。
うけ　つけ

山　下：きょうの午後、やってますか。
やま　した　　　　　　ごご

Are you open this afternoon?

S-5. How to ask about office hours

Use **やってますか** to ask if a place is open:

＜time / date＞　（は）、やってますか。　　　*Are you open 〜?*

You can ask how long they are open by saying the following: ⇨GN Ⅳ

| 何時から何時まで
なんじ | やってますか。
ですか。 | *How long are you open?* |

山　下：きょうの午後、やってますか。
やま　した　　　　　　ごご

169

```
--------------------------------------------
```

山　下：何時から何時までですか。
<ruby>山<rt>やま</rt></ruby> <ruby>下<rt>した</rt></ruby> <ruby>何時<rt>なんじ</rt></ruby>

受　付：午後は、2時から5時半までです。
We are open from 2:00 till 5:30 p.m.

To enquire about the office hours of a company, you can also use 営業時間.

営業時間 ┃ は何時から何時までですか。
　　　　 ┃ を教えてください。

For surgery hours, you can use 診察時間 or 診療時間 instead.

S-6. How to make an appointment

a. Once you have information on office hours, you can ask for an appointment slot with お願いします．お願いしたいんですが can also be used. ⇨L8CN S-2

じゃ、<time/date> ┃ お願いします。
　　　　　　　　　 ┃ お願いしたいんですが。

A：じゃ、あしたの午後、お願いしたいんですが。
Can I come tomorrow afternoon, then?

B：はい。それじゃ、4時15分に来てください。

A：4時15分ですね。どうも。

B：はい。お大事に。

If you can't make it at the time offered to you, give an alternative as shown in L6. ⇨L6CN S-5

b. To make an appointment for some specific purpose, indicate your purpose first as follows:

<topic>のことで <purpose>たいんですが。

For example, when you want to consult your adviser about your thesis, you can say:

論文のことで、ちょっとご相談したいんですが。
I'd like to consult you about my thesis.

c. After giving your purpose, you can ask about the person's availability:

いつ（何時／何曜日／……）が│いい。↗ 😊➡⬇
　　　　　　　　　　　　　　│いいですか。↗ 🖼

Or more politely:

いつ（何時／何曜日／……）が│いいでしょうか。↘ 🖼
　　　　　　　　　　　　　　│よろしいでしょうか。↘ 🖼⬆

Instead of（いつ）, you can also use **何時ごろ** or **何曜日**.

You can suggest a time yourself as follows:

＜time/date＞は│（どう）。↗ 😊➡⬇
　　　　　　　　│どうですか。↗ 🖼

Or more politely:

＜time/date＞は│どうでしょうか。↘ 🖼
　　　　　　　　│いかがでしょうか。↘ 🖼⬆

d. After making an appointment, you can finish the conversation with **よろしくお願いします**:

See the following example.

A：先生、論文のことで、ちょっとご相談したいんですが。

B：はい。

A：いつがよろしいでしょうか。↘

B：あしたの午後なら、いつでもいいですよ。

A：そうですか。じゃ、2時ごろはいかがでしょうか。↘

B：ええ、いいですよ。

A：じゃ、よろしくお願いします。

B：はい。

外国人はふつう名前をかたかなで書きますね。でも、ある人は漢字を使って、はんこを作ります。たとえば、「シャルマ」という名前は、「シャ」「ル」「マ」の三つの音に分けて、漢字をさがします。漢字の辞書には、次のような字があります。

シャ：	者	*person*		ル：	留	*stay*	マ：麻	*hemp*
	社	*company*			流	*flow*	間	*space*
	車	*car, wheel*					真	*true*
	写	*copy*					馬	*horse*
	射	*shoot*					魔	*demon*

シャルマさんは、「者」「留」「間」という漢字を使って、はんこを作りました。あなたは、どんな漢字を使って、はんこを作りたいですか。辞書を見て、いい漢字をさがしてください。

*ふつう usually
ある人　　あるひと　　some people
たとえば　　　　　　for example
音　　　　おと　　　sound
分ける　　わける　　to divide
さがす　　　　　　to look for
辞書　　　じしょ　　dictionary
次のような　つぎのような　as follows

第8課

許可を求める
きょか　もと
Asking permission

OBJECTIVES:

GRAMMAR

I . The **-nai** form of verbs: [V-nai]

II . The **-nakatta** form of verbs: [V-nakatta]

III . ～ないでください: *please don't ～*

IV . はい and いいえ: how to answer negative
questions

V . ～ている〈1〉: expressing a state of affairs

VI . ～ていない: *not (yet)*

VII . ～てもいい: *you may ～, it's all right to ～*

VIII . か *or*: connective particle

IX . とき〈1〉: *at the time of when*

CONVERSATION

＜General Information＞
1. Relationship between seniors and juniors
in Japan
2. A request for leave of absence

＜Strategies＞
S-1. How to start a conversation —5. Asking for
permission
S-2. How to introduce a main topic —3.
S-3. How to ask for permission
S-4. How to give a warning

Model Conversation

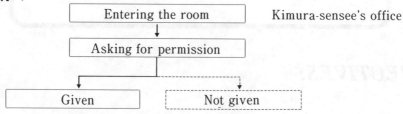

(1)

Characters ：Yamashita（山下）, Professor Kimura（木村）

Situation ：Yamashita-san needs to go and see a doctor today's afternoon, so he asks Kimura-sensee for permission to be absent from his seminar.

Flow-chart ：

```
        ┌─────────────────────┐      Kimura-sensee's office
        │  Entering the room  │
        └─────────────────────┘
                  │
                  ▼
        ┌─────────────────────┐
        │ Asking for permission│
        └─────────────────────┘
           │                 ┆
           ▼                 ▼
    ┌───────────┐      ┌───────────┐
    │   Given   │      │ Not given │
    └───────────┘      └───────────┘
```

―木村先生の研究室で―

山　下：（knock-knock）
木　村：はい。
山　下：失礼します。
木　村：やあ。
山　下：あの、ちょっとよろしいですか。
木　村：どうぞ。

＊　　　＊　　　＊

木　村：どうした。
山　下：あのう、午後のゼミのことなんですが。
木　村：うん。
山　下：きのうからかぜでちょっと熱があるんです。
木　村：ああ、そういえば、顔色が悪いね。
山　下：で、これから病院へ行きたいんですが。
木　村：うん。
山　下：ゼミ、休んでもよろしいでしょうか。
木　村：ああ、もちろんかまわないよ。
　　　　早くみてもらったほうがいいね。
山　下：どうもすみません。
木　村：いいえ。じゃ、お大事にね。
山　下：ありがとうございます。
　　　　じゃ、失礼します。

（2）

Characters：Yamashita（山下），Suzuki（鈴木）

Situation：Yamashita-san wants to make some copies in the seminar room.

Flow-chart：

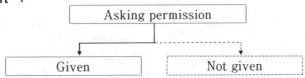

― コピー機の前で ―

山　下：すみません。

鈴　木：おう。

山　下：あの、ちょっとこれコピーしてもいいですか。

鈴　木：あ、いまソーターこわれているから、ちょっと使わないで。

山　下：そうですか。（To himself）困ったなあ。

鈴　木：午後には修理に来るからさ。

山　下：はい。じゃ、また来ます。

Report

　山下さんはきのう木村先生の午後のゼミを休みました。前の日から、かぜで少し熱がありました。それで、木村先生の研究室へ行って、「ゼミを休んでもいいですか。」と聞きました。先生は「早くみてもらったほうがいいね。」と言いました。

New Words and Expressions

Words in the conversation

やあ		Hi, Hello
ゼミ	zemi	seminar
きのう		yesterday
熱	ねつ	fever
顔色	かおいろ	one's complexion
悪い	わるい	bad
で		Therefore, So, =それで
これから		now
病院	びょういん	hospital
休む	やすむ	to be absent
ああ		Yes =うん/ええ/はい
もちろん		of course, certainly
早く	はやく	soon, quickly
コピー機	kopii き	photocopier
使う	つかう	to use
コピーする	kopii する	to photocopy
いま		now
ソーター	sootaa	sorter
こわれる		to be broken
修理	しゅうり	repair cf. 修理する to repair

＜Expressions in the conversation＞

失礼します。
しつれい

Excuse me. ⇨CN S-1

ちょっとよろしいですか。

Do you have a moment? ⇨CN S-1

〜のことなんですが。

It's about 〜. ⇨CN S-2

そういえば、

Now that you mention it,/Come to think about it,

顔色が悪い。
かおいろ　わる
　　　〜は〜が adj. ⇨L10GNIV

You don't look well./You look pale.

休んでもよろしいでしょうか。
やす

May I be absent? ⇨CN S-3

かまわないよ。	*All right, / No problem.* ⇨CN S-3	

みてもらったほうがいい。　　　　　　　　　*You'd better see a doctor.*

（医者に）みてもらう literally means *to get (a doctor) to examine someone.* ⇨
L14GNⅡ Here, it is used as a set phrase, *to see a doctor.* ／〜たほうがいい
⇨L12GNⅡ

熱がありますから、医者にみてもらってください。
Please see a doctor because you have a fever.

お大事に。　　　　　　　　　　　　　　　　*Take good care of yourself.*

This expression is used only to someone who is unwell.

コピーしてもいいですか。　　　　　　　　*May I take a copy.* ⇨GNⅦ

使わないで。　　　　　　　　　　　　　　　*Don't use it.*

This is a less formal variant of **使わないでください.** ⇨GNⅢ, CN S-4

修理に来るからさ。　　　　　*(They'll) come to repair it (so wait for a while).*

に indicates the purpose of going or coming.　〜に来る ⇨L14GNⅢ

① **コピー機の修理に来ました。**
(I) came to repair a copier.

② **センターへ日本語の勉強に行きます。**
(I) go to the Center to study Japanese.

Words in the report

前の日	まえのひ	*the previous day*
少し	すこし	*a little*
それで		*Therefore, So,*

＜*Expressions in the report*＞

〜に「……」と聞きました。　　　　　　　*He asked 〜 "......"* ⇨L9GNⅡ

MC

Grammar Notes

I. The -nai form of verbs: [V-nai]

Examples

① 田中さんは魚を食べない。　　　*Tanaka-san doesn't eat fish.*
　　たなか　　　さかな　た

② スミスさんは酒を飲まない。　　*Smith-san doesn't drink sake.*
　　　　　　　さけ　の

【Explanation】

1. The -nai form

　　[V-nai] is the plain equivalent of　[V-(base)]-masen, i. e. the plain non-past negative form of verbs. -Nai indicates negation like *doesn't* etc. in English.

　　-Nai changes to -nakatta（past）, -naide（-te form）etc., depending on the type of sentence.

2. Use of the -nai form

　　[V-nai] is used as follows:

1）in casual speech:

　　　　田中さんは魚を食べない。　*Tanaka-san doesn't eat fish.*

　　This is the casual equivalent of 田中さんは魚を食べません。

2）with endings that are attached directly to the plain form:

　　　ex. ～ そうです　　　　　⇨L19GNV
　　　　　～ んです　　　　　　⇨L5GNV, L7GNII

　　1. 田中さんは魚を食べないそうです。
　　　　They say that Tanaka-san doesn't eat fish.

　　2. 田中さんは魚を食べないんです。
　　　　(You see,) Tanaka-san doesn't eat fish.

178

II. The -nakatta form of verbs: [V-nakatta]

【*Explanation*】

[V-nakatta] is used as follows: ⇨GN III

1) in casual speech:

田中さんは魚を食べなかった。
た なか　　　 さかな　た
Tanaka-san didn't eat fish.

2) with endings that are attached only to the plain form:

田中さんは魚を食べなかったんです。

(You see,) Tanaka-san didn't eat fish.

III. 〜ないでください: *please don't 〜*

Examples

① **ここでタバコをすわないでください。**　　*Please don't smoke here.*

② **行かないで。**　　*Please don't go.*
い

【*Explanation*】

[V-te] **ください** is used to request someone to do something, eg. **すってください**, **行ってください**, etc. (⇨L5GN IV) To request someone NOT to do something, [V-naide] **ください** is used: **すわないでください** or **行かないでください**. In casual speech, **ください** is often omitted, as in ② above. ⇨CN S-4

179

[V-te] ください	[V-naide] ください

	[[V-nai]-te] → [V-naide]
すってください *Please smoke.*	すわないでください *Please don't smoke.*
着てください *Please wear it.*	着ないでください *Please don't wear it.*
来てください *Please come.*	来ないでください *Please don't come.*
してください *Please do it.*	しないでください *Please don't do it.*

The **-te** form of [V-nai] is [V-naide], although there is another negative **-te** form, [V-nakute], which will come up later (⇨L23GN I, II). For the moment, note the following:

[V-nai] has two **-te** forms.
(1) [V-naide]
(2) [V-nakute]

[V-nakute] **kudasai** is not possible.

○　すわないでください
✕　すわなくてください

Verb forms	[V-nai], [V-nakatta] & [V-naide]		
[V-(r)u]	[V-nai]	[V-nakatta]	[V-naide]
Group I	Drop final **-u** → Add **-anai**				
	iku *to go*	ikanai	ikanakatta	ikanaide
	kaku *to write*	kakanai	kakanakatta	kakanaide
	nomu *to drink*	nomanai	nomanakatta	nomanaide
	matsu* *to wait*	matanai	matanakatta	matanaide
	Drop the final **-u** → Add **-wanai** (**u** after vowel)				
	suu *to smoke*	suwanai	suwanakatta	suwanaide
	iu *to say*	iwanai	iwanakatta	iwanaide
	au *to meet*	awanai	awanakatta	awanaide

Group II	Drop the final **-ru** → Add **-nai**				
	taberu	*to eat*	**tabenai**	**tabenakatta**	**tabenaide**
	miru	*to see*	**minai**	**minakatta**	**minaide**
	okiru	*to wake*	**okinai**	**okinakatta**	**okinaide**
Group III	**kuru**	*to come*	**konai**	**konakatta**	**konaide**
	suru	*to do*	**shinai**	**shinakatta**	**shinaide**
	benkyoo suru		**benkyoo**	**benkyoo**	**benkyoo**
		to study	**shinai**	**shinakatta**	**shinaide**

* **-tsu** changes to **-ta.**

Ⅳ. はい and いいえ: how to answer negative questions

Examples

① **A : 鈴木さんに会いませんでしたか。**
すずき　　あ
You didn't see Suzuki-san, did you? or *You saw Suzuki-san, didn't you?*

B1 : (1) はい、会いませんでした。
No, I didn't. (lit. Yes, you're right. I didn't.)

(2) いいえ、会いました。
Yes, I did. (lit. No, you're wrong. I did.)

B2 : (1) はい、会いました。
Yes, I did. (lit. Yes, you're right. I did.)

(2) いいえ、会いませんでした。
No, I didn't. (lit. No, you're wrong. I didn't.)

② **A : いっしょに映画に行きませんか。**
えいが　い
Won't you come with us to the movies?

B : (1) ええ、行きましょう。
Yes, Let's go.

(2) あの、きょうはちょっと忙しいから……。
I'm sorry, I'm a bit busy today, so...

GN

【*Explanation*】

The Japanese way of answering with **はい/いいえ** *Yes/No* differs from English in that **はい** and **いいえ** don't indicate whether the answer is positive or negative but whether the speaker agrees or disagrees with the assumption made in the negative question.

A negative question can have several meanings. When saying **会いませんか**, for instance, the speaker may assume that you will meet, or won't meet; it can also be an invitation to meet. Which meaning is intended is normally clear from the intonation and situation.

In ①, A asks B 1 assuming that B 1 hasn't seen Suzuki-san. B 1 understands this from the intonation used and reacts to A's assumption:

(1) **はい、会いませんでした。**
Yes, your assumption is correct; I didn't.

(2) **いいえ、会いました。**
No, your assumption is incorrect; I did.

A's intonation could also imply he assumed B2 did see Suzuki-san. In that case, B2 would answer:

(1) **はい、会いました。**
Yes, your assumption is correct; I did.

(2) **いいえ、会いませんでした。**
No, your assumption is incorrect; I didn't.

When a negative question is used as an invitation, as in ②, the implication is quite different; if you accept the invitation, you can of course answer with **はい**, but if you don't, you will normally not use **いいえ**, but make some kind of excuse instead, as in (2):

(1) **ええ、行きましょう。**
Yes, let's go.

(2) **あのう、きょうはちょっと忙しいから……。**
Sorry, I'm a bit busy today, so....

Ⅴ．〜ている〈1〉: expressing a state of affairs

Examples

① お金が落ちています。
There's some money (that has been dropped).

② 鈴木さんは結婚しています。
Suzuki-san is married.

【*Explanation*】

1.　〜ている after verbs of action in general

　　[V-te] いる／います expresses a state resulting from the action of the verb, as illustrated in ① and ②.

お金が落ちました　→　remains　→
Money dropped.

お金が落ちています／落ちている
There's some money (that has been dropped).

結婚しました　→　remains　→
(He) got married.

結婚しています／している
(He) is married.

2. Verbs normally used in the 〜ている form only: 持っている・住んでいる・知っている

The Japanese verbs for *to have, to live at* and *to know*, are normally used in their [V-te] いる（います） form: 持っている, 住んでいる and 知っている. Note that the negative of 知っている is 知らない（知りません）.

<持つ>　A：奥さんの写真を持っていますか。
Do you have a photo of your wife?

B：いいえ、持っていません。
No, I haven't.

<住む>　A：どこに住んでいますか。
Where do you live?

B：大学の宿舎に住んでいます。
I live in the university dormitory.

A：シャルマさんも宿舎に住んでいますか。
Does Sharma-san also live in the dormitory?

B：いいえ、宿舎には住んでいません。
No, he doesn't.

<知る>　A：あの人を知っていますか。
Do you know that person?

B：はい、知っています。
Yes, I know him.

A：あの女の人は。
How about that woman?

▼　B：いいえ、知りません。
No, I don't know her.

Note that 〜ている is often shortened to 〜てる in conversation.

Ⅵ. ～ていない: *not (yet)*

Examples

① A：もう昼ご飯を食べましたか。
　　　　Have you eaten lunch yet?

　　B：いいえ、まだ食べていません。
　　　　No, I haven't yet.

　　C：はい、私はもう食べました。
　　　　Yes, I have already eaten lunch.

② A：この本を読みましたか。
　　　　Have you read this book?

　　B：いいえ、まだ読んでいません。
　　　　No, I haven't read it yet.

③ まだ、手紙を出していません。
　　　I haven't mailed the letter yet.

④ 準備ができていません。
　　　The preparation isn't finished.

GN

【*Explanation*】

1. ［V-te］いない compared with ［V-nakatta］

　　An action that has not been carried out or completed can be expressed with ［V-te］ いない, which indicates a state where an action has not (yet) taken place. Compare this to ［V-ta］／～ました and ［V-nakatta］／～ませんでした, which express a past event:

(1) Past event
　　A：きのう手紙を書きましたか。　　　*Did you write the letter yesterday?*
　　B：いいえ、書きませんでした。　　　*No, I didn't.*

(2) Present state
　　A：もう、手紙を書きましたか。　　　*Have you written the letter yet?*
　　B：いいえ、まだ書いていません。　　*No, I haven't yet.*

185

2. もう compared with まだ

As you can see from（1）and（2）above, **もう**＋ **[V-ta]** indicates that an action has been completed in the past（**もう** here means *already*）. By contrast, **まだ**＋ **[V-te] いない** indicates that an action has not yet been completed at the point the statement is made（**まだ** here means *(not) yet*）. This use of **まだ** is very common; other uses of **まだ** will be introduced later. ⇨L14GNⅣ

For now, remember carefully:

もう＋ positive ＝ *already*
まだ＋ negative ＝ *not yet*

Ⅶ. 〜てもいい: *you may 〜, it's all right to 〜*

Examples

① A：英語で話してもいいですか。
　　　May I speak in English?

　　B：はい、話してもいいですよ。
　　　Yes, it's all right.

② A：ここでたばこをすってもいいですか。
　　　May I smoke here?

　　B：いいえ、すってはいけません。（すってはだめです。）
　　　No, you mustn't.

③ 帰ってもいいですよ。
　　You may go home.

【*Explanation*】

[V-te] もいいですか is used to ask permission（① and ②）, while **[V-te] もいいです** is used to give permission（③）. To prohibit an action, **[V-te] はいけません** or **[V-te] はだめです**（②）is used. ⇨L6GNⅤ

[V-nakute] もいいです means *You don't have to 〜, It's all right if you don't〜*. ⇨L23GNⅡ

In all the examples, **いいです** can be replaced by the more formal **よろしいです** or **かまいません**. ⇨CN S-3

[V-te] もいいですか	*May I ~ ?*
[V-te] もいいです	*You may ~*
[V-te] はいけません／ [V-te] はだめです	*You are not allowed to ~*

も is optional: you can just say 帰っていいですよ in ③.
<ruby>帰<rt>かえ</rt></ruby>

VIII. か *or*: connective particle

Examples

① 自転車かバイクが買いたいです。　　*I want to buy a bicycle or a motorcycle.*
じてんしゃ　　　　　　か

② 手紙か電話をください。　　*Please contact me by letter or telephone.*
てがみ　でんわ

【*Explanation*】

In [N] か [N] , か gives a choice of alternatives, like *or* in English.

IX. とき〈1〉: *at the time of, when*

GN

Examples

① 子供のとき名古屋に住んでいました。
こども　　　　なごや　す
When I was a child, I lived in Nagoya.

② 頭が痛いとき、この薬を飲んでください。
あたま　いた　　　　　くすり　の
When you have a head ache, take this medicine.

③ 田中さんが元気なとき会いました。
たなか　　　げんき　　あ
When Tanaka-san was in good health, I met him.

187

【*Explanation*】

とき is a noun meaning *time*; like any other noun, とき can be modified by other nouns, adjectives or verbs, in which use the meaning of とき is *when*. In this lesson, we will look at the use of とき when modified by [N] [A] [NA] ; later we will see how とき is modified by verb phrases. ⇨L20GNⅡ

[N] のとき	子どものとき	*when I was a child,*
	病気のとき	*when someone is/was sick,*
[A-i] とき	頭が痛いとき	*when someone has/had a headache,*
	暑いとき	*when it is/was hot,*
[NA] なとき	元気なとき	*when someone is/was in good health,*
	不便なとき	*when it is/was inconvenient,*

Conversation Notes

<General Information>

1. Relations between seniors and juniors in Japan

Distinctions of seniority are important in Japanese society and play an important role in communication. (⇨ introduction) According to Confucianist morals, juniors must be respectful and obedient to their seniors (parents, teachers and other Highers).

Students are therefore expected to ask their teacher's permission for any extra activities they plan; this does not mean, however, that juniors must behave like slaves to their seniors; it is very much a give-and-take relationship, as seniors feel obliged to take good care of their juniors in return. Establishing a good relationship with one's seniors makes life in Japan much more easy and comfortable. Some more information about the relationship between seniors and juniors / Highers and Lowers will be given in L9GNⅥ, L10GNⅦ, L18GNⅠ, L19GNⅤ

Professor
Kimura

Assistant
Suzuki

Student
Yamashita

2. A request for leave of absence

In Japanese schools and companies, absence from class or work has to be reported to one's teacher or boss beforehand. An official request for leave of absence must often be submitted in writing, although an oral request is often acceptable. Illness (including a family member's illness), weddings, and funerals as well as an important appointment can be valid reasons.

I'm very sorry to say this, but...

What happened?

I want to be absent from class tomorrow.

Oh?

In fact, my grand mother passed away last week.

Come on! I've heard that excuse five times from you. How many grandmothers do you have?

＊**なくなる**　　　*to pass away*
＊**～回（かい）**　　　*～ times ⇨* L11GN Ⅶ

＜*Strategies*＞

S-1. How to start a conversation —5. Asking for permission

---

a. Visiting someone's room

When you visit someone's room, first knock on the door; if you are told to come in, enter the room saying 失礼します (*lit. Excuse me*).

① A：（knock-knock）

B：はい。どうぞ。　　　　　　　*Yes, come in.*

A：失礼します。　　　　　　　　*Hello.*

B：やあ、○○さん。🍴　　　　　*Hello, ○○-san.*

② A：こんにちは。　　　　　　　　*Hello.*

B：ああ、○○さん。　　　　　　*Oh, ○○-san. Please come in.*
　　どうぞ入ってください。

B：失礼します。　　　　　　　　*Thank you.*

b. Asking permission to talk to someone

If you are approaching someone who is busy, first ask permission to talk to them with 「ちょっとよろしいですか。 *May I disturb you for a moment?/Do you have a moment?*」.「ちょっとよろしいでしょうか。」 can be used for extra politeness, whereas among friends 「ちょっといい。↗」 is sufficient:

ちょっと	よろしいでしょうか。🈁⬆
	よろしいですか。🈁⬆
	いいですか。🈁➡
	いいかな。↗ 🇨➡⬇
	いい。↗ 🇨➡⬇

If the person is too busy to see you, s / he may say 「いまは、ちょっと。*I'm a bit busy at the moment.*」 and give you an alternative time.

① 🈁A：すみませんが、ちょっとよろしいでしょうか。　　　　⬆
　　　Excuse me, but may I interrupt you?

B：あ、いまは、ちょっと。3時ごろ来てください。　⬇

Oh, not right now. Please come around 3 o'clock.

A：はい。わかりました。　*Yes, all right.*　⬆

② 👤A：あの、ちょっといいですか。　➡

May I interrupt you for a moment?

B：ええと、いまはちょっと……。　➡

Let me see.... not right now.

A：あ、じゃ、またあとで。　➡

All right then, I shall come later.

B：すみません。　*Sorry.*　➡

③ ☺A：ねえ、ちょっといい。↗　➡

Listen, can I talk to you?

B：あ、ごめん。あとにしてくれる。↗　➡

Oh, sorry. Can you come later?

A：いいよ。　*O. K.*　➡

S-2. How to introduce a main topic —3.

When you want to discuss something intricate, it is useful to announce your topic. (⇨L5CN S-1, L6CN S-1) You can use 「<Topic>のことなんですが。*I'd like to talk about* <Topic>...)」. (⇨L7CN S-6)　The final が implies that the speaker wants the listener to indicate whether s/he wishes to continue the conversation:

① 👤学生：あのう、午後のゼミのことなんですが。　⬆
　　がくせい　　　　ごご

About this afternoon's seminar....

先生：うん。　*Uhum.*　⬇
せんせい

学生：実は、……　*In fact,....*（to be continued）　⬆
がくせい　じつ

② 👤　A：ええと、研究室のコピー機のことなんですが。　⬆
　　　　　　　けんきゅうしつ　　　　き

About the photocopier in the seminar room....

B：ううん。↘ そのことなら、あした聞くよ。　⬇
　　　　　　　　　　　　　　　　　き

Hmm.... Can we talk about that tomorrow?

192

A：はい。じゃ、よろしくお願いします。　⬆
Fine. I'll come tomorrow, then.

In casual speech, **けど** is often used instead of **が**.

③ 🈞 A：あのう、来週のテストのことなんですけど。　➡
About the test next week....

B：あ、それは事務室で聞いてください。　➡
Oh, ask about it in the office.

A：はい。どうも。　➡
I see. Thanks.

④ 🈞 A：ねえ、あしたの発表のことなんだけど。　➡
Listen, about tomorrow's presentation....

B：うん。　*Uhum.*　➡

S-3. How to ask for permission

a. Giving a reason

You can indicate your reason for asking permission as follows:

＜Reason＞んです。　　〜ても	よろしいでしょうか。🈞⬆
	いいでしょうか。🈞⬆➡
	いいですか。🈞⬆➡
	いい。↗ 🈞➡

*〜てもいい ⇨GN Ⅵ（〜でもいい ⇨L6）

① 🈞 学生：かぜでちょっと熱があるんです。あしたのクラス、休んでも
よろしいでしょうか。⬆

I have a fever because of a cold. Is it all right if I miss tomorrow's class?

先生：ああ、もちろんかまいませんよ。⬇
Oh, of course it's all right.

② 🈞 A：これコピーしてもいい。↗ ➡
Can I make a copy of this?

B：あ、いまはちょっと使わ<ruby>使<rt>つか</rt></ruby>わないで。こわれてるから。➡️

Oh, please don't use it now, because it's broken.

Alternatively you can signal what you intend to do and leave it to the listener to react:

<Reason>んで、V－たいん ┃ ですが／ですけど。😐
　　　　　　　　　　　　　　 ┃ だけど。🙂

＊～たいんですが ⇨ L7GN I

③ 😐 A：<ruby>資料<rt>しりょう</rt></ruby>がないんで、<ruby>図書館<rt>としょかん</rt></ruby>へ<ruby>行<rt>い</rt></ruby>きたいんですが。⬆️

I haven't got the materials, so I want to go to the library.... (is that all right?)

B：いいですよ。いってらっしゃい。⬇️

All right. Go ahead.

④ 🙂 A：ゼミで<ruby>使<rt>つか</rt></ruby>うんで、コピーしたいんだけど。➡️

I'd like to copy this because I need it for the seminar.... (is it all right?)

B：ううん。↗︎ でも、これ、こわれてるから....。➡️

Hmm.... but the machine is out of order... (so, you cannot).

b. Strategies useful with seniors

To make a difficult request of a senior, you have a choice of two common strategies.

One is to appeal to your senior's spirit of chivalry. You can take advantage of the relationship of mutual dependence that exists between seniors and juniors; if you present your difficulties to your senior in such a way as to get her/him to take the initiative, s/he will feel obliged to help you. Use 「<ruby>実<rt>じつ</rt></ruby>は、<difficult circumstances>んです。」 to explain your situation. Look at the following example:

<ruby>学生<rt>がくせい</rt></ruby>：あのう、あしたの<ruby>発表<rt>はっぴょう</rt></ruby>のことなんですが。

Excuse me, about my presentation tomorrow....

Bringing up the topic

<ruby>先生<rt>せんせい</rt></ruby>：うん。　*Yes?*

<ruby>学生<rt>がくせい</rt></ruby>：<ruby>実<rt>じつ</rt></ruby>は、けさ<ruby>数学<rt>すうがく</rt></ruby>のテストがあったんです。

Actually I had a math exam this morning.

Giving the reason

<ruby>先生<rt>せんせい</rt></ruby>：うん。　*I see.*

学生：で、先週からそのテストの準備でいそがしくて....。
がくせい　　　せんしゅう　　　　　　　　　　　　じゅんび

So, I have been busy with the preparation for

that test since last week, and....

先生：そう。↘
せんせい

Really?

学生：あまり準備ができてないんです。

I couldn't do much preparations (for my

presentation).

先生：ううん。↘　じゃ、しかたないね。

Hmm.... it can't be helped, then.

学生：もうしわけありません。

I am very sorry.

先生：うん。じゃ、来週やってよ。
　　　　　　　　らいしゅう

O. K. Do it next week.

学生：はい。どうもすみませんでした。

I will. Thank you very much.

> Explaining the
> circumstances
> and
> waiting for the
> professor's judgement

> professor's judgement

Note that the student in the above example never actually requests to have his presentation postponed; he merely explains the circumstances that prevented him from doing his preparation.

The other strategy is to use roundabout ways of making a request such as **できれば** *(if possible, if you don't mind)* and **〜していただけないでしょうか** *(Could you possibly do me the favour of 〜 ?)*. ⇨ L14CN S-1b

学生：準備ができていないので、できれば発表を来週にしていただけない
　　　　　　　　　　　　　　　　　　　　　　　　　はっぴょう
　　　でしょうか。

I couldn't do much preparation, so if possible, could you change my

presentation to next week?

先生：ううん。↘　しかたありませんね。

Hmm.... it can't be helped.

学生：どうも　すみません。

Thank you very mush.

A combination of both strategies can also be used.

CN

c. Approval and rejection

When a request is granted, this is indicated by expressions like **いいですよ** or **かまいませんよ**; the signals for refusing a request, however, are much less clear because Japanese usually avoid outright expressions of refusal. Therefore, you need to pick up various subtle indications of refusal:

1) Unnecessarily long pause or hesistant intonation

学生：あした休んでもよろしいでしょうか。

先生：ううん……、そうですね。↘

2) Conjunctions such as **でも、だけど、しかし**、etc. *But*

学生：来週にしてもよろしいでしょうか。

先生：でも、来週はもう予定があるから。
But we've already got something planned for next week (, so it'll be difficult).

3) Negative expressions like **むずかしい** (*difficult*), **こまる** (*problematic*), **むり** (*impossible*), etc.

学生：来週でもよろしいでしょうか。

先生：来週はちょっとむずかしいね。
Next week is a bit difficult.

4) Giving a proviso

学生：まだ資料がたりないんです。来週でもよろしいでしょうか。

先生：資料がたりなくてもいいから、やってよ。
It doesn't matter if you don't have enough materials, so go ahead with it.

There are several expressions of outright rejection or prohibition in Japanese, but these are largely restricted in use to adult/child interactions and other relationships of authority.

〜 [V-te] は | いけません。 *(You) are not allowed to* 〜　⇨GN Ⅶ
　　　　　　 | だめです。 *(You) mustn't* 〜

〜 [V-nai] ないでください。 *Please don't* 〜　⇨GN Ⅲ, CN S-4

d. How to finish the conversation

When your request has been granted, you can finish the conversation with **ありがとうございました** *Thank you.* You can also use **すみませんでした** which can mean *Thank you* or *Sorry to have bothered you.* ⇨まとめ1BⅡ4

In the latter meaning, **すみませんでした** can be used to finish the conversation as soon as it is clear that your request will not be granted.

学生：あした休んでもよろしいでしょうか。
Can I miss the class tomorrow?

先生：ううん↘、でも、あしたはテストがあるから。
Hmm.... but we'll have a test tomorrow. So....

学生：はい、わかりました。どうもすみませんでした。
I understand; sorry to have bothered you.

S-4. How to give a warning

a. Official prohibition

When something is officially prohibited, the person in charge can use his authority using **〜ないでください** (*Please do not* 〜 ⇨ GNⅢ). For example, a guard in a public garden or at a museum might issue a warning like in ① and ② below, and a bus driver or a train conductor might use ③ and ④:

① しばふに入らないでください。
Keep off the lawn.

② 館内で写真をとらないでください。
Don't take photos inside the building.

③ まどから手を出さないでください。
Don't put your hand out of the window.

④ 車内でタバコをすわないでください。
Don't smoke in the car.

If a stranger asks your permission, you wouldn't usually refuse with **ないでください**; this would be felt to be too direct/impolite. Instead, use **ちょっと** (⇨ まとめ2BⅡ 1c) in a hesitant tone:

⑤　A：タバコをすってもいいですか。　*May I smoke?*

　　B：あ、ちょっと……　*Oh, I'm afraid....*

（Avoid）B：いいえ、すわないでください。　*No, please don't smoke.*

⑥ A：ちょっと見てもいいですか。 *May I take a look?*

B：ええと、ちょっと…… *Sorry, I'm afraid....*

（Avoid）B：いえ、見ないでください。 *No, please don't look.*

Among friends, however, you can use the 〜ないで form as follows:

⑦ A：ちょっと見てもいい。↗ *May I take a look?*

B：あ、見ないで。はずかしいから。 *No, don't look.*
I'm too embarrassed.

b. Teacher's instructions

Teachers often give instructions in the classroom with 〜てください and 〜ないでください. A student's reply to the teacher's instructions is 「はい、わかりました。」.

① 先生：テストの時、辞書を見ないでください。
Please don't use a dictionary during the test.

学生：はい、わかりました。 *Yes, sir.*

② 先生：クラスで英語を話さないでください。
Please don't speak English in the class.

学生：はい、わかりました。

③ 先生：この漢字を読んでください。
Please read this Kanji.

学生：はい。……(Reads)

④ 先生：まだ名前を書かないでください。
Don't write your names yet.

学生：はい。

まとめ 2

A. GRAMMAR

Ⅰ. Time expressions
Ⅱ. About predicates
Ⅲ. Four uses of です
Ⅳ. Yes/No questions
Ⅴ. Uses of [V-te]
Ⅵ. About omission
Ⅶ. が and は: が in adjective sentences
　　　　　　　　and は indicating contrast

B. CONVERSATION

Ⅰ. Summary of Conversational Strategies

Ⅱ. Additional Information
1. Use of ちょっと
2. Use of じゃ
3. Quick responses
4. Final particles
5. Use of って

A. Grammar

Ⅰ. Time expressions

Months

1月（いちがつ）	*January*	7月（しちがつ）	*July*
2月（にがつ）	*February*	8月（はちがつ）	*August*
3月（さんがつ）	*March*	9月（くがつ）	*September*
4月（しがつ）	*April*	10月（じゅうがつ）	*October*
5月（ごがつ）	*May*	11月（じゅういちがつ）	*November*
6月（ろくがつ）	*June*	12月（じゅうにがつ）	*December*

Days of the month

1日（ついたち）	11日（じゅういちにち）	21日（にじゅういちにち）
2日（ふつか）	12日（じゅうににち）	22日（にじゅうににち）
3日（みっか）	13日（じゅうさんにち）	23日（にじゅうさんにち）
4日（よっか）	14日（じゅうよっか）	24日（にじゅうよっか）
5日（いつか）	15日（じゅうごにち）	25日（にじゅうごにち）
6日（むいか）	16日（じゅうろくにち）	26日（にじゅうろくにち）
7日（なのか）	17日（じゅうしちにち）	27日（にじゅうしちにち）
8日（ようか）	18日（じゅうはちにち）	28日（にじゅうはちにち）
9日（ここのか）	19日（じゅうくにち）	29日（にじゅうくにち）
10日（とおか）	20日（はつか）	30日（さんじゅうにち）
		31日（さんじゅういちにち）

Days of the week

日曜日 にちようび	月曜日 げつ--	火曜日 か--	水曜日 すい--	木曜日 もく--	金曜日 きん--	土曜日 ど--
Sunday	*Monday*	*Tuesday*	*Wednesday*	*Thursday*	*Friday*	*Saturday*

The hours

1時 （いちじ） *one o'clock*	**＊時** （じ） ji means *o'clock*
2時 （にじ） *two o'clock*	
3時 （さんじ）	
4時 （よじ）	＊Not **yon-ji** or **shi-ji**
5時 （ごじ）	
6時 （ろくじ）	
7時 （しちじ／ななじ）	
8時 （はちじ）	
9時 （くじ）	＊Not **kyuu-ji**
10時 （じゅうじ）	
11時 （じゅういちじ）	
12時 （じゅうにじ）	

The minutes

1分 （いっぷん） *one minute*	**＊分** （ふん／ぷん） fun/pun means *minute*
2分 （にふん） *two minutes*	（carefully note if **fun** or **pun** is used）
3分 （さんぷん）	
4分 （よんぷん）	＊Don't say **shi-fun**
5分 （ごふん）	
6分 （ろっぷん）	＊Don't say **roku-fun**
7分 （ななふん）	
8分 （はっぷん／はちふん）	
9分 （きゅうふん）	
10分 （じっぷん／じゅっぷん）	
11分 （じゅういっぷん）	
⋮	
20分 （にじっぷん／にじゅっぷん）	
30分 （さんじっぷん／さんじゅっぷん）／**半**(はん)	
何分 （なんぷん） *What time（minutes）?*	

まとめ

Other time expressions

きのう *yesterday*	きょう *today*	あした *tomorrow*	毎日（まいにち） *everyday*
先週（せんしゅう） *last week*	今週（こんしゅう） *this week*	来週（らいしゅう） *next week*	毎週（まいしゅう） *every week*
先月（せんげつ） *last month*	今月（こんげつ） *this month*	来月（らいげつ） *next month*	毎月（まいつき） （まいげつ） *every month*
去年（きょねん） *last year*	今年（ことし） *this year*	来年（らいねん） *next year*	毎年（まいとし） （まいねん） *every year*

朝（あさ）	*morning*	午前（ごぜん）	*a.m.*
昼（ひる）	*noon, afternoon*	午後（ごご）	*p.m.*
晩（ばん）／夜（よる）	*evening, night*		
いま	*now*		

きょうの午後	*this afternoon*	今朝	*this morning*
あしたの朝	*tomorrow morning*	ゆうべ	*last night*
来週の土曜日	*next Saturday*		
来年の1月	*next January*		

1. あしたの朝、電話してください。　　*Please call me tomorrow morning.*

2. 先週の土曜日に病院へ行きました。　*I went to the hospital last Saturday.*

Ⅱ. About predicates

				Plain form	Polite form
N o u n	**[N]** **[NA]**	Non-past	Pos.	－だ （学生／便利　だ）	－です （学生／便利　です）
			Neg.	－じゃない （学生／便利　じゃない）	－じゃありません （学生／便利　じゃありません） －じゃないです （学生／便利　じゃないです）
		Past	Pos.	－だった （学生／便利　だった）	－でした （学生／便利　でした）
			Neg.	－じゃなかった （学生／便利　じゃなかった）	－じゃありませんでした （学生／便利　じゃありませんでした） －じゃなかったです （学生／便利　じゃなかったです）
A d j e c t i v e	**[A]**	Non-past	Pos.	[A-i] （重い）	[A-i] です （重いです）
			Neg.	[A-ku] ない （重くない）	[A-ku] ありません （重くありません） [A-ku] ないです （重くないです）
		Past	Pos.	[A-katta] （重かった）	[A-katta] です （重かったです）
			Neg.	[A-ku] なかった （重くなかった）	[A-ku] ありませんでした （重くありませんでした） [A-ku] なかったです （重くなかったです）
V e r b	**[V]**	Non-past	Pos.	[V-(r)u] （行く）	[V(base)] ます （行きます）
			Neg.	[V-nai] （行かない）	[V(base)] ません （行きません）
		Past	Pos.	[V-ta] （行った）	[V(base)] ました （行きました）
			Neg.	[V-nakatta] （行かなかった）	[V(base)] ませんでした （行きませんでした）

まとめ

III. Four uses of です

です（the polite form of だ）can be classified into the following four types of use:

1) In the structure [N₁] は [N₂] です, です shows that the two nouns are equal:

1. シャルマさんは留学生です。 *Sharma-san is a foreign student.*

2. これは私の本です。 *This is my book.*

2) In the structure [N] は [NA] です, です makes the **na** adjective a polite predicate:

1. コンピュータは便利です。 *Computers are convenient.*

2. この部屋は静かじゃありません。 *This room isn't quiet.*

3) です is attached to **-i** adjectives to indicate politeness:

1. この荷物は大きい（です）。 *This luggage is big.*

2. 日本語はむずかしくない（です）。 *Japanese is not difficult.*

4) です acts as a substitute for a verb previously mentioned.（⇨L3GNII）Note that unlike in English, where prepositions such as *in* or *to* are often obligatory in the answers, many Japanese structure particles such as が, で, に, へ, can NOT used with です, whereas から and まで can:

1. A：田中さんはどこにいますか。 *Where is Tanaka-san?*

   B：（田中さんは）教室です。 *(She's in) the classroom.*

2. A：シャルマさんはどこへ行きましたか。 *Where's Sharma-san gone?*

   B：郵便局です。 *(To) the post office.*

3. A：だれがケーキを食べましたか。 *Who ate the cake?*

   B：私です。 *I (did.)*

4. A：どこから来ましたか。 *Where do you come from?*

   B：インド（から）です。 *(From) India.*

5．A：どこまで行きますか。　　　　*How far do you go?*

　　B：成田（まで）です。　　　　　*(To/As far as) Narita.*

Ⅳ．Yes/No questions

When answering a question, you can omit what is understood: in reply to *Are you going to see a film tomorrow night at 7:30?*, for instance, you can simply reply *Yes, I am.* In Japanese, the rules for this are as follows.

1) Always repeat the predicate, i.e. [NA]/[A]/[V], even in very short sentences.
2) Instead of repeating [N], you can substitute そう. Note that そう can only be used in noun sentences.

1. あれは本ですか。　　　　　　　　はい、そうです。
　Is that a book?　　　　　　　　　　*Yes, it is.*

　　　　　　　　　　　　　　　　　　いいえ、ちがいます。
　　　　　　　　　　　　　　　　　　No, it isn't.

2. これは便利ですか。　　　　　　　はい、便利です。
　Is this convenient?　　　　　　　　*Yes, it is.*

　　　　　　　　　　　　　　　　　　いいえ、便利じゃありません。
　　　　　　　　　　　　　　　　　　No, it isn't.

3. その荷物は重いですか。　　　　　はい、重いです。
　Is that parcel heavy?　　　　　　　*Yes, it is.*

　　　　　　　　　　　　　　　　　　いいえ、重くありません。
　　　　　　　　　　　　　　　　　　No, it isn't.

4. あしたこの本を読みますか。　　　はい、読みます。
　Are you going to read this book tomorrow?　*Yes, I am.*

　　　　　　　　　　　　　　　　　　いいえ、読みません。
　　　　　　　　　　　　　　　　　　No, I'm not.

まとめ

205

Ⅴ．Uses of ［V-te］

1. ［V-te］ください　　　ちょっと待ってください。
Wait a moment, please.

［V-naide］ください　　窓を開けないでください。
Don't open the window, please.

2. ｛S₁ ［V-te］｝、｛S₂｝　名前を書いて、はんこを押しました。
I wrote my name and put my seal.

3. ［V-te］いる　　　　　お金が落ちている。
(Here) is money (which was dropped).

［V-te］いない　　　　まだひるごはんを食べていません。
I haven't had lunch yet.

4. ［V-te］もいい　　　　ここでたばこを吸ってもいいですか。
May I smoke here?

Ⅵ．About omission

Elements that are obvious to the listener are often omitted, as seen from the examples below:

The part < > has been omitted.

1. Particles	① A：このかさ<は>いくらですか。 *How much is this umbrella?* B：それは1000円です。 *It is 1,000 yen.*	omit <は>
	② A：大きいのはあります<か>。↗ *Do you have a big one?*	omit <か>
2. Topic	① A：あの店は安いですか。 *Is that shop cheap?* B：ええ、<あの店は>すごく安いですよ。 *Yes, very.*	omit <あの店は>

3．Predicate	① A：**どこへ行くんですか。** *Where are you going?* B：**郵便 局 <へ行きます>。** *To the post office.*	omit <へ行きます>
	② A：**日本語はむずかしいですか。** *Is the Japanese language difficult?* B：**少し漢字が<むずかしいです>ね。** *Kanji are a bit.*	omit <むずかしいです>
4．Noun ＋ Particle	① A：**バスが来ましたよ。** *Here comes the bus.* B：**あ、<バスが>来ましたね。** *Oh, it's come.*	omit <バスが>
	② A：**ビールを飲みませんか。** *Shall we drink beer?* B：**ええ、<ビールを>飲みましょう。** *Yes, let's.*	omit <ビールを>

Ⅶ.  が and は：が in adjective sentences and は indicating contrast

1．が in adjective sentences

In adjective sentences, the subject particle **が** can indicate the speaker's realization of a fact, a matter, etc. Look at the pictures below:

ああ！
Ah!

さくらがきれいですね。
Cherry blossom is beautiful.

まとめ

**おなかがすき
ました。**
I am hungry.

ああ、魚がおいしい！
Oh, fish is delicious.

2. は indicating contrast

We saw that the discourse particle **は** indicates the topic of a sentence or a question. In some contexts, however, **は** can also indicate contrast:

ポークは食べません。
I don't eat pork.

チキンは食べます。
I do eat chicken.

リサさんには書きます。
I will write to Lisa-san.

？？さんには書きません。
I will not write to ??-san.

It is usually clear from the context whether **は** indicates a topic or a contrast.

208

B. Conversation

Ⅰ. *Summary of Conversational Strategies*

1. Factual Information

How to ask for information about a word

☐ ☐　a. Finding out how to read ：これ何て読むんですか。
　　　　　　　⇨L5 S-2a

☐ ☐　b. Finding out the meaning ：これ、どんな意味なんですか。
　　　　　　　⇨L5 S-2b　教室って何ですか。

☐ ☐　c. Finding out an English or ：〜は〜語で何ていうんですか。
　　　　Japanese equivalent ⇨L5 S-2c

☐ ☐　d. Requesting an explanation ：どうしてコンパなんですか。
　　　　　　　⇨L5 S-2d

☐ ☐　How to make sure you have ：事務室って、宿舎の事務室ですか。
　　　understood ⇨L5 S-3

☐ ☐　How to ask for a telephone number ：〜の電話（番号）｜わかりますか。
　　　　　　　⇨L7 S-1　　　　　　　　　　ごぞんじですか。
　　　　　　　　　　　　　　　　　　　　　　お願いします。
　　　　　　　　　　　　　　　　　　　　　　教えてください。

☐ ☐　How to deal with a wrong number ：あ、どうもすみません。
　　　　　　　⇨L7 S-3　　まちがえました。

☐ ☐　How to ask about office hours ：きょうの午後（は）、やってますか。
　　　　　　　⇨L7 S-5　　営業時間は何時から何時までですか。

☐ ☐　How to ask about a person's ：いつがいいですか。
　　　availability ⇨L7 S-6c　あしたの午後はどうですか。

2. Judgement

☐ ☐　How to correct others' mistakes ：いいえ、〜です。
　　　　　　　⇨L6 S-3　：いえ、そっち〜じゃなくてこっち。

3. Emotions

4. Actions

☐ ☐　How to ask for instructions ：書き方がわからないんですけど。
　　　　　　　⇨L6 S-2a　使い方を教えてください。

まとめ

209

☐ ☐ How to ask for advice implicitly　⇨L6 S-4　：ええと、はんこは持ってないんですけど。

　　いいえ、午後は休診なんですが。

☐ ☐ How to give an alternative　⇨L6 S-5　：じゃ、〜でも ｜ いいです。
　　　｜ けっこうです。

☐ ☐ How to make an appointment　⇨L7 S-6a　：じゃ、あしたの午後、お願いしたいんですが。

　：あしたの午後は、｜ いかがでしょうか。
　　　　　　　　　　｜ どう。

☐ ☐ Asking for permission　⇨L8 S-1a　：〜ても ｜ いいでしょうか。
　　　　　　　　　　　　　　　｜ よろしいでしょうか。

　　＜reason＞んで、〜たいんですが。

How to give approval and rejection

☐ ☐ 　a. Approval　⇨L8 S-3c　：いいですよ。
　　かまいませんよ。

☐ ☐ 　b. Rejection　⇨L8 S-3c　：でも、来週は予定があるから。
　　ううん、ちょっとむずかしいね。
　　ううん、こまったな。

　：〜ては ｜ いけません。
　　　　　｜ だめです。

　：〜ないでください。

☐ ☐ How to give a warning　⇨L8 S-4a　：〜ないでください。

5. Social formulas
☐ ☐ Asking politely　⇨L7 S-6d　：よろしく、お願いします。

6. Communication strategies
☐ ☐ How to introduce a main topic-1. 2.　⇨L5 S-1,L6 S-1　：あの、掲示板にこれがはってあったんですけど。

☐ ☐ How to introduce a question politely　⇨L7 S-4　：あの、ちょっと ｜ うかがいますが。
　　　　　　　　　　　　　　｜ おたずねしますが。

How to start a conversation-5

☐ ☐ 　a. Visiting someone's room　⇨L8 S-1a　：失礼します。

☐ ☐ 　b. Asking for permission to talk to someone　⇨L8 S-1b　：ちょっと ｜ よろしいですか。
　　　　　　　　｜ いいですか。

☐ ☐ How to end a conversation -3.　⇨L5 S-4　：じゃ、いいです

☐ ☐ Strategies useful with seniors　⇨L8 S-3b　：実は、先週からテストの準備で忙しくて。

II. *Additional Information*

1. Use of ちょっと

ちょっと is used very often in daily conversation, in a variety of ways.

a. The basic meaning of ちょっと is *a little*.

① きのうからかぜでちょっと熱があるんです。 〈L8 MC〉

② ちょっと待ってください。

b. ちょっと is also used often for making a request. When the actual request following ちょっと is clear from the situation, it is often left out.

① ああ、山下くん。ちょっと。 〈L1 MC〉
In this sentence、きてください is omitted.

② あの、ちょっとおたずねしたいんですが。 〈L7 MC〉

③ あの、ちょっとよろしいですか。 〈L8 MC〉

④ あの、ちょっとこれコピーしてもいいですか。 〈L8 MC〉

c. ちょっと is also handy for refusal because it sounds suitably hesitant and vague enough not to offend the person refused:

① ちょっとわからないな。 〈L5 MC〉

② あ、ちょっと使わないで。 〈L8 MC〉

③ きょうは、ちょっと……。

In reply to an invitation、きょうは、ちょっと…。 means *I don't think I can make it today.* ⇨L17CN S-3

2. Use of じゃ

じゃ or それじゃ（often pronounced そいじゃ in casual speech）often indicates a turning point in the conversation. In more formal speech、では or それでは tends to be used.

211

a. Used as follows, **じゃ** indicates an alternative:

① シャルマ：ええと、はんこは持ってないんですけど。

　事務員　：じゃ、サインでいいですよ。　　　　　　　〈L6 MC〉

② 受　付　：火曜日の午後は休診なんですが。

　山　下　：あ、そうですか。じゃ、あしたの午後は。　〈L7 MC〉

b. **じゃ** can also be used to proceed to the next stage of a conversation:

① After confirmation
　事務員：じゃ、ここに名前書いて、はんこ押してください。〈L6 MC〉

② After Sharma signed
　事務員：じゃ、この荷物。　　　　　　　　　　　　〈L6 MC〉

c. You can conclude a conversation with **じゃ**: ⇨L3CN S-3

① 山　下　:ううん、困ったな。ちょっとわかんないな。

　ブラウン:あ、じゃ、いいです。　　　　　　　　　〈L5 MC 〉

② After making appointment
　受　付　：それじゃ、4時15分に来てください。　　〈L7 MC〉

d. **じゃ** can also be used to say goodbye at the end of a conversation: ⇨L1CN S-3

　山　下　：それじゃ、シャルマさん、また。

　シャルマ：はい。じゃ、失礼します。　　　　　　　〈L1 MC〉

3. Quick responses

In Japanese conversation, various types of quick responses help to keep the flow of conversation:

a. あ（ああ↘）: Becoming aware

When you suddenly remember or notice something/some person, **あ** or **ああ↘** can be used as an initial response.

① シャルマ：はじめまして。アニル・シャルマです。

　山　下：あ、どうも。　　　　　　　　　　　　　〈L1 MC〉

② シャルマ：この辺に、電話ありますか。

　田　中：ああ、↘　食堂の自動販売機のとなりにありますよ。

　　　　　　　　　　　　　　　　　　　　　　　〈L4 MC〉

You can also use **あ** to show that you've understood:

③ 田　中：ほら、あのコーラとかジュースとかの……。

　シャルマ：ああ、↘　わかりました。　　　　　〈L4 MC〉

b.　はい: Short response

When someone calls you, you can respond with **はい**:

① 木　村：ああ、山下くん。ちょっと。

　山　下：はい。　　　　　　　　　　　　　　　〈L1 MC〉

② 山　下：すみません。

　局　員：はい。　　　　　　　　　　　　　　　〈L2 MC〉

When you hand something to someone, you can say **はい** and s/he will say **はい** in response to having received it.

③ 局　員：ええと、280円です。

　山　下：はい。（Paying）

　局　員：はい。（Receiving the money）　　　　〈L2 MC〉

はい can also be used in responses to instructions:

④ 田　中：私はビーフカレーとコーヒー。

　ウェイトレス：はい。　　　　　　　　　　　　〈L3 MC〉

⑤ A：ここに名前を書いてください

　B：はい。

c.　はい↘・ええ↘・うん↘ ⓒ: Positive responses

These can be used in response to questions, suggestions or requests:

① 事務員：ええと、インドのアニル・シャルマさんですね。

シャルマ：はい、↘ そうです。 〈L6 MC〉

② 山下：じゃ、いっしょに行く。↗

田中：ええ。↘ 〈L2 MC〉

These words can also be used as Aizuchi. ⇨L1CN4/まとめ3BⅡ2

d. え↗（ええ↗）・はあ↗・ん↗ ⓒ: Asking for repetition

When you don't catch or understand what someone has said, use these words with short rising intonation. ⇨L4CN S-3

① 事務員：いや、そこじゃなくて、こっち。

No, not there but here.

シャルマ：え。↗

What? 〈L6 MC〉

Said with long rising intonation, these words indicate surprise:

② A：さいふ、なくしちゃった。 *I lost my wallet.*

B：ええ。↗ *What?!*

e. いいえ（いえ）・いや ⓒ・ううん↘ⓒ: Negative responses

These can be used, with slightly raised intonation, to say No to a question:

① A：4階ですか。

B：いいえ、3階です。

② シャルマ：ここですか。

事務員：いや。そこじゃなくて、こっち。 〈L6 MC〉

Suggestions or requests can be refused point blank by using these words. However this is impolite. Recall that these words can also be used in response to thanks or apologies in the sense of *Not at all.* ⇨L4CN S-3

f. ううん↘ⓒ: Hesitation

ううん↘ can be used to indicate that you are unable to give an answer:

① 山下：ううん。↘ 困ったな。ちょっとわかんないな。〈L5 MC〉

ううん ↘ can also be used for turning down suggestions or requests indirectly:

  ② A：いっしょに行く。

    B：ううん↘　ちょっと……。

4. Final particles

In Japanese, there is a number of particles that are added to the end of a sentence. They show the speaker's attitude towards the listener and require the correct intonation.

a. か

In formal speech you can ask a question with か ↗ although short rising intonation by itself can also indicate a question（usually in casual speech）. However, after です, か must be used.

  ① シャルマ：これでいいですか。↗

    事務員　：はい、けっこうです。　　　　　　　　〈L6 MC〉

  ② ブラウン：場所、わかります（か）。↗

    女子学生：せんたく機なら、4階にありますよ。　　〈L4 MC〉

か ↘ is used with questions using でしょう（だろう）or ましょう（う／よう）：

  ③ A：木村先生はどちらでしょうか。↘

    B：事務室ですよ。

  ④ A：ちょっと休みましょうか。↘

    B：そうですね。

When you react to some new information（*Really/I see*）, you also add か↘ .

  ⑤ A：専門はコンピュータです。

    B：コンピュータですか。↘

  ⑥ 事務員　：じゃ、サインでいいですよ。

    シャルマ：ああ、そうですか。↘　　　　　　　　〈L6 MC〉

まとめ

215

b. よ

To make it clear that you are informing the listener of something, you add **よ**. The listener's attention can be attracted by **よ**↗.

① 山下　：ちょっと、郵便局まで。

　　田中　：あ、私もよ。↗　　　　　　　　　　　　　〈L2 MC〉

② 事務員　：重いですよ。↗

　　シャルマ：あ、ほんとうだ。　　　　　　　　　　　〈L6 MC〉

When you want to push your statement, you can add **よ**↘.

③ 山下　：ご専門は。

　　シャルマ：コンピュータです。

　　山下　：ああ、ぼくもコンピュータなんですよ。↘　〈L1 MC〉

Use **よ**↘ with care, as it can imply ignorance on the listener's part (*didn't you know that?*). For this reason, **よ**↘ shouldn't be added to the answer in cases like the following:

④ 山下　：ご専門は。

　　シャルマ：コンピュータです。

c. ね

ね is basically used to solicit the listener's agreement. **ね**↗ is used to confirm an assumption:

① 事務員　：ええと、インドのアニル・シャルマさんですね。↗

　　シャルマ：はい、そうです。　　　　　　　　　　　〈L6 MC〉

You can also show agreement with **ね**↗:

② A：ちょっと休みましょうか。

　　B：そうですね。↗

ね↗ can also be used as a friendly reminder, usually in casual speech:

③ 事務員：それから、はんこね。↗

You can use **ね**↘ when you are impressed or overwhelmed:

④ 事務員　：じゃ、この荷物。

　　シャルマ：わあ、ずいぶん大きいですね。↘　　　　〈L6 MC〉

⑤ Ａ：いい天気ですね。↘

　　Ｂ：そうですね。↘

ね↘ can also be used to indicate that you are unsure how to answer:

⑥ シャルマ：このへんに電話ありますか。

　　田　中　：電話ね。↘　　　　　　　　　　　　　〈L4 MC〉

⑦ Ａ：ちょっと散歩しませんか。

　　Ｂ：そうですね。↘　ちょっと……。

d. な

For a spontaneous indication of your feelings, **な** is often used, usually in casual speech（men prefer **な** instead of **ね**）.

In the examples below, **な** ↘ indicates perplexion and joy, respectively.

① 山　下　：ううん、困ったな。↘

　　　　　　ちょっとわかんないな。↘

　　ブラウン：あ、じゃ、いいです。　　　　　　　　〈L5 MC〉

② リ　サ　：（Giving Suzuki a music tape）

　　鈴　木　：うれしいな。↘　どうもありがとう。

　　　　　　I'm so glad. Thank you so much.　　　〈L22 MC〉

e. かな／かしら♠

To indicate that you are not sure about something, you can add **かな** usually in casual speech（women often use **かしら** instead **かな**）. Uncertainty or doubt can be indicated by **かな**↘ or **かしら**↘.

① 事務員　：1人でだいじょうぶかな。↘

　　シャルマ：ええ、だいじょうぶです。　　　　　　〈L6 MC〉

かな↗ or **かしら**↘ can be used to drop a hint:

② Ａ：あ、ぼくもあとでコーヒーもらおうかな。↗

　　Ｂ：はい。　　　　　　　　　　　　　　　　　　〈L3 MC〉

まとめ

5. Use of って

（っ）て is very common in daily conversation, and has a number of different functions:

a. Asking/giving information how to read or write something; this is an informal variant of と. ⇨L9GN

① この字、何て読むんですか。

② 何て書いてあるんですか。

③ 「たっきゅうびん」って読むんですよ。

b. Quoting someone's words

って（falling intonation）means *They say that.* or *It says....*

事務室に取りにきてくださいって。↘

The quotation is often given only in essence; in this case, in full it would read: 「事務室に取りにきてくださいと書いてあります。」.

って（rising intonation）means *'Does it say that....?'*.

事務室に取りにきてくださいって。↗

Does it say that I have to go to the office and collect it?

c. For clarifying or defining a word

This って is a contraction of というのは *that's called/what do you mean by～* ⇨L10 GNV

事務室って、宿舎の事務室ですか。

（*What do you mean by*）*office? The dormitory office?*

Appendix

I. Grammar Check

II. Answers to Grammar Check and
Model Conversation Check

I. Grammar Check

Grammar Check L1

Read the Grammar Notes for Lesson 1 and check how well you have understood them. Choose the correct statement.

1　A：専門は何ですか。
　　B：a）　はい、そうです。
　　　　b）　医学です。
　　　　c）　留学生です。

2　A：大学はどちらですか。
　　B：a）　はい、松見大学です。
　　　　b）　いいえ、松見大学じゃありません。
　　　　c）　松見大学です。

3　A：ジムさんは学生ですか。
　　B：a）　いいえ、そうです。
　　　　b）　ええ、そうじゃありません。
　　　　c）　いいえ、そうじゃありません。

4　a）　こちらは、私の友だちのリサさんです。
　　b）　　　　　　リサさんの私の友だちです。
　　c）　　　　　　私のリサさんの友だちです。

5　a）　アニルさんは学生です。リサさんは学生です。
　　b）　　　　　　　　　リサさんも学生です。
　　c）　　　　　　　　　リサさんと学生です。

6　a）　リサさんも私は学生です。
　　b）　リサさんの私は学生です。
　　c）　リサさんと私は学生です。

7　a）　大学院の学生です。
　　b）　大学院は学生です。
　　c）　大学院も学生です。

8　a）　アニルさんは専門の化学です。
　　b）　アニルさんと専門は化学です。
　　c）　アニルさんの専門は化学です。

Read the Grammar Notes for Lesson 2, and check how well you have understood them.
Choose the correct statement.

1　a）　アニルさんは東京を行きました。
　　b）　　　　　東京で行きました。
　　c）　　　　　東京へ行きました。

2　a）　田中さんは本に買いました。
　　b）　　　　　本を買いました。
　　c）　　　　　本で買いました。

3　a）　アニルさんは大学へ勉強します。
　　b）　　　　　大学で勉強します。
　　c）　　　　　大学に勉強します。

4　a）　アニルさんは田中さんと行きました。
　　b）　　　　　田中さんに行きました。
　　c）　　　　　田中さんで行きました。

5　a）　これ、航空便をお願いします。
　　b）　　　　　航空便にお願いします。
　　c）　　　　　航空便でお願いします。

6　a）　きのう東京へ行きます。
　　b）　　　　　行きました。

7　a）　田中さんは、はがきを5枚買いました。
　　b）　　　　　5枚はがきを買いました。
　　c）　　　　　はがきの5枚を買いました。

8　　　　A：きのう日本語を勉強しましたか。
　　a）　B：いいえ，しません。
　　b）　　　　しました。
　　c）　　　　しませんでした。

9　a）　だれは読みますか。
　　b）　だれが

Grammar Check L3

Read the Grammar Notes for Lesson 3, and check how well you have understood them.
Choose the correct statement.

1   a)   アニルさんは田中さんが本をもらいました。
     b)   アニルさんは田中さんに
     c)   アニルさんは田中さんを

2   a)   アニルさんは田中さんがお金を払いました。
     b)   アニルさんは田中さんに
     c)   アニルさんは田中さんを

3   a)   いつ　新聞を読みますか。
     b)   いつに
     c)   いつは

4   a)   食堂でカレーを食べました。
     b)   食堂は
     c)   食堂と

5   A：きのう何をしましたか。
     a)   B：映画を見ます。
     b)   見ましょう。
     c)   見ました。

6   A：だれが書きますか。
     a)   B：田中さんがです。
     b)   田中さん　です。

7   a)   大学で日本語を勉強をします。
     b)   日本語の勉強をします。
     c)   日本語　勉強をします。

8   a)   留学生はふたりです。
     b)   ふたつです。
     c)   にです。

9   a)   国は　英語を勉強しました。
     b)   国はで
     c)   国では

Grammar Check L4

Read the Grammar Notes for Lesson 4, and check how well you have understood them. Choose the correct statement.

1 a）ねこがあります。
   b）　　　います。

2 a）すみません。お手洗いはどこにありますか。　　どこですか。
   b）　　　　　　　　　　どこでありますか。
   c）　　　　　　　　　　どこがありますか。

3 a）リサさんは教室でいます。
   b）　　　　　教室にいます。
   c）　　　　　教室がいます。

4 a）先生は2階にあります。
   b）　　　　　　　います。
   c）　　　　　　　です。

5 a）何でケーキを食べますか。
   b）どのケーキを　　　which cake
   c）どれケーキを

6 a）このカメラはだれのですか。
   b）ここカメラは
   c）これカメラは

7 a）カメラはつくえの上にです。
   b）　　　　つくえの上がです。
   c）　　　　つくえの上　です。

8 　　A：あの人はだれですか。
   a）B：この人はアニルさんです。
   b）　　その人は
   c）　　あの人は

9 a）レストランには紅茶とかケーキがあります。
   b）　　　　　　紅茶　も　ケーキがあります。
   c）　　　　　　紅茶　が　ケーキがあります。

Grammar Check L5

Read the Grammar Notes for Lesson 5, and check how well you have understood them. Choose the correct statement.

1 　a) 先生に聞てください。
　　-b) 　　　聞ってください。
　　ⓒ) 　　　聞いてください。

2 　a) 帰りてください。　　　go home
　　ⓑ) 帰って
　　-c) 帰て

3 　a) かえりてください。　　　(かえる to change)
　　b) かえって　　　change
　　ⓒ かえて

4 　ⓐ 急ぐんですか。　　to be in a hurry
　　b) 急ぎんですか。
　　c) 急ぎますんですか。

5 　a) きのう行くんです。
　　ⓑ) 　　行ったんです。
　　c) 　　行きましたんです。

6 　ⓐ これ、何て　読むんですか。
　　b) 　　何って

7 　a) かたかなに名前を書いてください。
　　b) かたかなを
　　ⓒ かたかなで

8 　a) 行きませんから、時間がありません。
　　ⓑ) 時間がありませんから、行きません。
　　c) から時間がありません、行きません。

Grammar Check L6

Read the Grammar Notes for Lesson 6, and check how well you have understood them. Choose the correct statement.

1 a） 安いくないです。
   (b)） 安くないです。
   c） 安いじゃないです。

2 a） 私の部屋は静かないです。
   b）　　　　　静かくないです。
   (c)） 　　　　　静かじゃないです。

3 a） きのうの夜はうるさいです。
   b）　　　　　うるさいでした。
   (c)）　　　　　うるさかったです。
   d）　　　　　うるさかったでした。

4 a） あまりきれいです。 → always + negative
   (b)）　　　きれいじゃありません。

5 (a) A：大学はどうですか。
   b）　　　どれですか。
   c）　　　どこですか。
      B：おもしろいです。

6   A：ペンがないんです。
   a） B：じゃ、えんぴつがいいですよ。
   b）　　　えんぴつはいいですよ。
   (c)）　　　えんぴつでいいですよ。

7 a） 友だちを呼ぶ、　パーティーをしました。
   (b)） 友だちを呼んで、
   c） 友だちを呼んだ、

8 (a) ここにすわってください。
   b） ここで

9 (a)） つくえの上に置いてください。
   b） つくえの上で

225

Grammar Check L7

Read the Grammar Notes for Lesson 7, and check how well you have understood them.
Choose the correct statement.

1   (a) テレビが買いたいです。
    b) テレビに
    c) テレビで

2   a) コーヒーが飲むたいです。
    b) 　　　　飲めたいです。
    (c) 　　　　飲みたいです。

3   a) 朝ごはんは食べたいじゃないです。
    b) 　　　　食べたいないです。
    (c) 　　　　食べたくないです。

4   a) あしたは休みんです。
    (b) 　　　　休みなんです。
    c) 　　　　休みですんです。

5   　　A：いっしょに映画を見ませんか。
    a) B：今ちょっといそがしい。
    b) 　　　　いそがしいです。
    (c) 　　　　いそがしいんです。

6   a) カレー*karee*は安いですと、おいしいです。
    (b) カレーは安いですが、
    c) カレーは安いですも、

7   a) 銀行は9時からまで3時やっています。
    b) 銀行はから9時3時まで　　　*is open*
    (c) 銀行は9時から3時まで

8   a) けさ7時から起きました。
    (b) けさ7時に
    c) けさ7時で
    　　　on about
9   (a) 4日ごろに来てください。
    b) 4日にごろ

226

Read the Grammar Notes for Lesson 8, and check how well you have understood them.
Choose the correct statement.

1　(a)　きのう田中さんに会わなかった。
　　b)　　　　　　　　会うなかった。
　　c)　　　　　　　　会いなかった。

2　a)　英語で話しないでください。
　　(b)　　　　話さないでください。
　　c)　　　　話せないでください。

3　a)　きょうとかあした行きます。
　　b)　きょうや
　　(c)　きょうか

4　(a)　質問してもいいですか。
　　b)　質問するもいいですか。
　　c)　質問しますもいいですか。

5　a)　まどを開けます。
　　b)　まどを開けています。
　　c)　まどが開きます。
　　(d)　まどが開いています。

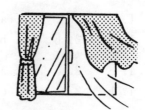

6　a)　小野さんは先月結婚します。
　　(b)　　　　　　　結婚しました。
　　c)　　　　　　　結婚しています。

7　　　A：もうごはんを食べましたか。
　　(a)　B：いいえ、まだ食べていません。
　　b)　　　　　　　食べませんでした。

8　　　A：あの人を知っていますか。
　　a)　B：いいえ、知っていません。
　　(b)　　　　　知りません。

9　a)　ひまとき、　何をしますか。
　　(b)　ひまなとき、
　　c)　ひまのとき、

II. Answers to Grammar Check and Model Conversation Check

1. Answers to Grammar Check

L1	1. b	2. c	3. c	4. a	5. b	6. c	7. a	8. c
L2	1. c	2. b	3. b	4. a	5. c	6. b	7. a	8. c	9. b
L3	1. b	2. b	3. a	4. a	5. c	6. b	7. b	8. a	9. c
L4	1. b	2. a	3. b	4. b	5. b	6. a	7. c	8. c	9. a
L5	1. c	2. b	3. c	4. a	5. b	6. a	7. c	8. b
L6	1. b	2. c	3. c	4. b	5. a	6. c	7. b	8. a	9. a
L7	1. a	2. c	3. c	4. b	5. c	6. b	7. c	8. b	9. a
L8	1. a	2. b	3. c	4. a	5. d	6. b	7. a	8. b	9. b

2. Answers to Model Conversation Check

L1	I.	1. b	2. c	3. a	4. c	5. b
	II.	1. b	2. a	3. b	4. c	5. b
L2	I.	1. c	2. a	3. c	4. c	5. b
	II.	1. c	2. b	3. c	4. a	5. b
L3	I.	1. c	2. c	3. a	4. a	5. b
	II.	1. b	2. b	3. b	4. a	5. b
L4	I.	1. c	2. c	3. a	4. c	5. b
	II.	1. b	2. b	3. c	4. b	5. a
L5	I.	1. c	2. b	3. a	4. a	5. c
	II.	1. b	2. c	3. a	4. b	5. c
L6	I.	1. a	2. c	3. b	4. a	5. c
	II	1. a	2. c	3. a	4. a	5. b
L7	I.	1. c	2. b	3. a	4. c	5. b
	II.	1. a	2. c	3. c	4. a	5. c
L8	I.	1. b	2. a	3. c	4. b	5. c
	II.	1. a	2. b	3. b	4. a	5. b

Index to Grammar Notes (L1~L8)

---

8 III
↑ ↑ — Item number
— Lesson number

Index to Conversation Notes (L1~L8)

Reporting something

事務室に取りにきてくださいって。 まとめ2BⅡ5b

Actions

Offering to do something for someone

Nと呼んでください。 L1S-2c

これ、おねがいします。 L2S-1a

＜thing＞を＜number＞ ｜ お願いします。 L2S-4
｜ ください。

これでおねがいします。 L2GI3a

こちらへどうぞ。 L3GI2a

もう少し待ってください。 L3S-4a

まだですか。 L3S-4b

Nの電話番号教えてください。 L7S-1a

Giving something

はい。 L2S-1

どうぞ。 L3S-2

Receiving something

あ、どうも。 L3S-2

Asking for instructions

………が分からないんですけど。 L6S-2a

Checking what you have done

これでいいですか。 L6S-2b

Asking for permission

あの、………で(も)いいですか。 L6S-5b

＜reason＞んです。……てもよろしいでしょうか。 L8S-3a

＜reason＞んです。～Ｖ－たいんですが。／ですけど。 L8S-3a

Giving permission

いいですよ。／かまいませんよ。 L8S-3c

Refusing permission

～Ｖではだめです。／いけません。 L8S-3c

～Ｖないでください。 L8S-3c

Asking for advice

ええと、はんこもってないんですけど。 L6S-4

Giving an alternative

じゃ、………でもいいです／けっこうです。 L6S-5a

Warning someone

～Ｖないでください。 L8S-4a

Suggesting

じゃ、………はどう。↗／どうですか。 L6S-5a

Making an appointment

Social formulas

Introducing yourself

Introducing someone

Responding to an introduction

Starting a conversation with a stranger

Expressing politeness

Greetings

Thanking

Communication strategies

Attracting someone's attention

Aizuchi

Starting a conversation

Ending a conversation

Introducing a main topic

Summing up

Asking to say something again

Checking that you have understood

Showing you do not understand

Gaining time to collect your thoughts

Compiled and Edited by:

General editor	Otsubo, Kazuo	大 坪 一 夫
Authors	Akutsu, Satoru	阿久津　　智
	Ichikawa, Yasuko	市 川 保 子
	Emura, Hirofumi	江 村 裕 文
	Ogawa, Taeko	小 川 多恵子
	Kano, Chieko	加 納 千恵子
	Kaiser, Stefan	カイザー シュテファン
	Kindaichi, Kyoko	金田一 京 子
	Kobayashi, Noriko	小 林 典 子
	Komiya, Shutaro	小 宮 修太郎
	Saegusa, Reiko	三 枝 令 子
	Sakai, Takako	酒 井 たか子
	Shimizu, Yuri	清 水 百 合
	Shinya, Ayuri	新 谷 あゆり
	Tochigi, Yuka	栃 木 由 香
	Tomura, Kayo	戸 村 佳 代
	Nishimura, Yoshimi	西 村 よしみ
	Hashimoto, Yoji	橋 本 洋 二
	Fujimaki, Kikuko	藤 牧 喜久子
	Ford, Junko	フォード 順子
	Homma, Tomoko	本 間 倫 子
	Yamamoto, Sonoko	山 本 そのこ
	Yokoyama, Noriko	横 山 紀 子
	Watanabe, Keiko	渡 辺 恵 子
Cover design	Robles, Maria Elizabeth	ロブレスM.エリザベス
Illustrator	Teshigahara, Midori	勅使河原　　緑

SITUATIONAL FUNCTIONAL JAPANESE
VOLUME ONE: NOTES

1991年12月16日　初　版第 1 刷発行
2000年10月10日　第 2 版第 5 刷発行

著　者　　筑波ランゲージグループ
発行所　　株式会社　凡 人 社
〒102-0093　東京都千代田区平河町 1 － 3 －13
菱進平河町ビル 1 F　　電話 03－3263－3959

© 1991, 1995 Tsukuba Language Group
Printed in Japan

	-(r)u f. (dic f.)	-nai f.	-ta f.	-nakatta f.	[V(base)]-masu	-te f.	-nakute f.	-tara f.
Group I	行く	行かない	行った	行かなかった	行きます	行って	行かなくて	行ったら
	書く	書かない	書いた	書かなかった	書きます	書いて	書かなくて	書いたら
	急ぐ	急がない	急いだ	急がなかった	急ぎます	急いで	急がなくて	急いだら
	飲む	飲まない	飲んだ	飲まなかった	飲みます	飲んで	飲まなくて	飲んだら
	呼ぶ	呼ばない	呼んだ	呼ばなかった	呼びます	呼んで	呼ばなくて	呼んだら
	帰る	帰らない	帰った	帰らなかった	帰ります	帰って	帰らなくて	帰ったら
	待つ	待たない	待った	待たなかった	待ちます	待って	待たなくて	待ったら
	使う	使わない	使った	使わなかった	使います	使って	使わなくて	使ったら
	話す	話さない	話した	話さなかった	話します	話して	話さなくて	話したら
Group II	食べる	食べない	食べた	食べなかった	食べます	食べて	食べなくて	食べたら
	開ける	開けない	開けた	開けなかった	開けます	開けて	開けなくて	開けたら
	見る	見ない	見た	見なかった	見ます	見て	見なくて	見たら
	いる	いない	いた	いなかった	います	いて	いなくて	いたら
Group III	来る	来ない	来た	来なかった	来ます	来て	来なくて	来たら
	持ってくる	持ってこない	持ってきた	持ってこなかった	持ってきます	持ってきて	持ってこなくて	持ってきた
	する	しない	した	しなかった	します	して	しなくて	したら
	準備する	準備しない	準備した	準備しなかった	準備します	準備して	準備しなくて	準備したら